ENGLAND AND WALES
IN A FLASH

Adam and Roger Colton

Roger Colton, PO BOX 44, New Romney, Kent, TN28 8YB

First published in Great Britain in 2003 by
Roger Colton, PO BOX 44, New Romney, Kent, TN28 8YB

British Library Cataloguing-in-Publication Data.
A catalogue record for this book is available
from the British Library.

ISBN: 0-9544771-0-3

Cover Design: Graham Perkins.
Front Cover: Dungeness (Kent), Old Lighthouse.
Back Cover: Hartlepool Headland, Red Light.

Printed in Great Britain by *Manuscript ReSearch Printing*
P.O. Box 33, Bicester, OX26 4ZZ, U.K.
Tel: 01869 323447/322552   Fax: 01869 324096

CONTENTS

PREFACE

'Around the ragged rock, the ragged rascals ran!'

This is the story of a mission.

A mission to visit all the lighthouses of Britain, and where possible, to circumnavigate them, i.e. walk, in a clockwise manner around them, as if in some ancient Druidic ritual. Do not ask why.

The mission will use the car as our main mode of transport, therefore lighthouses located off of the British mainland cannot be visited. At least not until people like your good selves enable us to hire or purchase a boat!

However, if the lighthouse is within view of the naked eye and can be filmed adequately with a video camera, we will say that we've visited it.

These are the rules.

When we say Britain, initially we mean England and Wales - Well, you didn't expect us to visit all those ridiculously isolated lighthouses in Scotland, did you? Especially considering that we live in South-East England, and spending the number of weeks it would take to get round the entire Scottish Coast off work would be a near impossibility. Maybe we should consider a career in politics, then we would have several months free for this kind of activity every summer!

Anyway, when I obtain a nice fat pay-cheque from sales of this first book, I should have sufficient cash to write a second book on all the Scottish lighthouses, and after that, who knows? Alternatively, this book could sell poorly and I will have to graft for a further 35 years.

It is hoped that this mission with be 'exhaustive' as opposed to being merely 'exhausting!'

Why lighthouses?

Why not?

We all like to look after endangered species, don't we?

CORNWALL AND NORTH DEVON

Fowey Ahoy!

1)   FOWEY (disused)

Right.

The first leg of this gargantuan mission was to be Cornwall. Thus my Father, Roger Colton (who initiated the idea from conception to reality), and myself set off in his, at the time, new car for the West Country, which from our house in the charming and attractive village of Hamstreet in Kent, is about 200 miles - the first 100 miles being decidedly un-charming and unattractive, including the delights of the M20, M25 and M3!

However, upon reaching the A303 you begin to feel that you are out of the vastly over-populated South-East. There was even a West Country farmer on the radio talking about the damage done to roads by snow-chains!

The A303 is a road, which can't make up its mind whether to be a major dual carriageway from London to Exeter, or a car-park. At the end of each section of dual carriageway comes the inevitable traffic jam as two lanes of traffic files into a single lane in order to pass through a village or around Stonehenge.

I've heard that there is even a plan to tunnel the road underneath Stonehenge. I would like to propose a cheaper solution; dual carriageway the road anyway and have Stonehenge as the centrepiece of a roundabout! (I nicked that idea from Ashford Borough Council. If you don't know what I mean, next time you're in Kent, check out the roundabout by the designer shopping outlet). However, this was early March and the journey down to Devon was relatively painless.

We found a roadside tea wagon for lunch, somewhere in the area where the road seamlessly becomes the A30. The Honiton to Exeter section was slow due to the construction of a new dual carriageway (now open), but after Exeter, the road excels at being a high speed conduit into Cornwall with notable views of first, Dartmoor and then Bodmin Moor.

We decided to head for Fowey for the first night – a quaint little fishing town near St Austell. We found a pleasant inn as we entered the town, and immediately decided to stay.

After a beer, we walked down the picturesque footpath past the church to the town centre with quiet afternoon birdsong as our accompaniment. Across the River Fowey, we could see the smaller village of Polruan which had a flotilla of fishing boats lined up along its shore. Had we wished to visit, Polruan could be reached by means of a ferry. Standing on Fowey dock on this predominantly sunny day, we savoured the stillness, with just the sounds of the gently lapping water and the footsteps of the locals going about their merry way through the town. Now I see why Otis Redding placidly enthused about 'Sitting on the dock of the bay'.

We headed out of the town past quiet residential dwellings, and the lane eventually wound its way down to a cove. At first, I thought we were just going for a walk but my Dad informed me that we were on our way to our first lighthouse. There was no turning back now; the mission had begun.

We headed off up the opposite cliff by means of a footpath and, upon reaching the top we assumed we were in the vicinity of our goal.

Having asked several walkers in the area, our hopes were slightly dashed as they denied all knowledge. We had found the ruins of St Catherine's Castle, but the lighthouse was strangely absent.

This small fort was built by Henry VIII to defend Fowey harbour, with regard to earlier bloody raids emanating from France.

Our eyes were drawn to a lone fisherman standing on the outermost rock at the base of the cliff. This wave-lashed vantage-point struck us as being a particularly perilous choice, but as we would discover on later jaunts, a glance at the tide tables has distinct advantages. No doubt this fellow was well aware of this fact.

Convinced that the map doesn't lie, we returned to the top of the cliff and criss-crossed a field several times, searching in a manner a little like in a Rupert Bear story, except that *he* always managed to find Ping-Pong to point him in the right direction! After climbing through a barbed wire fence, we trampled our way through undergrowth until, at last, we stumbled upon a redundant red structure, perhaps 12 feet high, shaped like a tin helmet and built into the cliff-side - hardly what the general public would describe as a lighthouse, hence the bewildered answers we got to our earlier requests for directions.

So we left the concrete plinth that it stood upon behind, hidden by bushes, and returned to Fowey for a steak, several pints of St Austell brewery's Tinner's ale, a few games of pool, several more pints of the aforementioned brew, a chat to some of the locals who by now were mentally ready to listen to the finer details of our challenge, several more pints of... (I think you get the picture), and a good night's kip.

I don't remember this being quite the way Rupert Bear used to end his adventures, but had a distinct feeling that I was going to like this mission!

'Peculier' Penzance

2)   MEVAGISSEY (harbour light)
3)   ST ANTHONY'S HEAD/ZONE POINT* (white/red flash every 15 secs)
4)   LIZARD POINT* (white flash every 3 secs.)

Note: This symbol (*) denotes a Trinity House lighthouse. I will let you know the relevance of this in due course. In addition I have stated the flash sequences where known. For a comprehensive list of specifications, may I suggest a visit to the Trinity House website at www.trinityhouse.co.uk ?

Now, where were we? Yes - Fowey.

What we discovered from our night in Fowey, (by the way, it's pronounced 'Foy'), is that people who live in Fowey, 'like' Fowey. This is understandable; it's a nice town, with no modern suburban sprawl, not much traffic (so its narrow streets are more than adequate), and a very obscure lighthouse!

After a good English breakfast, we pressed on, taking the A-road to St Austell, which follows the railway line for the last few miles.

St Austell appeared to be an average English town, in that what we saw of it, (the outskirts), was littered with all the usual DIY superstores etc... We then headed for Mevagissey, another fishing town, seeming slightly smaller than Fowey, with considerably smaller streets and more traffic. I can't imagine what it must be like at the height of the summer, as this was a drizzly day in March, and driving through the town was a task akin to passing a camel through the eye of a needle!

Worse still, we could find nowhere to park and had to turn round and do it all again from the opposite direction, this time with slightly more scrutinising eyes.

My Dad bought some fags and indigestion tablets - perhaps his stomach was not yet fully adjusted to large intakes of Cornish beer!

On this dull morning, the town centre quietly bustled with folk cheerily going about their daily business. We allowed them to continue, and headed out along the winding concrete quay-side, at the end of which stood a thin, octagonal, white structure of maybe 20 feet in height, with a black base and a balcony around the light compartment – our anonymous looking 'lighthouse number two'.

I'm now going to brag a bit. Since a very young age I have possessed a particular talent for navigation. At the age of five, I used to draw maps of imaginary road networks between imaginary places. At ten, I used to do the navigation when we went on family holidays. At 25, a colleague rang me up and asked me to go to Coventry with him. I had never been sent to Coventry before, but he trusted me to direct him without so much as opening a road atlas.

I have come to be renowned by my colleagues for an almost obsessive fascination with road numbers and have generally become regarded as the human equivalent of on-board satellite navigation! So the question is 'what went wrong in Cornwall?' For somewhere between Mevagissey and our next lighthouse at Zone Point, we got lost in the network of small Cornish lanes.

Eventually, having regained our bearings, the lane we were on became a car-park and there was a finger-sign directing us down a stepped footpath to the lighthouse – our first bone-fide lighthouse of the mission.

It was here that we first encountered something that would become a familiar scene to us - a locked gate with a notice, which read something like 'Property of Trinity House, Keep Out.'

For the uninitiated 'Trinity House' is the body that runs and maintains most of the major lighthouses of England and Wales.

They were originally a medieval guild of mariners. During this period there are believed to have been only 30-40 lighthouses in the British Isles, mostly beacons which were lit in chapel towers, etc. These eventually proved inadequate, and in the sixteenth century the Corporation of Trinity House was commissioned to erect new lighthouses as well as maintain the existing ones.

In Scotland the lights are generally owned by the Northern Lighthouse Board, and in Ireland (Both N & Rep. of) it is the Commission of Irish lights who maintain the lighthouses. These bodies are collectively known as the General Lighthouse Authorities, commanding an annual income of £73million. In October 2002, major shipping companies argued that the levy they pay towards the upkeep of lighthouses could be halved, and the Independent Light Dues Forum postulated the idea of merging the three into a single, more efficient unit.

So there we have it, a potted history, past present and future, and no doubt you are eager for me to get back to the job in hand and tell you about our next light.

St Anthony's lighthouse was built in 1835, and consists of a 62-foot high, white, octagonal tower with two black chimney-breasts at the top. I am informed that it was also the setting for the 1980's children's puppet series 'Fraggle Rock'. The lighthouse nestles below the cliff with, above it, a lookout position, important and much strengthened during the Second World War to protect Falmouth Harbour. The cliff-top is now the site of a hide for bird-watchers.

Falmouth Port is at the entrance to Carrick Roads, guarded on the east by St Mawes Castle, and on its west by Pendennis Castle. Henry VIII again!

We would come across these crenellated structures all the way along our journeys through the South Coast of England. Built during the period 1539-1545, this was a massive engineering feat for the time. Juxtaposed were many of our lighthouses. The lights for the furtherance of the nation's trade; the castles for the defence of these trading centres. Pendennis would be the most westerly we would encounter.

On we pressed to the King Harry ferry, a short cut across the River Fal. This wasn't the rusting hulk of a ship which we saw in the estuary, but a slab of metal that pulls itself along by gobbling up the chains which run underwater from one side of the river to the other.

Within minutes, it seemed like we were spending hours waiting for a gap in the traffic to pull out onto the A39.

Avoiding Falmouth, and just touching on the outskirts of Helston, we headed for the Lizard. The road, which was a slick highway around the bizarre area of Goon Hilly Down (a series of large white dishes which were used for early satellite defence projects), soon became a hilly road where coach-loads of tourists crawl along, and round, and up, and...

Then we were at the Lizard - the most southerly point on the British mainland. By now the sky was blue and the sun was shining. This meant that we had to walk right round the wall surrounding the 62-foot high, white, octagonal tower and its stately terrace of two-storey dwellings, for me to get optimum light for a bit of video-camera footage.

The first light here was in 1619, when Sir John Killigrew charged a toll of 10 shillings for the cost of the coal. In the seventeenth century it was common practice for lighthouse keepers to make a living in this way. At one point there were two towers here. The current lighthouse was built in 1812 and was converted from oil to electricity in 1878.

At the southernmost tip of the Lizard, a path wound down to a cove with some wooden boat buildings. I was expecting a signpost with distances to all kinds of exotic places, but I would have to wait till we got to Land's End for that.

We toyed with the idea of finding a B&B in the village of Mullion, but decided to continue to Penzance. Above the town the small hills appeared white. A closer look would reveal row upon row of protective polythene covering; beneath this, a crop of early potatoes.

Growing potatoes in March isn't really cheating nature but taking advantage of the increasing warmth in the early spring sunshine.

At the Lizard, we had been told that it was unlikely that the area would ever see a frost again. Indeed the very notion of taking a holiday in March had at first seemed adventurous, but here we were comfortably exploring the coastline, occasionally breaking into a sweat, over-dressed in our wax jackets.

It took us a while to settle on a place to stay but eventually found an inn where we even had the luxury of watching Channel Five!

Bizarrely, in Kent, we are not allowed to watch this channel unless we are prepared to fork out for non-terrestrial TV equipment. This is not because Channel Five's material is considered too harsh for our refined tastes, but because transmitting it in the South-East interferes with French radio signals. In return, I'd argue that their regular strikes interfere with the traffic flow on our M20. But, before we get into the predictable and age-old England versus France debate, I'll tell you how we spent our evening.

We wandered up from the seafront into the town centre and called into a pub, which had music playing at ear-splitting volumes. Upon ordering a couple of pints, we realised that it didn't serve food, but rather than waste good money, and more importantly, good beer, we stayed as the place filled with loud youths and eventually we concluded that it wasn't a suitable place for a couple of intrepid lighthouse explorers to mull over the day's proceedings.

After a meal in a restaurant where we sampled the local seafood platter, we returned to the Dock Inn where we were staying, for a game of pool and a couple of halves of 'Old Peculier', which at the time was over 6% proof and a perfectly adequate end to the night. No wonder the brewers had forgotten how to spell 'peculiar!'

Hayle Ale

(or 'As I was going to St. Ives')

5)   PENZANCE (harbour light)
6)   NEWLYN (harbour light)
7)   TATER DU* (main light: 3 white flashes every 15
     secs + fixed red/white sector light)
8)   LONGSHIPS* (white/red isophase every 10 secs)
9)   PENDEEN* (4 white group flashes every 15 secs)
10) ST IVES (harbour light)

The new day that dawned was a bright sunny one, and we had the luxury of having breakfast brought up to our room. The day ahead was to be an intense schedule, which began with a further exploration of Penzance. This consisted of another walk up to the town centre to find a post office and a circular route back to the dockside, where we found our way out to our first lighthouse of the day, at the end of the quay.

The round, white tower with a black base was a similar affair to the one at Mevagissey, although it appeared to be too thin for a normal-sized human being to fit inside. It also had a flat square like a mortarboard separating the tower from the light chamber. More notable was the ship, which passengers were boarding to travel to the Isles of Scilly.

A bit of info on the Isles of Scilly now:

There are five populated islands here and 19 other islands, plus many more rocks. The population is estimated at little over 2000. Situated 28 miles west from Land's End, they are a cornucopia for lighthouse enthusiasts. Furthest west is Bishop Rock lighthouse - one of the most exposed there is. Then there's Penninnis Head on St Mary's Isle (the largest of the Scilly Isles), the disused St Agnes light, and Round Island light on the northern edge of the group of islands. There is also Wolf Rock, out in the void half way between the Scilly's and Lizard Point.

All irrelevant to us on our strictly land-based mission, (although we were to meet an easy-going former keeper of Wolf Rock light some three years later at Glasson, Lancashire).

A short drive around the bay brought us to Newlyn, where roads were narrow and parking was difficult. A flight of steps led us down to the quay, at the end of which stood a round harbour light. Its base and top were red, and it had a balcony. This structure was much larger, both in terms of height and girth, than the light at neighbouring Penzance.

In South-West Cornwall, and in this area in particular, fishing is very important to the economy. Many porpoises used to become entangled in the nets. Since then, measures have been taken to avoid this problem.

Incidentally, the datum-line was fixed at Newlyn in 1921. This means that all our local heights we are so fond of quoting are relative to the mean sea-level at this westerly location.

There are views across Penzance to St Michael's Mount - an island that is linked to the mainland by a sand causeway at low tide. Several months after our visit, this area was famous for being about the only place in Britain where you could experience the total eclipse of the sun. It is interesting to note that it didn't herald the end of the world, as some people expected, and neither, come to think of it, did the passing of the millennium. I distinctly remember seeing a guest on daytime TV being asked "If by any chance, the world hasn't ended within the next year or so, will you come back on the show?"

The reply was something like, "I can guarantee that won't be necessary!" Unfortunately, we were denied the opportunity of watching him eat his words on live TV, as that particular show has now been axed - which I suppose for some people *is* the end of the world. Perhaps he was right after all!

We got stuck behind a tractor on the B-road leading to our next lighthouse, so we found a place to park and wandered around an ancient burial ground which dates back to the Neolithic period (early Bronze Age). We decided to take a footpath, which led towards the sea, but after trudging around a ploughed field, it became ridiculously overgrown. So we returned to the car and headed off up a farm track. The owner of the farm politely told the two trespassers that there was no access to the lighthouse via his farm and directed them back along the B-road to Lamorna Cove.

The lane down to the cove was very narrow and had a steep unfenced drop to the left of us. Naturally, passing oncoming vehicles was approached with extreme caution. At the bottom was a cafe, where a cup of tea and a light snack prepared us for the walk ahead. The South-West Coast Path runs for 613 miles, from Poole in Dorset, round every nook and cranny of the Devon and Cornwall coasts, to Minehead in Somerset. And it isn't easy terrain either - the bit we walked began by climbing up huge boulders, and was signalled by a painted arrow pointing towards the sky on the first rock!

For the next three hours or so, we would hear very little apart from the continual sound of waves breaking on the rocks below us. Once over the initial boulders, the path became easier to follow, and for about two miles we wound our way up and down the rocky cliffs, till a steep concrete drive with steps running down the middle led us straight down to Tater Du lighthouse.

It seemed apparent that this was not the only way to approach the lighthouse, as there were two workmen inside, and I doubt very much that they walked two miles of the Cornish Coast Path, complete with tools and equipment, to get here!

They were very friendly and gave us a guided tour inside and up to the top of the white-painted concrete tower, which musters a height of just under 50 feet rising from the square building at its base. There is a foghorn lattice on the front. Tater Du lighthouse stands on Runnelstone Rocks.

Built in 1965, this is the most recent 'new' lighthouse on mainland Britain. By this I mean that there was no lighthouse on this site previously. I would imagine that this statistic will remain unchanged, which underlines precisely the purpose of this mission:

'To visit all these lighthouses before they become a redundant feature of the coastline'.

You may or may not have noticed that every lighthouse has its own individual flash sequence. This is because they exist not merely to stop ships crashing into the shore, but also as a navigational aid. For example, a sailor seeing a white flash every three seconds would know he was in the vicinity of Lizard Point - 'turn left to dock at Penzance' kind of thing!

Marine navigation today relies heavily upon GPS (Global Positioning System), which using satellite technology can pin-point your exact position on the globe to within a matter of yards. So what will become of the lighthouses? Will they become redundant, fall into a state of disrepair and eventually be pulled down for safety reasons?

Or, will they become listed buildings, preserved as a reminder of our maritime heritage? On our travels, we would find examples of both. Tater Du's pre-eminence seems safe for the time being as it is one of the main GPS fixing centres, hence all the technical gadgetry that we saw inside.

We gave this lighthouse a 'difficulty' rating of high, a 'satisfaction' rating of good, and were back at the car an hour and a half later, with the roar of the sea replaced by the gentle trickle of the waterfall, which happened to be by the public toilets (the power of suggestion?). We made good use of this little oasis of facilities, then headed off for Land's End.

Land's End, in terms of statistics, is far less notable than the Lizard; it is merely the most westerly point on the mainland of *England*. (The most westerly point of mainland *Britain* is Corrachadi Moor in Scotland).

Upon arrival, it successfully masquerades as a theme park, complete with parking fee. Visiting Land's End without paying the fee is simply not an option (unless you are of an Olympic standard in walking), as the last mile or so of the A30 is lined with double yellows on both sides, until it disintegrates into the aforementioned car-park.

By the way, the A30 is the fifth longest road in the UK stretching 273 miles from London to Land's End. OK - the top four are the A1, A9, A6 and A38.

We parked the car and wandered through the various attractions, which were closed for the winter season, and soon found ourselves at the famous sign:

'John O'Groats 874, New York 3147, Isles of Scilly 28 and Longships lighthouse 1½' - just close enough for the zoom lens on my video camera to pick up.

This granite lighthouse is 115-foot high, 62-foot round at the base and is now topped with a flat landing-pad for helicopters. The tower was built in 1883, replacing earlier towers of 1795 and 1843. The first tower was built by a Mr Smith who was rewarded with the right to charge a toll on shipping for a limited number of years. It sits alone on its rock, exposed to the Atlantic Ocean.

There was another arm on the famous Land's End sign which, for five pounds, could be occupied by the distance to the place of your choice. So it was irresistible to us to give the smashing village of

Hamstreet in Kent a second moment of prominence. Our village had never mustered an appearance on any sign further than eight miles away before, so with a distance of 351 miles, we hoped to galvanise our village in the consciousness of a wider audience than ever before. That's of course, until somebody else comes along with the intention to immortalise their home town for a mere fiver!

You may be asking what our village's first moment of prominence was. Well, this was back in 1991, when a set of four stamps were issued to commemorate 200 years of the Ordnance Survey. Hamstreet was one of the first areas to be mapped and just happened to fit rather nicely onto a square the size of a postage stamp. The result; for a brief period a map of our village could be seen in the top right hand corner of every letter posted in the UK - magnificent!

John Craven even came and did a 'Countryfile' special on the event, as people dressed up in the clothes of 200 years ago and buried a time capsule, to be opened in another 200 years.

Moving swiftly on, our next lighthouse to visit was Pendeen Watch, which was a few miles past St Just.

It was easy to find, with a finger-post directing us down a lane which headed straight to the 56-foot high, round, white tower with a green base and single-storey dwellings. It was built in 1900 and appeared very well looked after. Situated near the Pendeen Watch House, its light is 190 feet above sea level and is visible for twenty miles.

The road to St Ives went through a very peculiar area like nowhere else we'd seen in Cornwall, or indeed Southern England. With stone walls across the rugged, red, earthen landscape, it reminded me of the Yorkshire Dales viewed through rose-tinted spectacles! The road meandered around stone farm buildings and the journey came to an abrupt halt to let some chickens across, and they weren't in any hurry either!

Just around the next blind corner we were confronted by an oncoming vehicle being driven like a bat out of hell, which set us pondering as to not, *why* the chicken crossed the road, but, did it reach the other side?

Our intention was to find somewhere to stay in St Ives, so we parked up, and while still bewildered by the sudden return to civilisation from the back of beyond, we did something unforgivable - we cheated!

A quick glance across the bay revealed an unexpected lighthouse. The plan was to find lodgings and add it to tomorrow's schedule, but upon looking around the town we could find nowhere within our price range that met all of the criteria we demanded. Soon we were the other side of the headland that overlooks the town, watching surfers in the western bay. So we returned to the car and trained the camera lens on the 1830, standard, white, quayside structure, which was almost identical to the one at Mevagissey. Please bear in mind that this pier was built by John Smeaton – an important name in lighthouse circles that we will come across aplenty later.

The next coastal town we came across was Hayle, a much less tourist orientated place than St. Ives, where we quickly found a cheap and cheerful pub to stay in. Here, we enjoyed three pints of Guinness, which went down like silk, and were cooked an evening meal especially. There was live music too, although it seemed that half the evening was taken up by setting up the performer's equipment! However, the second half of the act, which consisted of midi-based entertainment, went down well; people danced enthusiastically, we drank as much beer as our stomachs could hold and retired to our trench-like beds.

Of course this was tempting fate, and a restless night ensued. My father swears blind that he went on a route march along a labyrinth of corridors in search of the lavatory. The only consolation was that after this trek, his slanting bed of yore miraculously no longer seemed to trouble him!

Well, what do you expect for sixteen pounds?

Boy Racing in Bude

11) GODREVY ISLAND* (white/red flash every 10 secs)
12) TREVOSE HEAD* (one flash every 7½ secs)

There are variations on the traditional British breakfast which can be noticed as you travel round the country. For example in Yorkshire, you are far more likely to encounter a piece of black pudding on your plate than in Sussex. In Ireland, you may find yourself tucking into a Boxty pancake with your bacon and eggs. In Scotland, they eat porridge with salt. Hayle too has its own variation:

A Hayle breakfast would appear to consist of all the other items crammed into a corner of the plate occupying about twenty percent of the space, with a huge swathe of baked beans sprawled over the remainder. Nevertheless, it was very filling, and no doubt the economical price for our night's stay had something to do with making bulk purchases of 'value' supermarket own-brand beans!

Before long, we were embarking on another hard day's lighthousing, and our next one was a mere five miles away just off the coast on Godrevy Island.

We turned off the B-road in the lush, green, 'Red River' valley. Soon we were in National Trust territory, which inevitably meant parting with some collateral before we could park the car. We wandered along the grassy cliff-top and were soon at the closest point to view the white, octagonal, 1859-built structure just across the water. During the year it took to build the lighthouse, a lightship was stationed here. There was once an additional lower fixed light on this 85-foot high tower, which was reputedly the inspiration for Virginia Wolf's aptly named novel 'To the Lighthouse'.

Before long, we were back on the road, traversing a fairly wild, moor-like landscape, then descending to Portreath - a small village complete with the all-essential surfing shop! The village nestled in a picturesque bay between cliffs, where many of the aforementioned store's target-market could be seen catching the waves.

Within a few miles, we had caught up with our old friend the A30 again, which at this point was in 'major dual carriageway' mode, streaking its way past Camborne and Redruth. Then, off we came onto was a fairly fast A-road to Newquay. We headed northwards towards Trevose Head, which would be our final lighthouse in Cornwall, on a scenic B-road which bumped its way up and down various hills, until at last the large headland at Trevose could be seen looming ominously before us.

Soon the wallet was open again, as the lane became a narrow toll-road with passing places, purposefully heading in a straight line up the hillside in front of us.

A tarmac footpath gently led down from the obligatory car-park to the 88-foot, white, round lighthouse. This one was built in 1847, and until 1882 there was a lower light as well. This was sited about fifty feet in front of the lighthouse. The flash sequence here has changed several times, most recently in 1995 when the revolving of the optic was slowed from once every five seconds to once every seven and a half seconds. The red screens were also removed to give a clear light.

As we walked into the courtyard, we were startled by a loud shout of "OI - NO!" from the balcony. The shouts did not seem to be directed at us, but at the hillside above us, where at an educated guess, some indecent act had taken place by somebody who didn't bargain for aerial viewing!

A wave of satisfaction washed over us now, like the waves that crashed over the treacherous rocks below us, foaming over the rugged terrain. We had completed our first leg of the mission - the twelve lighthouses of the Cornish Coast, so we reclined for a while on the grassy knoll, contented.

But twelve lighthouses is never enough! We had achieved this much quicker than we had envisaged and now that the dream of visiting every light in England and Wales seemed a more plausible reality, we were eager to add the three lights of North Devon to our agenda - we had become compulsive pharophiles. (Pharophile = one who likes lighthouses).

The remainder of the day was spent trying to find somewhere to stay. Our standards had risen; we were looking for somewhere that we wouldn't have to leave to get an evening meal; somewhere with soft, flat beds, and a breakfast that consisted of less than fifty percent baked beans!

First, we tried Padstow - a small town at the bottom of a cliff with a modest range of little shops.

Secondly, we tried Wadebridge - a larger town, bypassed by the

A39, boasting more shops and even a cinema.

We were taken aback by this, as at the time, our home town of Ashford, in spite of having over 50,000 inhabitants, didn't possess this luxury.

Perhaps Ashford even had the distinction of being the largest town in Britain without a cinema. The way things are going now, it will probably soon be just the largest town in Britain, full stop!

I've exaggerated a bit, yes, but the place does seem to be growing at an alarming rate. The problem is that there are 58 million people in the UK and only 26 million houses. People are no longer content to live in households of 2.2, (I know I wouldn't be, it sounds painful!). They prefer to live alone, or at the most in couples. As a result the South-East has got to find room for another million homes.

So as the southern boundary of Ashford moves inexorably closer to our poor, oblivious village, with its ever-larger supermarkets draining the trade from our local shops, the appeal of de-camping to Shropshire, or Cumbria, or even a remote lighthouse on the Cornish Coast, becomes greater!

Anyway, Wadebridge has no such pressures, and Ashford now has a splendid twelve-screen cinema. So I will put the soapbox away and return to the plot!

Still with nowhere suitable to stay for the night, we proceeded along the A39, which is apparently known as the 'North Atlantic Highway' in this area; I simply know it as the ninth longest road in Britain, spanning 214 miles from Falmouth to Bath.

This was a genuine 60mph road, with the obvious exception being the bit through Camelford.

Soon we were turning off for Bude - the most northerly town in Cornwall. We found a very spacious hotel to stay in, and my Dad quickly went into 'rigor mortis' mode, no doubt brought on by a combination of yesterday's walking and today's driving.

I decided to have a wander around, and found something of a rare commodity in these small Cornish towns - a music shop. The notion of being over an hour's drive from the nearest place to purchase a CD is anathema to me, I thought music was an indispensable part of modern life. Perhaps the people here are just too busy surfing!

The sound of children enjoying the cool sunshine of an early spring evening could be heard as I strolled along the river bank to the sea, and by the time I returned to the hotel, my Dad was sufficiently invigorated to venture out to try the pubs of Bude.

The first one we went in was full of bikers and loud youths with vocabularies as colourful as a 1970's stage outfit! More about that shortly.

We then found a quieter establishment where we plied the jukebox with cash in return for some classic Beatles' songs and hits like 'Whiter shade of pale'.

Then it was back to the hotel for a roast dinner of the self-service variety. We shared the dining room with a coach-load of elderly tourists. This gave us a (rather prejudiced) insight into the kind of people who like to visit Bude.

Having had sufficient alcoholic intake on the previous three nights, we declined to join the other guests in the ballroom, fearing that it might turn into a lively shindig; although that did not look very likely at first glance!

Instead we ended up watching an amusing programme on the top ten 'glam-rock' bands of all time, which was far funnier than any of the so-called comedies that are transmitted these days in the name of humour.

Watching the likes of Slade, T-Rex, etc. prancing about in outrageous seventies clothing would have probably proven too much for our more senior fellow residents, so it's just as well that they stayed in the bar!

Having settled down with the idea that Bude was a quaint little 'granny' town, a contrasting side began to emerge. It was time for the pubs to kick out and hordes of tanked-up youths began to fill the streets. The sound of highly-revved motorbike engines mingled with loud drunken shouts in the cool night air. This lot would make Gary Glitter and chums seem like a string quartet in a nunnery!

Then came the boy-racers; stereos turned to the max so that the drone of the bass became the only decipherable musical sound, feet poised over the throttle, a few blips, then they're off - tearing through the streets leaving a pound of rubber on the road at every corner, accelerating through the gears with dump-valves hissing like a turbo-charged pressure cooker!

It's a pastime I've never really understood. Every town seems to have its circuit. One-way systems are the best - you can tear round them at four times the speed limit, with no threat of having to slam on the brakes to miss an oncoming car. Then one day, at the age of twenty-five, comes two revelations:

1)   That there are actually roads outside of one's home town to be explored, and,

2)   That this 'accelerate then brake' kind of driving burns rather a lot of fuel!

From then on, one has reached the age of affordable motor insurance, and a car becomes what it was intended as - a means of getting from A to B!

So as the sound of internal combustion engines gently submerged into the night like the passing of a storm, sleep could at last become a viable proposition!

All this in the town that Sir John Betjemen described as the country's 'least rowdy resort!'

Foreland Fatigue

13)   HARTLAND POINT* (6 white group flashes every 15 secs)
14)   BULL POINT* (3 white flashes every 10 secs)
15)   LYNMOUTH FORELAND/COUNTISBURY HEAD* (4 white flashes every 15 secs)

A new day dawned and breakfast was another self-service affair. After a little bit of 'Kilroy' to stimulate the mind about some pressing current affair, we were ready for the off. So we fired up the motor and hit the 'North Atlantic Highway' - a rather high-faluting title for a road which was now more of a test for one's cornering techniques.

We soon dived off onto back lanes and headed for Hartland Point via Hartland village. There was a lane which took us 'straight to the point' once it had wound its way past a series of farms in a valley, reaching its natural conclusion, quite predictably, as a car-park.

Being in the middle of nowhere on an overcast blustery day, we thought we may escape the terminal fee, but no sooner had the ignition key been turned off, than somebody leapt out of a wooden hut politely asking for some dosh!

After ignominiously parting with the dough as requested, and looking at the 'Property of Trinity House - No Unauthorised Access' sign on the gate, which barred us from using the easy route to the lighthouse, we headed off up a fairly steep cliff-top path.

As we stood by a transmitter/beacon surrounded by a wire fence, we got our best view of the 1874-built, 59-foot high, white lighthouse, which was isolated from us on the rocks below. Both the round, balconied tower which had a little dome on top, and its flat-roofed, cube-like, two-storey keeper's house, were surrounded neatly by a wall, which resembled an arch shape pressed flat onto the rock from which the buildings rise.

Erosion has been a problem here, as it was necessary to break rocks from the cliff behind, so they'd fall on the beach and form a barrier. We also saw a shipwreck rusting away a little to the south of the lighthouse. The wind howled around us, and when we returned to the car and shut the doors, it was respite for the ears and time to straighten our hair out. Speaking of 'straight', it wasn't too long before the A39 had resumed its 'expressway' character, bypassing Bideford and leaping over the River Torridge on a viaduct.

Barnstaple had the feel of a largish town, akin to how our home town of Ashford used to be, after its days as a small market town; but before it decided to go 'international'. Talking of Ashford, (yet again), we passed a tiny village of the same name on our way to Braunton. The road we were on, the A361, doesn't quite make the top ten of Britain's longest roads, but is nevertheless an epic route, running from Ilfracombe to, more or less, Rugby.

Beyond Braunton we found ourselves driving along a valley bounded by wooded hills. We were unsure whether to approach our next lighthouse, Bull Point, from the east or the south. We eventually chose the latter, opting against trudging across miles of ploughed fields on the eastern side. Unable to turn the car around, due to the perilously small width of the lane, we continued via the village of Lee.

Eventually, we found our way to Mortehoe - the starting point for our next hike as the lane was prohibited to traffic.

After passing a caravan site, the lane wound its way through heathland up, and round, and down, and a mile or so later - there it was; an unusual lighthouse of a grey stone colour, with three fog-horn dishes on the front of its 36-foot high chubby tower. The original lighthouse here dates from 1879, but in 1972 ground movements sent fifteen metres of cliff crashing into the sea. This was followed by a further fifteen metres subsiding. Walls cracked and part of the engine room/fog-signal station collapsed.

As a temporary measure, the redundant lighthouse at Braunton Sands (about 10 miles south), which was being maintained as a piece of heritage by Nature Conservancy, was borrowed back. Eventually in 1974, the reconstructed lighthouse at Bull Point opened at a cost of £71,000. As for Braunton Sands lighthouse, we would spend a whole day searching for it a year later, because nearby Crow Point beacon appears as a lighthouse on several maps and features on Trinity House information handouts.

About fifteen miles west of Bull Point lies Lundy Isle - a thin sliver of land, about three miles from top to bottom, with three lighthouses: north, south and most notably, west, a light which was reputed to have been seen at a distance of 45 miles. Best of all, cars are prohibited on the island, which in these days of pollution, global warming and congestion must be literally 'a breath of fresh air'.

In contrast, I'm about to talk roads again. I promise this will lessen as the book goes on, but the A39 really *is* a remarkable road. Seeming to have given way to a B-road at Blackmoor Gate (a rare example of hierarchical submission), the route meanders its way to Lynton and Lymouth. There is an option to go into Lynton; and the official route, which goes all round the sun to meet the moon, resembling a highland pass as it snakes through the wooded valley, finally reaching Lynmouth to present you with a 1in4 hill to climb.

Lynmouth is a very attractive place, although notorious for its fatal flood of 1953, when torrential rain saturated the high land above the town, causing the water to run off at an alarming rate. This channelled into a raging torrent, carrying rocks and boulders down the River Lyn and destroying a substantial part of the town.

Climbing up onto Exmoor, we parked the car at Countisbury and prepared for our final lighthouse of the day; and indeed, of this first stage of the mission - Foreland Head. If this hadn't been the finish of the mission, then the mission would have finished us! We trekked across bleak moorland, facing the onslaught of freezing gusts. Then a long steep descent eventually led us to a road, which if we'd had known, could have saved our feet several miles. There was another shorter route, but this involved descending a steep slope of scree. Obviously, having seen my black office shoes with worn away soles, some hikers had recommended that we steer clear of this.

The descent by road was almost as long again. These cliffs are reputedly the highest in England, at over a thousand feet, so I suppose a little discomfort to the legs was inevitable. The white, 50-foot, 1900-built lighthouse, has a round, balconied light compartment with a lattice window. The top of the structure seemed no higher than the terrace of keeper's dwellings on the cliff-side that it nestles beneath. We too viewed this lighthouse from above, being separated by a gate and the all too familiar 'keep out' sign. The base of the lighthouse is still in excess of 170 feet above sea-level.

Having savoured the tranquillity of this isolated spot for a few minutes, it was now time to face up to the climb, back up the steep lane, back up the steep steps, back up the steep path, back up the even steeper grassy hillside, across the moorland and back to the car. Phew!

During this time-consuming ascent, the sun came out, and combined with the high level of physical exertion, a stiff wind in our faces and my Father's dependency on the plant Nicotina, it was a considerable relief to reach the car to ease the sound of his wheezing mixed with breathless muttered oaths.

So that was it - the fifteen lighthouses of Cornwall and North Devon. The rest of this holiday was a slow retreat home - across Exmoor, down the 1in4 hill into Porlock's narrow street, back up the other side, through the more mundane parts of Minehead, and through the attractive little village of Carhampton to Washford, where we decided to break our journey for the night.

In hindsight, a little hasty. For three and a half years later, thinking we had completed the mission, we would discover to our horror that Watchet quay (barely two miles north-east of our inn) has its own lighthouse.

Our room overlooked Washford station, on the North Somerset Steam Railway, which runs from Minehead to just short of Taunton. When we were tired of looking at steam trains, we could view the horrendous queue on the A39; and when we became tired of that, there was the TV. Being Sunday, 'Songs of praise' seemed the most appropriate option – a soothing end to a hectic day.

We retired to the bar for the evening and I tentatively tried a half of Scrumpy. I'm not a great cider fan. Most of the smooth ciders that you get in pubs tend to be a bit too sweet for my liking. They also tend to catch you out when it comes to assessing how much of it to drink. A few pints and you could be tasting it again later, if you see what I mean. (Value for money, I suppose!).

But this was quite drinkable and had a more raw flavour. The yokels in the bar certainly had no qualms about drinking the stuff - it seems to be the regulation drink here, and the standard recommended consumption is 'lots of it!'

After we had finished our steak and cider pie, the scrumpy-fuelled yokels seemed to become more raucous, as if someone had just turned the volume up. So we had a wander up the road on foot, but soon realised we were in a one-pub village and returned to the bear-pit for a final pint or so; and kip.

One simply cannot accomplish the kind of achievement we had done without some serious psychological scars! For in the night I had a dream - I was stuck at the bottom of a cliff and my Dad was at the top. There was no way out, with rock faces encircling me like a well-shaft. I began shouting for help, and such was the trauma of this dream that I awoke still shouting. So a warning to anybody of a nervous disposition who wants to follow in our footsteps – don't!

* * * * *

The next day we drove home via Taunton, where we tried to find a tape of Somerset's chief musical export – the Wurzels. Having searched every music shop in town, the collected works of Adge Cutler and Co. were still strangely elusive and I had to settle for a video of a John Cleese film instead.

Could it be that modern Somerset music-lovers aren't actually fans of this cider-swilling, dung-spreading, country-loving band. Perhaps they are less familiar with such classics as 'Drink up thy zider' 'Good old Zummerzet' and 'I am a cider drinker' than I am.

I wonder if the locals in Washford ever gather round the bar to sing a few lines of 'Combine harvester' or 'Drink yer zider up.' Perhaps not.

Here's an interesting fact now. On the third of May 1967, about a month before the Beatles released Sergeant Pepper, their engineer Geoff Emerick was not available to them. Instead, he was recording a live 'Adge Cutler and the Wurzels' album at the Royal Oak, Nailsea, Somerset.

According to Mark Lewisohn's book 'The complete Beatles recording sessions', beforehand they had indignantly told him "You can't go to Somerset to record the Wurzels rather than the Beatles!" His reply was firm, "Yes we can. It's booked and that's that!"

However, it is remotely possible that I have uncovered a little more to this story. Upon purchasing a recent Wurzels compilation which features some of the live tracks, I noticed that a snippet of the audience laughter at the end of the track 'Twice daily' sounds remarkably similar to the laughter at the end of the track 'Within you, without you' on Sergeant Pepper, apparently added by the song's composer - the much-missed George Harrison. I may be entirely wrong, but could it be a wry response to forfeiting their engineer for a couple of days to the country-boy outfit?

Sadly Adge Cutler died in a road crash in 1974, two years before chart super-stardom for his group and three hits, reaching no.1, no.3 and no.32 respectively.

We hit highways no.358, no.303 and no.3 respectively!

I'm sorry, I'm at it again!

THE SOUTH COAST

Quizzed in Brixham

16) BRIXHAM PIER (harbour light)

A year passed, and the next stage of the mission was to be South Devon, Dorset, Hampshire and West Sussex. We were slightly more ambitious than last year, in that we went in early February - a month where snow has been common, and bad weather is the norm. February 2000 was no exception.

On the day before we left, the forecast had predicted that a huge band of rain would sweep across the country from west to east, and for once, it was right!

So off we set, out of the still-dry county of Kent, for the West Country. I had predicted that the band of rain would hit us before we reached the M25, and it became apparent that I'd made a prediction that would put certain weather forecasters and their hurricane-denying words of October 1987 to shame. The rain would not leave us until we were in deepest Devon.

Severe spray from the wheels of lorries gushed across the windscreen as we cruised down the M3, with the wipers being about as effective as using a paper towel to soak up the River Severn! Effectively, this was driving by guess at seventy miles per hour.

Having survived the 'tidal wave on the windscreen' test, we were now faced with the 'how long are you prepared to sit in traffic on the A303 at Chicklade' test.

Our patience failed us, as did that of the lorry driver in front of us. Truckers generally know the best evasive action to avoid decaying at the wheel in traffic jams, so we followed this one through a network of country lanes, rejoining the road at a point that the stationary swathe of traffic had yet to reach.

In the interests of nostalgia, continuity and convenience, we used the same roadside tea-wagon as last year, and had the same bacon and egg sandwiches and tea, in the same drizzly and overcast weather. But two things weren't the same - the graffiti from the loos had gone (not necessarily a good thing, as some of it was quite entertaining), and this time the new section of the A30 beyond Honiton was not only open, but already being declared as 'the noisiest road in Britain' by a multitude of protest signs. An old saying about locking a stable door and a bolting horse springs to mind. Perhaps the old farmers should get out there with their snow-chains and run up and down it a few times, not that I'm suggesting wanton damage to this pristine concrete surface as a means of obtaining a new quiet tarmac layer!

From Exeter, the dual carriageway makes light work of the approach to the Torbay conurbation, until it enters the vast swathe of urbanality at Newton Abbot, and never really recovers. And so to Brixham.

We expected Brixham to be of a similar size to Fowey, but it is actually much larger. The road system is rather hostile to non-locals, with all roads leading into a bizarre-looking multi-storey car-park. With the town centre being pedestrianised, the harbour area is marooned behind it, with this car-park acting like an inescapable black hole at the centre of the town. We ended up in a network of extremely narrow streets juxtaposed at angles designed to obliterate one's bearings, which suddenly dump you back out where you started, on the main road into town.

So we temporarily gave up on Brixham and headed for Kingsweir. We followed a bus that seemed illogically large for the lane-like road that led us up out of the town. Then we wound our way down a very green, unspoilt valley, before the road skewed into a one-way system to enter the small picturesque town, which is the terminus of a steam railway that runs down from Paignton. Finding no suitable place of rest to be open at the time, we decided to return to the metropolis of Brixham, parking in the area around St Mary's Church with the intent of walking to our first lighthouse of this second leg of our mission. It was to be found at the end of the quay.

We were much further from the town centre than we thought. It was one of those situations where you think 'it's bound to be just round that next corner' and what's round there? Another corner, of course!

The pedestrianised High Street was lined with all the usual shops and estate agencies, beyond which was the harbour, filled with fishing boats; and there, hidden by the quagmire of masts and sails, on the end of a long jetty, was the lighthouse, modestly beckoning us to walk another mile.

The light was slowly fading - another bad point about going on holiday in February - by 5pm it's dark.

The wind increased as we headed along the jetty, further out into Torbay. Unfortunately, there is little to say about the lighthouse, which is a standard, white, quayside structure, which first shone its light in 1839. We touched it, filmed it and savoured it, then began the mammoth walk back amidst the seagulls and fishermen.

Walking evidently stimulates the mind, for it was now that we were able to find a driveable route to the harbour area via the east cliff. We found a B&B overlooking the sea, and after parking in the tightest space imaginable which was bounded by iron poles and chains, we wandered down to a popular drinking establishment and ate a fine, hot curry.

I have one criticism of these chain pubs - that the bar is so often a massive free-for-all when it comes to being served. Whether there are just a handful of people waiting or a vast crowd, there seems inherent, a level of fairness that makes even the ref. at the 1986 World Cup match between England and Argentina seem like a master of diplomacy!

The credentials for quick service are:

a)   being female, blonde and having a genetically perfect physique, or

b)   being male, pushy and having the appearance of being 'a bloke you wouldn't want to mess with!'

Meanwhile, the boozy old men sit at the bar, content to wait (after all, they've got all day!), and the non-aggressive males and less attractive females become increasingly uptight, as simmering discontent begins to wind them up like a clock-spring.

After ten minutes of waiting while others waltz up to the bar to receive instant service, this anger begins to reveal itself in one's facial expression and exasperated sighs. The bar staff then say "I'll be with you after I've served three more blondes and two more hard-nuts". Then you can put in your order and, eventually, twenty minutes after you first walked up to the bar, you receive your drink which, having built up such a thirst, you down in under a minute and then contemplate repeating the entire process again!

That said, the meal was very good value, and soon we were off to another pub which had a ceiling covered in pots and pans. This public house was located above the side of the harbour wall, a short walk from our B&B lodgings.

A small digression at this point, because it would be easy to imagine if we were making this walk some two hundred years earlier, this area would be alive with 'press gangs'. The press gangs roamed the maritime ports looking for likely lads to join the Navy, by whatever means of inducement, for service at sea, to newly opened routes to the colonies, or for defence against whatever nation happened to be posing a threat to the British Isles.

They were greatly aided by a parliamentary act of 1704, which stated that 'idle persons, rogues, vagabonds and sturdy beggars' were legitimate targets. This act, not repealed until 1815, after the defeat of Napoleon, meant that any person faltering inside of; or not scuttling away from, a dockside pub could very well find themselves next day sailing out of the harbour, heading for the 'Indies'.

But today, this was not our fate. Instead it was quiz-night at the pub, and despite our protestations, we were 'pressed' into service and before we knew it, we were seated at a table with sheets of paper before us, being mercilessly asked questions on all manner of obscurity!

We would have won, had it not been for the tiebreak question at the end. It would have been nice to win, as we could have left the pub as legends - instead, we were finally allowed to leave as two anonymous visitors from Kent who happened to like lighthouses!

Plymouth Repose

17)   BERRY HEAD* (2 white group flashes every 15 secs.)
18)   TEIGNMOUTH (harbour light)
19)   START POINT* (white group flashing, 3 times every 10 secs)
20)   PLYMOUTH HOE (redundant Eddystone light)
21)   PLYMOUTH SOUND (breakwater light)

A new day dawned, and during breakfast we discovered that the owner of the B&B that we were staying in was a fisherman. It seemed that we had found the perfect person to ask about lighthouses. Out came a plethora of charts and seafaring maps which we chewed over at the breakfast table, desperately trying to look intelligent after our rigours of the previous evening, and hoping not just to leave them smeared with bacon-grease and marmalade! We failed on both counts.

Some interesting facts about Brixham did emerge, however. Apparently, as a fishing port, the town has the second highest turnover in Britain, at over £15million a year. This seemed a little hard to swallow, but we *did* trust his information that there was no lighthouse to be seen at Kingsweir, which made our first port of call today Berry Head.

The cliff-top lane led us past expensive looking dwellings for a mile or so, before quite predictably becoming, yes, you've guessed it, a 'pay and display' car-park! There is a Napoleonic fort at Berry Head, and as we walked between the stone turreted walls trying our best not to fall in the massive puddles, a rainbow shone in the sky - a kind of by-product from the decision making process concerning whether to brighten up or rain all day.

This stumpy, white lighthouse was built in 1906. It is shaped like a buoy and is surrounded by a metal fence. The lens was originally turned by the action of a weight falling down a 150-foot deep shaft; and its light has mustered a range of twenty miles, in spite of its status as the shortest lighthouse in the UK (approx. 16 feet). The weather vane on top is barely higher than the little white block building behind it.

We were also told that it is the highest light in the UK - a statement that seems as flimsy as the cliff that it stands upon, a mere 180 feet above sea level. Over the following years we would visit other lights, (both working and redundant), that would appear to be based at far loftier altitudes.

This is the problem with these bizarre and dubious word-of-mouth facts. It seems that everybody tries to promote their own village, town or features in their area by coming up with such hyperbole. For example, how many places have claimed to be the smallest town in Britain? I can name two within a twenty mile radius of my home. Winchelsea near Rye, and Fordwich near Canterbury are both vying for the title, and probably both are unaware of the other one's claim on it!

I am even guilty of using such hyperbole myself. Was it not just a few chapters ago that I postulated that Ashford could have been the largest town in Britain without a cinema? And what can I come up with for my home village of Hamstreet? Going back to the Ordnance Survey postage stamps thing again, I could describe it as the most thoroughly 'licked' village in England! See how easily it's done? So we left Brixham and its windswept headland behind, vowing to take all future such claims with a pinch of salt.

Having left Brixham, we plunged down into the suburbs of Paignton and Torquay. Paignton had a heavily congested one-way system at its centre, and Torquay lived up to Basil Fawlty's claim that it is 'the English Riviera' with its streets lined with palm trees. Somewhere around the centre, we lost the A-road and had to negotiate our way through the suburbs without the comfort of a familiar number to follow.

The short stretch of open countryside which followed surprised us. Then the road plummeted down the hillside to the picturesque bridge between Shaldon and Teignmouth. After a few false attempts to get to Teignmouth seafront involving turning down industrial estate type dead-ends, we found the lighthouse, which appeared to be made from stone blocks, and looked like the kind of mock castle tower that you would find in a fun-fair. The first light was emitted here in 1845, and as Forrest Gump would say "That's about all I have to say about that!"

Just across the water, we could see another lighthouse-looking structure on the Shaldon side of the River Teign. Thus, for the first time, we were encountered with the quandary, 'When is a lighthouse not a lighthouse?'

Answer: When it's a beacon.

Quite what the distinction is, I am not sure. After all the lighthouse at Fowey was little more than a beacon. So we decided that the Ordnance Survey would be our oracle. We would visit everything shown as a lighthouse on OS maps, and would ignore everything shown as a beacon. So if anybody reading this wants to dispute the inclusion or lack of inclusion of a structure, don't write to me, write to the Ordnance Survey! And if at any point in this book our distinctions differ from the oracle, put it down to poor map reading!

Having covered myself against future legal intervention, I shall now continue my story.

The road to Newton Abbot ran alongside the railway line and river, albeit slightly higher up. The route across to Totnes was painfully slow due to the heavy lorry in front, and the route onward to Kingsbridge was an undulating affair.

Those of you who aren't interested in roads will have to bear with me for a minute, because the bizarre numbering system around Kingsbridge is worth noting. The A381 seamlessly becomes the A379 a mile or so north of the town, with unclassified lanes being their only link to the town. Yet, another section of the A379 becomes the A381 in the town itself. It's a little like that magic trick where two assistants are put in boxes, sawn in half and put back together the wrong way, except with roads, of course!

We had a wander around Kingsbridge with the intention of finding somewhere to stay, (a little premature at 1pm, I thought). After a snack, we moved on to Salcombe, which seemed to be a dying fishing port, with most shops closed for the winter and a population that seemed to be largely elderly. It reminded me of a poor man's Padstow.

So it was back to Kingsbridge and out on another axis to Start Point.

We turned off the main road onto one of those ridiculously narrow lanes, where meeting an oncoming vehicle results in having to reverse for about a mile and a half to the nearest passing place; only to find that when you drive on, he would have only had to reverse fifty yards for you to pass him. Unbelievably, as we came to the T-junction at the end of the lane, an articulated lorry was turning into it. Someone who would even attempt to drive such a large vehicle down a blatantly unsuitable road like this has to be treated with respect for their highly skilled driving prowess!

40

Soon we were at Start Point, and from the windswept car-park a path led away down the cliff-side with a stone wall alongside it, which snaked around the headland like a miniature Great Wall of China. There were nice views across Start Bay to the sandy beaches of Hallsands, Beesands and Torcross.

This whole area has been a victim of tidal erosion. Whole villages along the bay have disappeared into the sea and the process continues, as cliff-top homes one by one tumble into the brine. Even the gate to the lighthouse has a sign stating that the area and buildings beyond that point are liable to collapse, indeed the unstable ground had claimed the fog signal building in December 1989.

The 92-foot, white lighthouse was built by James Walker in 1836. Its light compartment is thinner than the stout, round tower it adorns and there are two keepers buildings at its base. It was automated in 1992/93 at a cost of over £82,000. - Not a bad investment for a lighthouse perched on the brink of oblivion.

And that was it. Back to the car, back to the main road and back to Kingsbridge. Yes - Kingsbridge again. In this area, Kingsbridge *is* the centre of the universe! No matter where you go, you have to pass through it.

We had a quick look around Modbury - a large village or small town with three pubs. We went in one of these for a well-earned Guinness and were told that back in the seventies there were twelve pubs here - another hard to swallow fact, but one I believe to be true.

Life in Britain, it seems is increasingly not about 'long shadows on county grounds and warm beer' as John Major quoted in a particularly prosaic moment; neither is it about cream teas on summer lawns. Modern Britain can be summed up as dashing to the supermarket, filling a trolley with mass-produced goods, paying an anonymous cashier with a piece of plastic and charging home again before it all defrosts; then cracking open a four pack of beer and watching some instantly forgettable junk on TV!

We are not surprised when a place like Modbury loses three quarters of its pubs in twenty years. We are not surprised to see a place like Salcombe more or less closed for business all winter, yet bizarrely, this is the lifestyle we choose. We are selling our country for a pocket of silver.

Plymouth however, seems to be thriving. It is a large city without the large city feel. 270,000 people call it home, yet the roads are relatively uncongested. The area around Plymouth Hoe is very tranquil, and right in the middle of the parkland stands Smeaton's red and white striped, round tower, which tapers upward in a slight curve. This structure was a monumental leap in lighthouse design.

This lighthouse was originally sited fourteen miles out to sea on Eddystone Rocks. It was in the seventeenth century that a need for rock lighthouses was first postulated. Construction faced a number of problems. First, getting the raw materials out to these small isolated islands; and secondly, constructing a tower where the light is high enough to remain above the waves even in the most violent storms, without it falling down again.

Eddystone was the first British rock lighthouse, the only previous one being a twelfth century construction at Meloria off the West Coast of Italy, which had since perished.

Henry Winstanley built the first Eddystone light in 1696-98. He perished along with his ornate tower during a particularly fierce storm in 1703. Next up was John Rudyerd. His lighthouse opened in 1708. This one was destroyed by fire.

It was John Smeaton who elevated construction from this 'build it one year, watch it crumble into the sea the next' situation. His tower was built from blocks which could only be removed in the reverse order of construction. He was the first to use dovetailed joints in stone. His light shone for 123 years, from 1759 until 1882, after which the top half was retired to Plymouth Hoe; and the fourth and final Eddystone light, built by James Douglass took over the reins. This light now has a flat, square heli-pad on the top of its tower.

Smeaton's red and white striped tower at the Hoe is now open to the public in summer, and is widely recognised as the blueprint on which many other lighthouses are based.

Smeaton was also the first person to call himself a civil engineer, and the crest of the Institute of Civil Engineers has a small representation of his lighthouse at the top of it.

Some three miles out to sea another lighthouse can be seen standing on the breakwater across Plymouth Harbour. This could just about be identified as a grey tower, similar in shape to Smeaton's tower, through the fourteen-times magnification of my zoom-lens. First light on Plymouth breakwater: 1844.

The sun had briefly shone on us, but soon the clouds were back, and a steady shower ensued as we began to search for somewhere to stay.

There were plenty of hotels and guesthouses to choose from, and we settled on the Imperial, where I had a succulent medium-rare steak that was cooked exactly as I wanted it.

Too often you ask for 'medium-rare' and it comes out 'well-done', which makes me wonder what 'well-done' must be like - you are probably just presented with a plate of ash!

The proprietor was friendly and talkative as we reclined in the bar drinking our ale. There was a man there who had lived in this comfortable hotel continually for seven years. This seemed to us a particularly languorous lifestyle and made us slightly peeved with envy.

Another regular was a long-distance lorry driver. Soon a debate erupted about the use of computers. The lorry driver said that his job had been vastly simplified by using a spreadsheet for expenses, and was emphatic that computers would soon change everything. The hotel owner disagreed and I'm afraid that at the time, I had a tendency to side with him. This seems particularly pithy as I sit typing these words on a 'state of the art' PC, which a friend of mine has devoted vast amounts of time perfecting and installing for me.

The debate progressed nomadically to the Internet.

Now, at the time of this discussion only a mere seven percent of the British public had access to it, yet the amount of adverts for Internet-related companies on TV was phenomenal. Companies that didn't even exist yet were declaring massive future profits. Every news bulletin seemed to contain some reference to the net and it was being promoted as a medium that would reform our whole way of life. It all seemed just a little overblown to somebody who had yet to experience it. At this particular point in time the 'information superhighway' seemed more like the 'misinformation M25!'

Yet, gone were the days when a net was something you catch fish with, a web was something a spider makes and www.co.uk.backwards-slash/forwards-slash, etc. were just a bunch of meaningless hieroglyphs!

Perhaps I was just longing for John Major's pre-computer-age Britain of 'green suburbs and dog-lovers', where people drink afternoon tea, every village has a full selection of shops, and everyone goes to church. Oh, and by the way, John Major once stayed at the Imperial Hotel - there was a framed picture of him with the hotel owner on the wall, which made us feel comfortable and serene. Maybe this was just an illusion!

Burrowing in Braunton

(or 'A wasted journey')

A new day dawned and a splendid breakfast awaited. Upon leaving the dining room we noticed a map on the wall which showed a lighthouse in North Devon that we'd apparently missed. Being the committed lighthouse enthusiasts that we were, the idea seemed a travesty, and this glimpse at the map catapulted us off in the direction of North Devon - again!

So, after about six miles of Plymouth suburbs, we found ourselves on the outskirts of Dartmoor. The village of Yelverton was picturesque and, after a steady climb, we were crossing the bleak expanses of the moor. At Princetown we decided to visit a shop for the day's nutritional supplies and to relieve our bladders of the remains of last night's ale!

Princetown was a very grey place. The air was bitterly cold. It seemed a suitable place for Dartmoor prison, which overlooks the small town ominously. Who knows what grizzly characters lurked behind those stone walls.

It didn't seem long at all that we were across Dartmoor and heading through greener scenery to Moretonhampstead. This led me to wonder if there are actually any vast expanses of untamed wilderness in Britain left. On the map Dartmoor looks like a huge barren area, yet we were across it in under half an hour.

Perhaps the best way to appreciate scenery is not to use a car at all, so it passes by more slowly. Still, this is certainly not an area I would want to cycle due to its hilly nature; and walking inevitably leads to that popular hobby of climbing the summits of hills and mountains, which in turn, leads to parting with large amounts of cash for boots, clothing and equipment.

As far as travelling by car is concerned, to experience true bleakness, one probably has to travel to the top of Scotland. Having never been there myself, for all I know the A9 could be lined with all the usual supermarkets and DIY stores like everywhere else.

Next, we headed for Winkleigh, via a series of lanes re-classified as B-roads, and B-roads re-classified as A-roads. It all became so confusing that at one point we got lost. It seems a popular thing in Devon to re-number roads and still display the old number with a line through it. I'm not sure what exactly is gained by this; the road through Winkleigh resembled a lane, but I've no idea whether it was a B-road, C-road, cattle trail, motorway or whatever!

We eventually found ourselves on a particularly curvaceous trunk road, which followed a river valley to Barnstaple, which was familiar territory to us, as was Braunton.

We tried to find a lane leading to the lighthouse, and ended up driving round a load of back-streets. The first really bad sign was when we asked somebody how to get to the lighthouse, and found their response to be about as informative as a railway station information screen!

Eventually, we found a lane leading out to Braunton Burrows, which became a toll-road. The man at the toll-house told us that he thought there *was* a lighthouse. This seemed encouragement enough to part with some cash and drive on.

The road soon degenerated into a mass of potholes and terminated beside a sign prohibiting naturist activities, (the furthest thing from our minds on a chilly February day!). We then trekked along sand-dunes and dropped down, almost vertically, to the beach. At first, my Dad stayed on the dune, but when I was merely a speck in the distance, he decided to follow. He shouldn't have bothered:

As I rounded the head of the dunes, right at the end was a metal framework structure with a small light on top. This looked like the skeleton of a lighthouse, complete with balcony - in fact unquestionably, a beacon.

Across the channel two other lights flashed in unison. They looked more like lighthouses, but on the map, they were shown as beacons near the village of Instow. To reach them, we would have to drive about twenty miles, even though they were under a mile away as the crow flies. Speaking of the crow, the place where we stood is known as Crow Point.

Returning to the car, I then noticed that the lighthouse on the map was not where we had just been at all, and that a path made out of wooden slats led away in the direction it should be. An access path, perhaps?

So off we set again. Eventually this path disintegrated into beach, and as we wandered around a large wooden groyne with the wind howling at us, a mass of broken bricks came into view. It reminded me of the scene out of '2001' where the astronauts explore the barren landscape of the moon and discover a huge monolith - the remnants of an ancient civilisation?

The landscape was almost surreal as we trampled over these remains, which clearly formed a square base with a round hole, about the right size for a lighthouse tower to rise from. But where was the tower? Were Nature Conservancy unable to reclaim and maintain it when it was rendered redundant due to the reconstruction of the lighthouse at Bull Point in the early 1970's?

Sadly Braunton Burrows lighthouse has clearly disappeared forever.

And so, it was back to the car and back to Braunton for a quick pasty and milkshake, while we reflected on what had been an eighty mile long waste of time!

There seemed to be a foot and cycle path connecting Braunton and Barnstaple. However, the A361 was our conduit between the two 'B' towns. After Barnstaple, it revealed itself to be a splendid modern trunk road, which cut its way to South Molten and Tiverton in the same 'bridge and bypass' style of our own Hamstreet bypass - the A2070 in Kent.

So good is the A2070 that motorcycle magazines actually recommend using the road for speed trials. The bikers obviously heed this advice, as large numbers have been arrested for travelling at speeds in excess of 150mph on this road.

In Britain, we don't celebrate our roads enough. Think of all the American songs there have been written about roads. The blues song 'Highway 51' and of course Mr Dylan's 'Highway 61 revisited'. You can even 'get your kicks on route 66'. The nearest thing to any of that in Britain is down to those West Country bards 'the Wurzels' again, with their classic hit 'Rock around the A38!'

Mind you, the M25 has made it into a Chris Rea song - who can forget 'The road to hell'?

After a graceful sweep down off of the hillside, we left this monument to modern road-building and headed into Tiverton, which had terraced houses, industrial estates and a confusing road system.

We bought a few items of nominal value in a supermarket, purely to make use of the free parking while we explored the town. After much searching, we found a pub, which we decided to reside in, in spite of clear signals that the woman in charge was giving off that she really didn't want the aggro. I call this 'service with a snarl!'

A routine was now beginning to emerge. After each exhausting day, we would arrive at our room gasping for a cup of tea. My Dad would frantically fill the kettle and infuse the bags with an army-like precision. Then we would relax with our feet up on the beds, allowing the intake of tannin to lull us into a 'comatose' state of rest for a few hours, after which we would be ready to search for a suitable place to eat, with the usual scrutiny and lack of decisiveness. This evening's foray was no exception.

Tiverton is a small town with a lot of history, much of it bloody, going back to the War of the Roses and beyond. Tiverton's own MP, Viscount Palmerston enjoyed two terms as Prime Minister in the mid-nineteenth century. It seemed that after this, the town did not grow at the rate of its neighbours, Taunton and Exeter.

The town, of course, has the ubiquitous one-way system, shopping centre and newly-built houses. However, this evening, both the town centre and the local hostelries were quiet; and we soon found out why.

Round a corner, by the river, we found another westerly outpost of a national pub chain. The range of beers and competitive pricing of ale and meals mean that, in a local environment, small traders have to run to keep pace. It was doing brisk business.

As we enjoyed fish and chips, a steady stream of expletives was emanating from a gang of young males hanging around the fruit machine.

It seemed odd to hear such frequent use of the 'F' word in West Country accents. I used to think that London and the South-East shared the monopoly on this word's usage, with northern cities like Newcastle and Glasgow coming a close second. But no, its use is ubiquitous - an indispensable facet of the English language, to be sprinkled liberally in every sentence from Land's End to John O'Groats; and to precede every noun from Dungeness to Dunnet Head!

And while we're on the subject of this particular profanity, did you know that its first recorded use was as early as 1503? So next time you think it's 'hip and trendy' to misuse such diction, try to envisage a bunch of sixteenth century farmers cussing their way through the day as they furrow the earth!

I was particularly astonished when several years ago, I read an article in the Times on the fifty most offensive swearwords. Actually seeing some of those words printed, without the aid of asterisks, in a broadsheet newspaper seemed, at the time, like the end of civilisation! Of course I was wrong: the world is still spinning and the words are being spun into use more and more. Still, you won't find any of them in this book. If that's what you want, perhaps you should buy a Bill Bryson!

We returned to our lodgings and guiltily slunk past the bar, where we had not even purchased a drink this evening, to our room.

The night was stormy and the effects of this were far more intrusive than both the loud water movements rumbling through the pipes, and the high revs, squealing brakes and one hundred decibel 'techno' coming from the boy-racing fraternity.

The inn-sign groaned, clanked and vibrated in the wind. At times it seemed that it would be whisked away, taking half our bedroom wall with it. Perhaps it was some retribution for our lack of generosity.

The sign survived. So did our wall.

Lymington Liaison

22/23) PORTLAND BILL (old high and low lights - both
        redundant)
24)   PORTLAND BILL* (4 white group flashes every
        20 secs)
25)   PORTLAND HARBOUR (breakwater light)
26)   ANVIL POINT* (white flash every 10 secs.)

The next day the chastened men ate a hearty breakfast and were soon on their way to Honiton.

By now, you may have noticed that I have more than a passing interest in roads. I'm not the only one. On local news reports I've seen a man who paints pictures of bridges on the A27; the author of a book all about the A272 called 'Ode to a road'; and two men who have videoed the whole of the M25. I actually bought that video out of curiosity, and found myself catapulted into the seedy world of road-movies. No, not movies like 'Easy rider' and 'Duel'; I'm talking movies like the 'B2067' and 'A28!'

For I found myself inspired to set my camera up on a tripod in the passenger seat of my car, and film various routes in my local area for posterity. As time went by, I perfected this bizarre hobby by taking into account such things as light-direction, traffic-flow and 'optimum speed to reduce camera-wobble!'

There are now whole programmes on TV covering this field of entertainment - 'Police stop', 'Police camera action', 'Police arrest speeding motorcycles on the Hamstreet bypass'...

OK, I made the last one up, but it has potential doesn't it?

The very first time I tried to film such a journey, it had been a day of torrential rain and floods. We came flying round a corner on a major trunk route with camera rolling, to find a middle-aged woman with parked car, changing her trousers in the middle of the road! Little did she expect to be making her film debut strolling around in her underwear in the middle of the Folkestone to Honiton trunk road! This brings me neatly back to Honiton - a small town of around five thousand inhabitants (compared with Folkestone, at the eastern end of this major route, which has fifty thousand inhabitants).

The A35 begins with a steep hill, climbing its way up out of the Honiton Valley, then gliding through some very attractive countryside via Wilmington - a quaint Devon village with thatched-roof cottages. Axminster is bypassed with a flourish, but for us, things slowed down considerably around Charmouth and never really picked up again. Around here you can see the back of 'Golden Top' which is claimed to be the highest cliff on the South Coast.

Turning off at Burton Bradstock, the blind summit 'switch-back' type road soon descended steeply to Abbotsbury, a very attractive place where all walls are stone. This was preceded by a smashing view of Chesil Beach - an eighteen mile long bank of shingle which leaves the shore at this point, isolating a watery lagoon behind it all the way to the Isle of Portland. Soon caravans dominated the landscape and we found ourselves in Weymouth.

Portland is an island with three lighthouses and at least three suicidally dangerous drivers. During the next hour we would be subjected to the worst mannered motorists that we encountered anywhere in our ten thousand mile adventure that this tome encompasses.

Now this team of driver and video-man/navigator have driven some two thousand miles in the USA and have noticed how disciplined and patient American drivers are. This may be due to the fact that if you exceed a twenty minute parking regulation by five minutes you are severely reprimanded by a gun-toting official, so perhaps a more serious offence like speeding could lead to a 'once in a lifetime' encounter with 'old sparky!'

On Portland, however, this is clearly not the case:

Firstly, before we even crossed onto the island, a boy-racer flew by us, not just breaking the 30mph speed limit through the suburbs of Weymouth, but smashing it to smithereens and driving all over the pieces!

Then, in Fortuneswell, a lorry tried to pull out in front of us, but as the next stretch of road was a long steep hill, we thought it not unreasonable for him to wait a few seconds. He responded by leaning on his horn for about two minutes, punching out a steady rhythm, punctuated with long blasts of up to thirty seconds in length. Maybe if we had listened to the pattern of long and short blasts more carefully, we would have realised he was spelling out something very rude in

Morse code that could have well topped the list in a recent swearing survey!

Next, at Portland Bill, some young Herberts in a BMW overtook us at about 60mph round a blind bend. This was unquestionably a gamble akin to playing Russian roulette with the Grim Reaper!

Finally, coming back off the island, we pulled over to view the lighthouse on Portland Harbour breakwater. As I crossed the road, at least half a minute from impact with the nearest car, I received an angry blast of the hooter from about a quarter of a mile away!

Once again I had to revise my views on bad behaviour. Like swearing, London and the South-East do not have the monopoly of lunatic drivers. In fact, these Dorset boys could eat our mobile maniacs for breakfast!

Bad attitude isn't confined to the roads either. We called into a shop at Easton for some refreshments, and when my Dad asked for the latest lottery result, it was met with the silent handing over of a piece of paper and the kind of scowl you would expect if you had just ram-raided the shop with a manure lorry!

Anyway, like I said, there are three lighthouses at Portland Bill.

Before encountering the main lighthouse, we passed the old upper and lower lights that it replaced. The upper light consists of a squat tower with its light compartment appearing as if behind black bars. The lower light is now used as a bird observatory, and is a tall, white tower with a handful of windows at various levels.

This pair were built in 1869 to replace earlier towers which were often not lit until two hours after sunset, much to the consternation of the sailors. The original patent for a lighthouse at Portland was issued in 1716.

And so to the southerly tip of the island where the present 1906-built lighthouse stands triumphantly. Its 135-foot tower, which narrows with height, is white with a red middle band. The flash sequence is unusual in that you will see between one and four flashes depending on your position at sea.

We had first visited this promontory almost a decade previous. At that time, there was a small, sandy car-park with no charges, set among undulating grassland with a little refreshment cabin - a pleasure to behold after the drive around the stone quarry sites.

It was the pleasing sight of the red and white lighthouse planted amidst this scenery that first sowed the seed that propagated into this mission. However, there is now a huge 'pay and display' car and coach park. This bland concrete oblong does nothing to enhance the wild windswept location.

As we rounded the lighthouse by foot along the cliff-edge, we found that the Portland weather was toady, as inhospitable as four of its drivers and one of its shop assistants! Soon the icy blasts were ushering us back to the car for a pork pie, with a slight sense of disappointment that the lighthouse centre had not been open to provide some respite.

As for Portland Harbour light, this is a tall, round, white tower situated at the southern end of the offshore breakwater, which can be seen from the main road crossing onto or off of the island. Another zoom-lens job, inaccessible to landlubbers like ourselves. First light here: 1851.

Back on the mainland, after a mile or so of suburbs, one descends Boot Hill to Weymouth dock area. Here rail lines run along the roads like tramways, where trains used to run passengers to the ferries for the Channel Islands and St Malo, France.

The seafront is a sweeping curve from the clock-tower to the hills at Preston. Soon the caravan parks are well behind us and we're back in thatch-country.

Bypassing Wareham, the village of Corfe is like a haven in the barren heathland, with its ruined castle overlooking from its high mound.

Swanage is a smallish town with a picturesque bay. From here, we climbed up the hillside along a lane to Durlston Head Country Park, which has a car-park, toilets and a shop. A sign enticed us away from such attractions with the simple words 'To Anvil Point Lighthouse'.

We could see the lighthouse almost straight away, but between our 'Holy Grail' and us, was a valley, which the path had to skirt around. We passed the remains of an old stone-mine. Here, a cart was pulled up and down the track, which ran deep into the mine, by a horse turning an axle to wind or unwind the rope. The trouble was that sometimes the rope was allowed to unravel itself and many men plunged to their deaths.

As we pressed stoically on, a strange thing happened; a large yellow ball appeared in the sky and began emitting light and warmth.

What's more, the sky had turned a bizarre blue colour, and by the time we realised that we were experiencing a rarely-seen phenomena known as 'sunshine', we were at the 1881-built lighthouse which was opened by Neville Chamberlain's Father.

It was surrounded by a stone wall and had a stumpy, white tower which mustered 40 feet in height. In front was a separate foghorn structure, like a stone lattice.

The plan was to find somewhere to stay in Swanage, but it was still early in the afternoon and, although my Dad and myself had a difference of opinion about the amount of time we should spend in 'rigor mortis' mode (i.e. chilling out on a hotel bed), we eventually decided to bite the bullet and get the ferry to Poole.

This was another 'King Harry' style ferry, which took us across the mouth of the second largest natural harbour in the world. To our west was Brownsea Island - the location of Baden Powell's first scout camp, and also one of the few places where the red squirrel continues to thrive.

Strong currents drifted in from the English Channel as this slab of metal transported us from the marshland at Studland, to the area that a newspaper report of August 2001 stated as the fourth most expensive area for property in the world. This was Sandbanks, a salubrious area with a hotel lined bay.

Within minutes we were driving through 'granny-city' or the retirement conurbation of Poole, Bournemouth and Christchurch. The leafy suburbs of Bournemouth maintained the middle-class feel of Sandbanks, but once one has left the efficiency of the A338 for the slow-moving traffic jam through Christchurch, that perception dissipates a little, along with the prospect of getting Hurst lighthouse in before it gets dark.

The problem is, that Hurst is located a mile out to sea on a long spit of shingle. It would be the equivalent of walking half-way to the Isle of Wight. So my Dad abandoned his policy of 'once we reach Bournemouth, we may as well drive home', and after looking at the attractive village of Milford-on-Sea, we headed for Lymington. Here, we found ourselves at the mercy of an assertive salesman. One minute we were asking the price of a room, and the next minute, before we'd had time to think about it, we were signing bits of paper and being told where to park the car.

Nevertheless, it was a very comfortable place to stay and the rooms were all named after previous inhabitants of varying degrees of fame. It even had an electric gate to welcome us.

OK, time to settle down in front of the television in our room to watch the news. Now, in Kent, we were used to getting a two minute weather report, being delivered at about five hundred words-per-minute, with the weatherman seemingly incapable of responding to any good-natured jibes that the presenters made before his appearance. And, no matter how dire the forecast was, it would end with a non-committal 'sunny spells!'

But here, in Lymington, we were watching the self-same forecaster being broadcast 'live', taking his time and even enjoying a bit of lively banter with the newsreaders! So with lively banter in mind, we headed down to the bar for a pint.

Having walked several lengths of Lymington High Street, we found ourselves at the dock. Here, the boats were of a different ilk to the ones we saw at Brixham, or Fowey. These were the kind of boats that cost the same as a small house.

We were startled as a train thundered across the harbour in the dark to its terminus, like some ghostly apparition, and so we dived into ours - the nearest alehouse.

My Dad found it equally surprising, when rather than opting for the usual gargantuan portion of red meat, I enjoyed two starters - a prawn cocktail and the pate. And that was dinner.

And so back to base for a final pint before bed.

A young drunk decided to approach us with some friendly chat, asking where we were from. When we said 'Kent', he made the intelligent observation that it sounds like a very rude word that topped a list of profanities in a recent survey, yet has apparently been around since the year 1203! Apart from that he had no further recollections of the county.

The barman was unaware that this had been the best entertainment since the lively weather forecast a few hours ago and tried to lure him away from us, telling him to go to another pub where there was a 'great disco!'

Glancing through the back door, we could see the 'great disco' in action, with patrons dancing frenetically, waving their arms and legs around in a completely uncoordinated fashion, flailing maniacally somewhere near the brink of hyper-ventilation!

We watched as various limbs appeared and disappeared randomly in the doorway. The fact that we could hear nothing of the musical catalyst for this behaviour made it seem a little like watching an old silent movie at three times the normal speed. Eventually, we allowed our friend to join the revelry and retired gracefully to bed.

Shoreham 'Lights'

27) HURST POINT* (4 white/red flashes every 15 secs)
28) SOUTHSEA
29) LITTLEHAMPTON (harbour light)
30) SHOREHAM-BY-SEA

During our night in Lymington, the phenomenon known as 'sub-conscious lighthouse-induced stress' manifested itself again. This time it was my Dad's turn, having a dream in which everything he encountered was named after 'Smeaton!'

Then, over breakfast, a liberal dose of caffeine proved sufficient to relinquish this phobia and obliterate Smeaton's name from our minds for long enough to gain an insight into Lymington during working hours.

As we reclined with our bacon and eggs, we saw busy people merrily strolling to work, but there was something unusual - everybody was alone. Apart from a woman with a pushchair, we didn't see a single couple, group of colleagues, pair of friends or family, in the whole half hour we sat there observing. And who knows, the pushchair was probably empty anyway!

Our observations were brought to a halt by us realising that we were the only two there and the three staff were becoming fidgety!

Lymington did not feel at all like a town of nearly forty thousand inhabitants, but more like a middle-class country town of eight thousand. We saw no chain stores, industrial estates, one-way systems or run-down tenement blocks, and certainly no long, drawn-out suburbs either on our way in or out of the town. Where do all these people live? Underground?

And so, it was back to Hurst Point. We parked up, and for the next hour we would hear little but the rhythmic sound of our feet tramping in unison, as we made our way along the deserted shingle bank.

At the end of the mile long spit stood Hurst Castle which, to be honest, looked nothing like a castle, least of all a Henry VIII castle. The truth of the matter is that huge walls were built in the nineteenth century as part of our defence against Napoleon III, engulfing Henry's little round castle and extending a considerable distance either side. The result wouldn't look out of place in ancient Greece, being a huge superstructure with square inlets giving it a pillar effect, and smooth parabolic corners.

As for the lighthouse, it consisted of a 85-foot high, round, white tower. It dominates the landscape in the same manner that Portland Bill does, in spite of being smaller. It is also less tapered and slightly older (1867). The base is painted 'Trinity House' green.

The first light to be built here was in 1733. Later it was decided that a low light would be required as well as a high light. The purpose of having two structures is to guide vessels safely into the harbour. If the lights appear directly above one another, then the ship is on course.

The problem is that shingle shifts over the years, and eventually a replacement low light had to be built to show the new 'safe route'. Both of these lights were actually built onto the castle wall. This means that they stick out like a sore thumb to the traveller that has his eyes open. How *we* missed them remains a mystery; so busy were we following the disused rail tracks across the grass that we forgot to look up. We would be back at a much later date.

There are a few dwellings at the end of this spit which is a popular place for walking. As we left, around a dozen people passed us, walking in purposeful silence, as if drawn to the lighthouse by a pre-programmed plan!

Across the Solent we could just about see the red and white striped tower of Needles lighthouse on the Isle of Wight, situated at the end of a series of chalk-stacks, once a natural extension of the cliffs.

We would not be crossing onto the Island with its quadrangle of lights: Needles to the west, St Catherine's to the south, Nab tower just five miles offshore to the east and Cowes to the north. Tempting though it was, we stuck doggedly to the outline for the mission, which held us like an invisible force to the mainland. Apologies to the 125,000+ residents of the island; if I am granted the opportunity of writing a sequel to this volume, I promise we shall visit your lighthouses first. Even if the book is on the lights of Tunisia or Morocco!

Next stop: Portsmouth.

On our way we passed through Brockenhurst and Lyndhurst, a town which could teach Lymington a lot about congested ring-roads, in spite of having a mere fraction of the population.

By the way, to get a true feel of the New Forest, head out on the B-roads towards Beaulieu. I discovered this on a trip to Lord Montague's museum, one of several pilgrimages I made with a mate of mine to see a 'DeLorean'. This is the car that controversially received backing by the British government, in the hope that it would boost employment in Northern Ireland. To a certain extent it flopped, with only four thousand ever rolling off the production line. However, the 'Back to the future' series of films has immortalised it in the minds of millions. - If only John DeLorean had added the time-travelling optional extras that enable this stainless steel legend to defy the laws of physics every time it reaches 88 miles per hour!

Unfortunately for my mate and myself, the gull-winged, stainless steel legend was nowhere to be seen; but it did provide me with a second glance at the area and, yes, Lyndhurst was still clogged with traffic!

Soon, we had passed Southampton and were heading into Portsmouth. Southsea is an attractive resort, where a large green separates the seafront from the usual hotels, etc. Southsea Castle was built by, (come on - you should know by now), Henry VIII. The lighthouse is actually built onto the castle wall and this 1823, black and white striped addition rises a mere eighteen feet. Had he lived 276 years longer, Henry could have not only seen it, but actually entered it from within his own castle.

We left via the congested eastern side of Portsea Island and after Chichester, decided to give the A259 a bash - a grave mistake! Three massive jams ensued as we inched our way towards Littlehampton.

We had some difficulty locating this lighthouse, but eventually found it at the mouth of the River Arun, having parked and walked some distance, mingling with the elderly residents enjoying the late afternoon sunshine.

I'm not sure if we can legitimately call this a lighthouse at all, because it is merely a white structure with no round body to it. The light is viewed through an oblong window in the top section, which sits on a single cross-shaped leg, at a guess, thirty feet above the beach to the south; the river to the west; and the fun-fair and town to the north. There has been a light at Littlehampton since 1848, I hardly think this plasticky looking structure is the original! Similarly modern was the splendid coastguard lookout-station next to it.

After another thirteen miles of jam-ridden A259, we would find ourselves at Shoreham. At one point we tried to find a short cut through the back-streets of Worthing, but soon found ourselves behind a school-bus which, in turn, was stuck behind about thirty motorists who should have let their children use the bus.

And I asked myself this question, 'why is the Sussex coast so popular for retirement?'

After forty-five years of hard graft, I would prefer to spend my autumn years somewhere more rural, for the urbanality is almost unbroken from Littlehampton through Worthing, Shoreham and Brighton to Rottingdean and Peacehaven. Perhaps the appeal is the closeness to both the sea and amenities. I don't know, but the traffic system is clearly heaving under the strain of thousands of small cars making short journeys at slow pace through unspectacular suburbs.

Upon reaching Shoreham, we dived off up a one and a half mile long dead-end on the wrong side of the River Adur and observed that the lighthouse stood right beside the A259 itself. So we returned to that infamous road, parked, and filmed the reasonably tall tower, which appears to be built from stone blocks and has its own Portaloo next to it.

As we viewed this latest innovation in coastal sanitation, a group of youths wandered up and asked for a light, and soon they were merrily puffing away on something that didn't smell at all like tobacco!

There has been a light at Shoreham since 1825. There was a light for them in 2000!

And that was it.

Thirty lighthouses.

The entire South Coast covered, from Brighton to Bridgewater.

NORTH SOMERSET AND SOUTH WALES

Barred in Bristol

31)   AVONMOUTH (harbour light)
32)   PORTISHEAD/BATTERY POINT
33)   PORTISHEAD/BLACK NORE* (white group
        flashing twice every 10 secs)
34/35)   BURNHAM-ON-SEA (high light - now private
        dwelling, and low light)

The notion of South Wales in late October is not synonymous with most peoples' idea of 'fun in the sun'. So, being on isolated headlands in South Wales the week after the comparatively dry South-East had the worst floods in living memory, would appeal to most about as much as a bacteriological infection!

However, when you are exploring lighthouses you cannot be choosy; North Somerset and South Wales was the next area to cover, and October was the month, and surprisingly, the weather was quite favourable.

So off we set out of gloomy Kent, into drizzly Surrey and on into dreary Berkshire, when suddenly, half way through overcast Wiltshire, the sun made a brief appearance around Swindon - that old railway town that has reinvented itself as a centre of technology and, needless to say, the location of the Honda car factory.

We were not tempted to venture off of the M4 and see what our home town (which has a remarkably similar background) may be like in ten years time; and sure enough, the sun disappeared as quickly as it had appeared, as if its sole purpose was to entice us there and enlighten us (if you'll excuse the pun).

Soon, we found ourselves in the industrial area of Avonmouth, with its chimneys belching plumes of smoke into the sky, refining oil into fuel for trips such as ours. Somewhere in the midst of all this were, allegedly, three lighthouses, all located at the end of breakwaters.

So, as the A4 terminated at a roundabout, we headed straight for the dock entrance, where an official promptly came out of his office and declared it a 'no go' zone. We explained our humble objective to visit all the lighthouses in England and Wales and were told that there were none to be seen here and that the nearest was at Portishead.

Unperturbed, we meekly turned the car around and headed towards the Severn Bridge, trying every left-hand turn to get out onto the riverside. We were greeted by high steel-wire fences every time.

We then tried to reach the dockside via the village of Avonmouth, but found that this rather grim community of terraced houses was imprisoned by yet more wire fences on all the sides that led to the water's edge. So we were forced to abandon our attempt.

This particular trip occurred shortly after the country was ground to a halt by fuel-tax protesters, blockading oil-refining ports such as Avonmouth. At the time, it seemed as though this would be the first of many protests, therefore we assumed that when the next one happened, we could slip in with the pickets and take a bit of camera footage of the lighthouse, whilst trying to look inconspicuous by shouting things like "Down with fuel tax" and "Don't rip us off, Mr Chancellor". Then hopefully, we would be able to slip back out again unnoticed and unscathed.

Of course no further protests have taken place and we are still plotting a way to get into the place.

So, it was off over the M5 bridge crossing the River Avon and into Portishead, which I had imagined to be a similar affair to Avonmouth - industrial and not at all nice, but we found it to be a pleasant, green town. Now I understand why a well-known music group would want to name themselves after this place. Perhaps I should start a music group and call it 'Avonmouth' and sing 'green' protests songs about industry and pollution!

We drove around narrow, rural lanes on the headland above the dockside, parked by a pub and wandered down some steps to a wide breakwater, which we reached by climbing through a gap in the fence. The area was filled with people fishing, who had no doubt got here via the same unorthodox route.

The sun was shining on us as we peered across the estuary into the mist and gloom that still shrouded Avonmouth. Suddenly, a white topped, lighthouse-looking structure caught my eye; and thinking about the guard at the port, uncharitable words like 'liar' and 'jobsworth' came into my mind, and I had to push this bitterness aside because there were two lighthouses to be found in Portishead and neither of them were here.

So we headed for Battery Point, an area of coastal parkland, and upon leaving the car and walking up some steps, we were greeted by this square based beacon-like structure which was surrounded by scaffolding. I heard a mother saying to her child "Look at the lighthouse", which is not a description I would give it, but nevertheless, as with the one 'Avonmouth' tower we'd spotted from across the water, I got the camcorder out and immortalised its presence on eight millimetre acetate tape!

Next, Black Nore.

As we drove past green parkland with a slight autumnal yellowing to its foliage, we became confused by the one-way streets - one of the few things that Ordnance Survey 'Landranger' maps don't show. My Dad observed that 'the leaves were on the turn' while *we* kept making wrong turns.

We parked down a residential road and found our way down to the cliff-path through the suburban dwellings. After a short walk, we found it - the most lighthouse-looking structure we'd seen so far on this, our third leg of the mission – 36 feet tall, round, white in colour and basically the top half of a lighthouse on stilts! There was a ladder leading up into it via a roof-hatch, or a floor-hatch, depending on how you look at it. It was built in 1894.

We took a different route back to the car on a footpath, which passed beside the grounds of a large mansion-type building called 'Hidden Village'. Perhaps they should rename Avonmouth 'Hidden Lighthouse!'

We headed through a picturesque valley towards Clevedon and onto the M5, which was a more interesting stretch of motorway than the kind we were used to, mainly due to large hills like Brent Knoll that seemed to rise up like islands out of a flat 'sea' of fields.

And so to Burnham-on-Sea. Heading northwards from the town centre, the 'high' lighthouse could not be missed. Now part of a private dwelling, this round, white structure rose confidently up from the suburban roadside scene. It is similar to Hurst Point in appearance and size, but almost thirty years older with a construction date of 1830.

We then found a footpath leading to the beach, which was about one third of a mile west of the lighthouse. At first, we assumed that the sea had receded, but the buildings along the front did not seem particularly modern. We later found out that there have been both high and low lights here since 1832. The low light resembles a large box, complete with roof and windows, on nine legs in the middle of the beach, with a red stripe running vertically in the middle of the front, and a black stripe diagonally across the back.

One of the lighthouses here was built by an enterprising curate, who then charged a toll fee to passing ships. With the return from this, he established two wells and Burnham briefly became a spa town.

Out in the Bristol Channel 'Steep Holm' and 'Flat Holm' rose out of the sea, as if the scene travelling down the M5 had been replicated, except with water replacing the fields. Across Bridgewater Bay to the south-west, Hinkley Point nuclear power station could be seen.

We headed into the town centre and parked in the unusually named 'Technical Street' to explore the adequate High Street. We were surprised at the size of the centre, as Burnham isn't mentioned at all on road signs travelling down the M5 until you reach the exit for the town. We then had a hot-dog from the pier before leaving the sunny seafront for Weston-Super-Mare.

As we entered the town whose most famous export is John Cleese and perhaps, whose most famous visitor was Bill Bryson, there was a queue of traffic of epic proportions trying to get out of the place. The reason they'd all been there - an annual event comprising of 750 motorcycles racing up and down the beach.

We quickly found a very pleasant hotel and our room had a good view of WSM pier; and when we were tired of looking at the view, it had a huge pair of curtains that ran the entire length of the wall, to shut it out!

The stairs did unusual things too; a stairway would start going down and end up going up - fine in the daytime, but after six pints of Guinness?

Which brings us to the bar...

Seated with a pint of the aforementioned Irish brew, we found out that the motorcycle event covered the whole weekend and that many of the bikers regularly stayed in the hotel.

Apparently, the bikers were much better behaved than the rugby teams that had stayed there. Among *their* pranks were; jamming the lever down on a fire extinguisher and putting it in the lift so that when the door opened, an unsuspecting guest would get covered in foam, and; running around naked on the lawn outside, except for a flaming piece of paper inserted into the lower terminus of the alimentary canal!

Apparently, when the proprietor apologised to the other guests for this lurid behaviour, they insisted that he allow it to continue as it made great entertainment!

Thankfully, there was no such viewing tonight (except perhaps on late night Channel Four!). We decided to venture out for food, and after circumnavigating the town several times, we settled for a pub right next to our hotel. Isn't that typical?

After a Chinese chicken concoction, we retired to our hotel bar, where classic sixties and seventies hits were being played. This was enough to keep us there for another two pints, as we looked forward every three minutes to finding out what the next song would be. Yes, songs were three minutes long in those days, and a hell of a lot better value for money, in my opinion! I am a mere twenty-something and find the modern singles chart to be as dull and uninteresting as the combination of the weather and the M4 had been on the way down!

These days you have a choice: manufactured bands singing manufactured songs to computer-simulated backing, or the bland regimented thump accompanied by a naff synthesised melody that is known as 'dance music'.

Perhaps we have achieved about all we can in the field of mainstream popular music. Unlike Don McClean, I don't view 'the day the music died' as the death of Buddy Holly, but the week that a certain all-girl group had their first number one! I don't like to knock things that are clearly popular, but it just doesn't interest me. Mind you, I don't expect much of the singles-buying market will be particularly interested in lighthouses either. Or roads!

However, I am not alone. Music lovers in the U.S. seem to agree with me. For during April 2002 we were rewarded with the fact that the American singles chart did not contain a single UK artist for the first time since 1963. It would appear that the latest pre-packaged, cling-film wrapped balladeers are not cutting the mustard across the water in the same way that our genuinely energetic groups did forty years ago.

Which brings me to my Dad's party piece 'House of the rising sun', which I expected to issue forth from the speakers at any point. Alas, this was not to be, and my Dad could save his embarrassment for another eleven months. (Whitley Bay, prepare yourselves!).

And so, as the last orders bell sounded, we had to drag ourselves away from this blissful aural time-warp and get a good night's sleep in, in readiness for Wales.

Mumbles & Grumbles

36)   FLAT HOLM* (island light – white and red group flashing every 10 secs)

37/38) EAST & WEST USK (West Usk now a private dwelling)

39)   BARRY ISLAND (harbour light)

40)   NASH POINT* (redundant low light)

42)   NASH POINT* (upper light - white and red group flashing twice every 15 secs)

42)   PORTHCAWL (harbour light)

43)   MUMBLES HEAD* (rock lighthouse - 4 white flashes every 20 secs)

A new day dawned and our pre-cooked breakfast of the 'pick as many items as you wish' variety contained that rarity, black pudding. This set us up for the day, which began with us venturing out with camera and tripod poised towards the Bristol Channel to focus on a white obelisk which was glinting in the sun - Flat Holm lighthouse. Last night we had seen its light flickering across the five or six miles of water, this morning we could clearly identify the almost 100-foot tall, round tower. The first light here was in 1737, the light now is high-tech and solar-powered.

Somewhere further out into the Bristol Channel there is also a Trinity House light called Monkstone. This is near to Lavernoch Point in South Wales and due to its off-shore nature, wasn't on our list to visit.

So off we set through the WSM suburbs which seemed to go on interminably, with Victorian houses giving way to 1930's housing, 1930's giving way to 1960's, and so on until we reached the mandatory red-roofed little boxes that you will see on the edge of virtually any sizeable town in England.

And so, to the M5, which after a scenic stretch crossing the hills, was soon bridging its way over the River Avon, from which we gained a fleeting but tantalising glimpse of two of the port-side lights.

Somewhere amongst the jumble of cranes and industry, there is even a retired octagonal lighthouse, according to my set of 1920's cigarette cards. Perhaps the reason my most up-to-date information comes from a time when George V was on the throne, people danced to the Charleston and Britain still had an empire that would make even the Romans green with envy, is because nobody has ever got in there since!

Perhaps it's like 'Area 51' in the US where staff are sworn to secrecy about what lies within. For those who have never seen an episode of the 'X-Files', 'Area 51' allegedly contains proof that UFOs exist, but the FBI doesn't want to share its captured flying saucers with the public due to the hysteria such knowledge would create. Still, there was nothing inter-galactic about the UFOs here - they were merely 'Unidentifiable Flashing Obelisks!'

My mind began to fill with uncharitable expressions strangely accompanied by the image of the guard at the port who had told us that there were no lighthouses to be seen! How dare he put the safety and security of the port before a grandiose mission such as ours! These thoughts lasted for the duration of the M49 and were interrupted by my Dad's triumphant rendition of a Welsh anthem as we traversed the newer of the two bridges over the UK's longest river - the Severn, into Wales.

Coming down off of the M4 like a jet-aircraft landing in another country, it is hardly surprising that we missed the lighthouse at Black Rock near Sudbrook, a little to the north of us. A return visit would one day be in order! Instead, we found ourselves in a bizarre area where rural lanes and fields intertwine with wide roads and industry. At one point the lane we were on abruptly terminated at a kerb, which was the pavement beside a larger road, clearly designed for heavy traffic travelling to the nearby steelworks.

We crossed this paradoxical landscape of sheep and pylons, trees and chimneys to Nash, beyond which the road abandons its course. A friendly Welshman told us the best place to park, and we set off walking along the stony tracks over 'Wetlands Nature Reserve'. Opened in March 2000, this was one of those strange areas that you often get around power stations, which seem to exist purely to show how nature and industry can survive together. For behind us stood three power station buildings which bore a resemblance to Battersea in the way their tall chimneys rose from square brick towers.

Unlike Battersea though, these buildings have not been used as the centrepiece for a 1977 Pink Floyd album cover, however there is a 'rock' connection, and that lies with the west lighthouse which we could view from across the River Usk, (which at 65 miles long is the UK's twentieth longest river).

According to an article in the Times (Sept 2000), an expert in music copyright law who used to work for Polygram owns the two-storey circular house, which surrounds the 28-foot high tower. The article also mentioned that the wedge-shaped rooms are rented out to guests for B&B. This is becoming an increasingly popular use for redundant lighthouse buildings. This one was decommissioned as long ago as 1922.

On our side of the river stood a more anonymous structure, East Usk light; at a guess, twenty feet high, it is surrounded by a white fence and has no accompanying buildings. The kind of thing you would expect to see on the end of a quay; a small, white, round light with a balcony around its light compartment.

So, it was back around the gravel pit lakes to the car. As we neared Newport, we expected to be crossed by a new M4 Southern bypass. It appears that this has not been constructed and the only distinguishing feature of the existing M4 was a short tunnel around the back of the town.

Soon precipitation began to precipitate, tongues tutted and windscreen wipers were activated. Well, it was Wales after all!

The last time I was in Wales was in 1982 at the mere age of seven. It was sunny the day we drove there and sunny the day we returned. In between, it rained heavily non-stop. To a seven year old who couldn't swim this meant a very real fear of floods; in the same way that global warming, climate change and rising sea levels bring a very real fear to a young man in his late twenties who still can't swim! Anyway, what do you mean 'climate change'? The climate clearly hadn't changed here in eighteen years!

Next up was Barry Island. At first we thought we'd missed our exit, but there are actually two A4232 exits; one they decided to show on the map and one they didn't!

Soon we were heading into Barry, which seemed to have a long suburban approach. After a strangely unnecessary one-way bit as we descended to sea-level, we crossed to Barry Island - famous for being the site of the first Butlins holiday camp. The island still retains a railway station. We crossed under the line, parked the car amidst the terraced houses, observed that the skies were now cloudless and set off walking down a narrow road to the dock.

Across the boat-filled harbour, we could see the lighthouse on the end of a stone jetty but could not find a way onto it. We asked a fisherman for advice and found him to be genuinely fascinated by our mission, and if we could have taken advance payment for this book, I'm sure he would have swiped his credit card for us there and then!

As this sea-dog reeled off the names of lighthouses that we should have visited, we responded with a 'yes,' 'no' or bemused 'where?'. He seemed to have a particular fascination with Trevose Head, which he name-checked at least three times! Soon, we were being led through private property and found ourselves on the jetty. The lighthouse was white, partially rusted and the usual quayside size and height. We had to view it through tall metal railings erected, presumably, to keep nosy people like ourselves from reaching the end of the jetty, which appeared to be in an advanced state of decay.

Speaking of rails, there were rusted rail tracks running the length of this breakwater. We wondered if long ago, coal had been transported here from the Welsh Valleys to be loaded onto ships. The fisherman was adamant that this was not the case and recommended popping into the local library to check out a publication on the town's history. Had we been with Bill Bryson, I'm sure we would have heeded this advice. Instead, we returned to the car and consumed a pork pie and milkshake!

For our reader, who may consider the last remark to have been made in a flippant manner, it would appear that the railway track had been extended from Barry Island station in the late 1890's via a 280 yard long tunnel, (now bricked up), to provide a connection for boat services to Bristol, the last of these running as recently as 1971.

Out into the Bristol Channel, behind the lighthouse, we had gained a second view of the light on Flat Holm, which is actually in Wales. It seemed rather lacking in achievement that we had been viewing this from the other side first thing this morning. All in all, as the crow flies, we had covered but a mere fifteen miles; a fact to make us down our strawberry flavoured milk-drinks as if they were a yard of ale, and head off to Nash Point.

The B-road was a fairly speedy affair, with only one winding section around a large industrial building and under a stone railway bridge.

Llantwit Major was confidently bypassed and soon we were back on lanes around St.Donats and Marcross, from which the lighthouse was sign-posted.

There was a steep ravine to the right of the lane. Then we rounded a corner and were greeted by the obligatory car-park, which we ignored, opting to park in the actual lighthouse compound.

There are two lighthouses here and the one we parked beside was the shorter of the two. Similar to the 'bird observatory' low light at Portland, it is a white, round tower over eighty feet in height. There are three windows at various levels and the flat top with balcony would indicate that the light section has been removed since it was made redundant at around 1900.

Passing the adjoining dwellings, half-way between the two towers on the grassy cliff-top is a small square building with the foghorns on top. A quick glance through the window allowed us to view the immaculately clean engines that power the compressor for the horns.

Both towers were built in 1832 after a passenger steamer was wrecked here in 1830. The easterly one is taller at 120 feet and has its own dwellings beside it. Unlike the low light, this tall, white tower (resembling Hurst Point lighthouse) has been modernised.

The blustery wind gave the 'cone' warning system good use, and at the end of the compound, a sign warned us of the 'dangerous cliffs'. This was basically an invitation to climb over the wall to look at them; in the same way that a weather warning will tell us not to drive in snowy conditions, but as soon as the white stuff falls, it is irresistible to go out to explore this temporarily white landscape - especially these days when, in the South-East it is becoming an increasingly rare sight.

However, I feel it is not yet the time for me to get the soapbox out about the climate change issue, because I think the sea conditions at Porthcawl will speak for themselves.

I remember very little about the journey to Porthcawl except that the skies were recharged with rain. The soothing music on classic FM was lulling me to sleep. It was one of those 'sleeps' where your eyelids close as if they have got lead weights attached to them and each time you suddenly realise they are closed, you open them with a jump, feeling wide awake again, but within seconds are repeating the action with your head beginning to flop about like a limp chicken

71

leg! This can be quite embarrassing on railway stations when you may inadvertently find your head about to rest itself on the shoulder of the boozy old man sitting next to you!

Still, the weather at Porthcawl was enough to waken the dead. Huge waves gushed forcefully over the top of the breakwater. The sea on the western side of it was a swirling quagmire of white undulating waves and foam. Amazingly, there were two people out on the end of the jetty, but we weren't going to follow their example and run the gauntlet of raging torrents pummelling up the side and over the top of the short pier.

The lighthouse on the end was a standard 'quayside' structure and was white with a black base.

As for the town, it was an attractive little place, almost resort-like in the area where we had parked. We were also surprised at the amount of 'granny' bungalows as we left via a more suburban western route.

Within minutes, we were streaming down the M4, which is interesting around Port Talbot, where it is squeezed between the mountains and an industrial chimney-lined dock area. It then strides over the River Neath, beyond which we descended from the motorway to go through Swansea, which for a city of its size was remarkably easy to drive through.

My Dad was still asking when we would be getting towards the city centre long after we'd been right through it. The road had seamlessly changed from the A483 into the A4062 and we were heading for Mumbles Head via a spacious green suburb.

In terms of traffic flow, I would put Swansea on a par with Plymouth - a big city without the big city feel. The number of towns and cities in the UK with a population of over a quarter of a million is in the high thirties. Plymouth is one of them although Swansea is not.

The sweeping bay to Mumbles via Black Pill and West Cross was quite attractive, as the sun had decided to grace us with its presence again.

Now, Mumbles lighthouse stands on a rock, just off of another rock, just off of a big rock called the Welsh Mainland. At first, it appeared that a bridge connected all three, but as we got closer we realised that it was actually a pier several hundred yards before the headland - an ideal place to park and view. There were cafes, amusement arcades and some firmly locked lavatories around the entrance to the pier, which a small monetary charge perturbed us from venturing onto.

The now solar-powered lighthouse is tapered, white and octagonal; a vintage 1794 structure restored in the 1970's. If you imagine a 55-foot high, eight-sided cone with the middle third of it removed, you will have a pretty good idea of the shape of this one. If however, you are not a geometry expert on drugs, you may wish to take a visit yourselves!

For vehicles, there is one way into the pier area and one way out. I think that the warning that the exit is via a steep hill is a bold understatement. 'No vehicles, except light cars with a strong engine and an extremely good handbrake' would be more appropriate.

Once at the top, we turned right and the road resembled a rocky pass for a few hundred yards before dropping back down to the sweeping bay back to Swansea. The nearby little town of Oystermouth was a very tourist orientated place, yet we could find nowhere to stay. It had pubs and restaurants by the dozen but there seemed to be no available accommodation; so we foolishly headed out into the rural void known as the Gower Peninsular, expecting to find suitable lodgings in every small village or hamlet that we came to. All we actually found was Swansea Airport, heathland and a network of narrow lanes.

Amazingly, in this sparsely populated area, cars proliferated by the score, especially at all the usual places like blind bends and narrow pinch-points. We drove through Gowerton and Gorseinon, which seemed a rather grim little town of Victorian terraces. By now, extreme tiredness was beginning to kick in, so we bit the bullet, hit the M4 and headed for Camarthen.

Along the M4 we'd seen lots of signs for counties we didn't know existed: 'Monmouthshire', 'City and County of Cardiff', 'City and County of Swansea' and now 'Carmarthenshire'.

In 1974, they decided to reorganise all the counties. Now, just as we are getting used to Gwent, Glamorgan and Dyfed, the old titles and boundaries make the biggest comeback since Rolf Harris sang 'Stairway to heaven!'

What I don't understand is that South Wales is not that densely populated, yet every town of any size has its own district or 'shire'. In Kent, we are used to a single county with well over a million people and perhaps several hundred thousand more on the way. Perhaps we should follow the Welsh example and strategically place signs along the M20 for each of our towns: 'City and County of Maidstone', 'City and County of Ashford', 'City and County of Folkestone', 'Dovershire!'

Not that I am advocating another shake-up. I know how much heartache the last one caused. People feel very strongly about these administrative boundaries and what they should be called. If you mention 'Humberside' to a Yorkshireman, you may as well just politely ask him for a black eye!

Having worked in a post-room for a company that involves itself in direct mailing, (that's 'junk mail' to you and me), I regularly encountered returned mail with things like 'North Somerset, not Avon' or 'Metropolitan counties have been abolished, I do not live in Tyne and Wear!'

Worse still, is when a letter went out addressing a couple as 'Mr and Mr'. It came back to us with the addition "Mr and Mrs please - we are not gay!"

Then of course there's the weird and disturbing things that people send in just to use the enclosed pre-paid envelope. These have included a middle-aged man's extremely disturbing portfolio of his twisted masochistic activities, and more tastefully, a hand-written working-out of the square root for a ten-digit number. Both prompted the question "Why?"

Right - Camarthen.

We found a nice inn with a spacious room in the main High Street, and after a succulent medium-rare steak washed down with a surprisingly smooth and refreshing pint from the local Felinfoel brewery, we stumbled across the latest innovation in pub entertainment - an Internet machine.

Now, I realise that I spoke a little cynically about the information superhighway a few chapters ago, but this may have been a kind of turning point in my encounter with technology!

First we put in fifty pence which obtained us seven minutes of 'What do we do?' 'Nothing's happening', 'Hit return', 'Type in anything and see what happens!' 'Move the mouse', 'Try clicking on search', etc.

After complaining that it was broken and getting a refund, the machine was switched off and on again, and in went another pound.

By now, we'd realised that the Internet is an exercise in patience, (at least it was in October 2000, which on a technological timescale is now aeons ago). It was futile to keep typing in different things and hitting keys; the proper course of action was to type in a website and wait... and wait... and wait... and at last something comes up. Usually 'site not recognised!'

Soon we were sampling the delights of the Trinity House website, which was very informative. This site contains a page of pictures showing all the Trinity House lights (and it was amazing how many we recognised already), along with plenty of historical info and technical data.

Having perused this haven for lighthouse fanatics, I tried to log onto one of my mate's websites. The result was a complete lock up and shut down of the computer! Perhaps the material on his site was just too much for the computer to handle. He later informed me that this was not the case, which was probably a blessed relief, as standing in a pub, not knowing what kind of deviancy may flash up on the screen has a high potential for embarrassment!

And this is perhaps as good a reason as any for a tentative approach to embrace this technology. It seems that many people seem to be fatally lured into browsing all manner of illicit material, (and I know, I've met enough of them). Perhaps this is in a curious, 'slowing down to look at an accident' kind of way, yet this unfortunate reputation the Internet has acquired is not enhanced by the many so-called 'entertainment' shows which are little more than an aimless trawl through the plethora of moderately disturbing sites.

All in all though, I think machines like this in pubs are a good idea - in terms of time, they are far better value for money than playing a fruit machine, and if used properly, could provide hours of idiosyncratic fact-based conversation, which has got to be an improvement on the usual 'TV soaps and football' stuff.

Searching Saunderfoot

44) FISHGUARD (harbour light)
45) STRUMBLE HEAD* (4 white flashes every 15 secs)
46) ST ANN'S HEAD* (white/red flash every 5 secs)

Camarthen could rival Tiverton for its night-time disturbances all-be-they fleeting. This is a place where they sweep the roads at five in the morning. And when I say sweep, I mean the loud monotone drone of machinery complete with flashing lights which could even rival the disco we watched from a distance in Lymington!

Mind you, I often find that such disturbances, rather than keeping me awake, help me to really appreciate the joys of sleep. Normally, one minute you are laying down at the end of a hard day, the next minute you are getting up to the prospect of another. A little light and noise helps you to appreciate the warmth and comfort of a nice bed.

Breakfast was unusual in that it contained no liquid. The two cups of tea we ordered never *did* materialise. We made no fuss, for we were keen to drive off down Camarthen's pristine High Street and continue our mission into the westernmost part of South Wales.

The scenery reminded me of Southern Ireland actually, with the A40 doing a very good impression of the N21 (yes, I know about Irish roads too!). Basically what I'm describing is a long queue of traffic undulating through a very pastoral landscape, crawling along the single carriageway to Fishguard like an overweight anaconda! In the end, rather than follow this slow convoy, we dived off up a B-road, which my Dad drove in fine 'rally' style, covering it's 24 scenic miles expediently, crossing the Preseli mountains and descending to Fishguard.

Now, the Preseli range is famous for supplying the blue stone slabs which were transported to Stonehenge on Salisbury Plain some 3,500 years or so ago. It is still a mystery as to how these huge blocks were moved a distance of around 180 miles and erected on a wind-swept plain in Wiltshire. When a few years ago, this feat was attempted to be replicated using only materials that were available to these ancient Bronze-Age peoples, the stones promptly sank in the Bristol Channel. Perhaps these primitive natives were a little more advanced than we give them credit for.

Fishguard was quite pleasant apart from the traffic filling its narrow streets. The port is situated a mile or so north-west of the town, and is reached via a modern looking A40 approach.

We parked near the marine centre and got straight down to business, walking out on the stone jetty. However, we could see that this was going to be fruitless. Most of the maps we were using showed the skeletal beacon, which looked like a short radio transmitter, as a lighthouse; but we remained unconvinced, and left this beacon sitting on its fat stone cylinder, and returned to the car.

At the end of the pier, we seemed surrounded by a still, calm greyness, with the lugubrious sky stealing all colour and form from the hills surrounding the bay. As we walked back, we met an elderly couple out walking. We got chatting about our itinerary for the day and learned something about lighthouses. The man told us that the light we were going to see at Strumble Head revolves on a heavy bed of mercury. This is, in fact, the norm for major lighthouses, as using a metal that is liquid at room temperature allows a perfectly smooth rotation with virtually no friction.

But before we could visit Strumble, there was another harbour light to check out at Fishguard, this one being on the end of the much longer breakwater running out from the ferry port.

The growth of Fishguard and the construction of its pristine new road bypass is due to the increase in sea traffic between here and Rosslare in Ireland. What we didn't realise is that it is easier to get into a maximum security prison than to get onto the breakwater, unless you have a valid ticket for the ferry-crossing.

Our attempts to reach it were futile. Parking in a road which just disintegrated into the grounds of a hotel, the closest we could get to view the chubby-looking structure, with bottom half stone-colour and top half white, was from within a caged footbridge crossing the railway line and the queuing lanes for the ferry. Steps led down to a short platform jutting into the harbour, presumably for disconsolate fishermen to sit upon.

Research revealed what our eyesight couldn't. The light is around 100 years old, is octagonal and built of concrete. There is a balcony around the round white section and another balcony around the light compartment. Its light is 60 feet above sea level, although a considerable proportion of this height is made up by the jetty it stands upon.

So it was back to the area known as Goodwick and off up a very steep climb into the rocky-topped outback known as Pen Caer.

We could see our next lighthouse from several miles away, sitting proudly on its bleak headland, turning its back on the patchwork quilt of green fields behind and staring confidently into the watery nothingness.

We parked up, and my Dad opted for the road-walk winding down to the steps while I cut across heathland. The steps led down to a ravine with a caged bridge across it. This time a metal-bar gate prevented our access, and we could only dream of running our hands along the bridge's hand-rail which used to carry a supply of oil across the ravine and into the basement.

Originally, goods including food, and even the lighthouse keeper himself had to be winched across the ravine on a boson's chair.

Steps zigzag up from the other side of the bridge to this rock lighthouse which was completed in 1909. It is round and white with a light compartment that appears somewhat elongated, seeming to account for a a good proportion of the tower's 55-foot stature. There are flat-topped keepers dwellings at the base.

The 4½ ton revolving lens was originally powered by a heavy weight descending on a cable. This needed to be rewound every twelve hours.

Converted to electricity in 1965, this is an energetic little light, we assume for the ferry traffic passing Strumble Head, flashing four times followed by a short gap, which was comforting on this gloomy day.

The wind blustered us back to the car, and off we set through the rocky-topped hills. Have you ever noticed how it is that you do not pass a car, person or rabbit for miles on a lonely country road yet, the minute you stop to pick a daffodil, World War III breaks out?

I insisted on stopping to video the view of Strumble Head from a distant hilltop; what I should have videoed was my Dad extricating himself from the lane-side bushes into which he had dived to avoid the flotilla of 4X4's engaging in their own personal hilltop sprint!

At the village of Letterston we stopped for our staple diet of pork pie/pasty and milkshake. Here we heard our first bit of Welsh being spoken by an old man in the shop.

The assistant switched instantly and efficiently back into English language mode to serve us. It was good to actually hear Welsh being spoken somewhere other than on the Welsh television channel S4C.

Without wishing to upset anybody (in the way that Ann Robinson did when she dared to dish the dirt on the three million-strong Welsh population), I wondered how many people in Wales actually use Welsh as their natural first language. After all, in this Celtic land the road signs are twice as large, containing a Welsh 'translation' for all place-names and instructions, right down to every last 'Slow/Araf' painted on the road.

Perhaps the cost of this is offset by the extra tourism it brings. After all, you feel that you are in a different country when you encounter such a proliferation of a non-Anglo tongue, albeit only on road signs. Maybe this was the reason that I would feel it necessary to watch whole Welsh-speaking programmes in a Saundersfoot guestroom the following evening! This was not merely to (perhaps ignorantly), laugh at the absurd sound of people shouting angrily in Welsh, but to savour the fact that I was in the land of the dragon, leeks and St David.

That neatly brings me to quickly list the lighthouses of South Wales that we would be unable to view properly from land, because out past the *town* of St David's is Ramsey Island beyond which stands the lighthouse of South Bishop.

About 20 miles further out to sea is another rock light at Smalls.

We were heading for St. Ann's Head (the south-west corner of Wales) and to our west would be Stockholm Island whose lighthouse we would only be able to distinguish as a white speck.

Finally, around the corner and just off the coast near Tenby, there stands a light on Caldey Island.

Concluding that section, which was a little like Jim Bowen on the darts quiz Bullseye inviting losing contestants to 'take a look at what they could have won', you now find us heading for St Ann's.

As we turned onto the A40, it seemed strange to think that this was the same road that forms Oxford Street in central London. But then it is the sixth longest road in the UK after all!

We bypassed Haverfordwest and picked up the B-road, which rambled its way across fourteen miles of unpretentious rurality, eventually running along a marshy tributary of Milford Haven to the little village of Dale, which has a long one-way system extending out into the countryside.

St Ann's Head was a couple of miles further along the lane, which in spite of running all the way down to the lighthouse, had a sign instructing us to park in a field about a mile away. We approached, somewhat dolefully on foot. I don't remember there being a Welsh translation of *this* sign!

The walk was a blustery one, heading straight towards the old coastguard lookout tower, which has had its rooms converted into guest accommodation. My powers of deduction suggest that this was used to be the high light, which closed in 1910. The lighthouse we sought was the rebuilt low light of 1841 - a hundred yards or so further.

Many people had walked down this lane to view it, but we were the only ones who assumed a divine right to ignore the 'No Public Access' sign and enter its courtyard for closer scrutiny.

The octagonal tower was a 42-foot dwarf. It had a rounded light compartment with a lattice window. The two-storey terrace to our left looked quite stately, and to our right stood the round foghorn building, beyond which there was a little heli-pad.

The first lighthouse here was established as long ago as the 1660s. Although supported by voluntary dues, its mercenary owners decided that it would be a 'nice little earner' to extract the odd fee illegally. The price they paid was the closure of their structure. This spirit of hostility is still in evidence today, and the stares of the workmen inside made us feel a little uneasy, growing in intensity once the video camera came into use!

As we wandered back to the car, the Trinity House helicopter flew off in the direction of Stockholm Island. Soon we were back in our Korean-manufactured cocoon, negotiating our way through the network of little lanes to Milford Haven, with its multitude of chimneys serving as a navigational aid like some industrial Mecca in this relentlessly pastoral and sparsely-populated corner of Wales.

'Classic FM syndrome' (i.e. soothing music inducing mid-afternoon tiredness) began to kick in again, so in the interest of staying on the road we decided to opt for a bit of pumping Radio Two instead!

There was an exorbitantly priced toll-bridge over Milford Haven to Pembroke. Believable signs warned of strong side-winds as we crossed. Then, after a fairly bland stretch of A-road, we found ourselves turning off for Saundersfoot.

Saundersfoot is an attractive seaside village, with its bustling harbour area and one-way system, (of which we did a complete circuit before parking), leading the visitor to believe it is a larger place than it is. Here we encountered the most unusually named road since 'Technical Street' which was 'Wogan Terrace'. This instantly brought to our minds the Irish presenter, who's dry and eccentric one-liners add a little bearability to the Eurovision Song Contest! And let us not forget his version of the floral dance which was usurped by the strangely more popular 'Bridgehouse and Rastrick' version in 1977!

The harbour and main centre nestles between two hills. Herein lies a cornucopia of gift shops, hotels and restaurants. One of these is called 'The Lighthouse' and has two blue and white striped models at its entrance.

In spite of giving us the impression that somewhere we would find a life-size replica, these would be the only lighthouses we would see in Saundersfoot. What we *did* find was just a round stone hut with a light on top at the end of the more southerly jetty/harbour-wall. There was a stone cylinder in the water, which looked as if it could have once been the base of a lighthouse, but upon venturing into a shop to enquire, we were told that there has never been a proper lighthouse here.

However, there were once two short stretches of railway here, both with an unusual gauge, precluding them from being joined into the main network. One such stretch ran from the harbour along the now shop-lined street below the northern cliff to serve the iron works.

Wishing to build up *our* iron for tomorrow's expedition, our minds turned to food, in particular - a nice juicy steak. We had a shorter than usual encounter with the black Irish stout this evening and retired to our guest-house on the hill early. A little Welsh television served as background noise while we perused our misleading maps and atlases that swore blind there was a lighthouse here.

Speaking of swearing, in the non en-suite bathroom an amusing advertisement for a lavatory cistern as patented by Thomas Crapper was proudly displayed. I had always assumed that the obvious slang word had been derived from his surname; a widely held misconception. In fact it originates from the Middle English word 'crappe' - for chaff - worthless rubbish. That's quite enough of that 'chaff' for the moment, to continue....

This amusing poster demanded filming, as seeing this was about the funniest thing that had happened to us in Wales.

Still, my video camera is no stranger to lavatories! No, I have not been corrupted by the Internet into misuse of my camcorder; I have merely picked up rather a lot of these sanitary receptacles inadvertently as a result of a desire to video our hotel rooms for posterity. As most rooms invariably contain a bathroom, and most bathrooms invariably contain a loo, they just seem to find their way onto tape! Hence the ritual showing of the video to the family after each trip usually prompts a few sniggers from the audience.

Of course this footage means that should this book fail to sell, I now have a backup plan - something purely for the eccentric British market along the lines of 'Hotel lavatories of the UK!' I might even win that annual competition for the most bizarre book title. And when I run out of interesting things to write about them, I could fill the remainder of the pages with stills from the video!

Perhaps not.

Gower Glances

47) WHITFORD POINT (disused)

Today we had breakfast with Beethoven, bacon with Brahms or tea with Tchaikovsky - I'm not sure which. Brushing my alliterative skills aside, I am basically saying that this morning, rousing classical music accompanied our breakfast.

We immortalised our names in another guest-house visitor's book as we left, and hoping that last night's lack of lighthouse had been just another one of those bad dreams resulting from the mental stresses of this mission, we wandered down to the harbour again, to make sure an 80-foot, blue and white striped lighthouse hadn't appeared overnight!

So to Saundersfoot, I say 'sorry' for not officially including your rounded stone hut in my tally. I am afraid that lighthouse number 47 is going to have to be Whitford Point.

Whitford was to be the big finish to this leg of the mission. An article in the Times had previously made us aware of this one, and we felt as though we knew it already.

So it was into the car, out of Saundersfoot and off to St.Clears, which is one of those odd places that appear on a disproportionately large number of road signs from a disproportionately long distance away. One of those places that, when you finally get there, you are surprised that you have just spent the last three hours counting off the miles to a nondescript hamlet.

The most famous of these non-destinations is of course Scotch Corner on the A1, important only because this is where the A66 decides to sever off westwards. We have one of these places in Kent too. Ours is called 'Brenzett' – a roundabout in the middle of Romney Marsh, with the Las Vegas-like attractions of a filling station and a 'Little Chef!' Even the sheep here look bemused!

It wasn't long before we were back in familiar territory, bridging the river to Gowerton and the Gower Peninsular. Once again, it seemed that the entire area's scant population had all taken to the roads at the same time, and as we headed further away from civilisation, we got our first glimpse of the rusty lighthouse, which appeared to be situated way out in the estuary of the River Lougher, or Afon-unpronounceable if you prefer!.

The road constricted itself into a single-track lane surrounded by farms, and when we realised that we could drive no further, we parked in the official car-park (a field), and braced ourselves for an epic walk.

Off we set down the lane following a tractor. The lane became a woodland track as it descended to sea-level, then wound its way through woods. It was a little disheartening when, after a mile or so on foot, a couple of vehicles passed us. Still, once we were past the house, we were on own, beyond all vestiges of the ubiquitous motorist.

The wind rustled the leaves until we found ourselves on marshland, which gave the breeze nowhere to go except to rattle round our ears. Then, as if to tease, we found ourselves led back into woodland again, then dunes and then - totally lost!

Regaining our bearings, we got to the beach 'proper', still over half a mile away from the derelict cast iron structure. Wisps of sand scurried along past our feet. Then came the rocks - uneven grey boulders and stones with little pools of water in between. It was as if we were walking across a giant bowl of 'grape-nuts' trying not to fall in the milk!

As we neared the lighthouse, the scale of its height became increasingly apparent - this was a giant of a lighthouse, 130 feet in height - perhaps the tallest we had seen so far. When the tide is in, the bottom of this structure is submerged by the sea. The newspaper article (16/02/2000) centred around the fact that it was for sale at the nominal fee of one pound, the only condition being that the proprietor spends £100,000 on its restoration - more of a hangman's noose than attached strings!

Apparently, it has one room and electricity, but no running water. Visitors are advised not to stand beneath it due to its decrepit nature - it has not been in use since 1926, was built in 1865 (replacing the original 1854 wooden structure), and is listed as an ancient monument.

As the sun briefly made its appearance, the rusty, cast iron panels had a brown shine to them, contrasting with the blue sky. It was interesting to observe the high water mark where the panels change colour, several feet above our heads. The remnants of ladders hung from the shell of its octagonal balcony.

Had we read the newspaper article more thoroughly, we may not have ventured out here at all. Apparently, the shore contains unexploded shells from its days as a firing-range in the war.

Reluctantly, we turned our backs on this neglected structure, and took a different route back to the car, walking for miles along the sandy beach, oblivious to what may lie the other side of the high dunes. Then finally biting the bullet when we thought we seemed close enough to the hills, we clambered over and eventually found our way back to the main track, and the car.

Finding a garage, we headed for the chiller and homed in on the pasties and milkshakes. From here on, I shall refer to these pink, brown or yellow milk drinks as 'Yuk!' This is as a matter of convenience and encompasses all brands and makes of this refreshing and nourishing product!

Why 'Yuk?'

Because 'nonsense' words beginning with 'Y' are used by at least two manufacturers as a brand name for these bovine beverages, and we don't want to recite any brand-names, do we?

Downing our 'Yuk,' we settled into our seats for the long haul home, adding a little variation by using the old Severn Bridge, now redesignated as the M48. In the early nineties, this 1966 construction was still the ninth longest bridge in the world (and the third longest in the UK after the Humber and the Forth). Nowadays, with so many other countries taking on ever-more ambitious bridging projects, it fails to even feature in the world top twenty.

The M4 reached a standstill as we neared the M25, so we opted for a detour around Windsor. The surprisingly rural scenery around Runnymede gave a distinct air of wealth and regality.

Then it was onto the four-lane free-for-all known as the M25; and home, with that usual feeling you get when you've been away, expecting things to be somehow different. Perhaps the addition of a new housing development, the modification of a road or even the appearance of a new shop? As this book goes on, I would realise that the complete opposite of this last possibility is unfortunately far more likely.

It's as if being away distorts time. Because the past few days have been so eventful, one expects things to have been as busy back at home, where in fact life has just sauntered along as uneventfully as during any other time-period of that length.

As that great Welsh crooner Tom Jones once sang, 'The old home town looks the same...'

EAST ANGLIA AND THANET

Crabby Cromer

48/49)   RIVER NENE (Guy's Head and East Light)
50)   HUNSTANTON (redundant)

The scene: Britain gripped by the next crisis.

No, not more floods or fuel tax protests, but foot and mouth disease.

Yes - 2001: The year that Stanley Kubrick's film of the Arthur C Clarke novel envisioned humanity challenging the very notion of space and time itself; leaving this weary planet behind to colonise the vast expanses of space, with the limitless bounds of science and ingenuity powering us forward into a new era of human evolution.

In reality, this was the year a whole nation was brought to a halt by blisters on the legs of farm animals! A country unable to explore its own countryside for fear of spreading the disease, or indeed, for fear of incurring a five thousand pound fine!

So, it was with this in mind that we set off to explore our next batch of lighthouses - from the Wash, around East Anglia and into our home county of Kent.

Luckily for us, most of these lights would be in the kind of locations we had recently become accustomed to, i.e. ones which don't involve trekking over vast expanses of rural land to get there.

So, off we set up the familiar route of the M20, onto the London orbital car-park and up through the breadbasket of England on the M11, past the swelling expanse of Cambridge and off into the true rurality of the Fens.

The levee of the New Bedford River was a huge bank to our left as we traversed the fertile plains. We curved round the low-rise hills at Sutton, then up to Chatteris, along its neatly curving bypass and onto the dead straight A141, which streaked off to a slightly raised horizon, a bit like one of those American roads you always see in films.

Soon we were coming into Wisbech, with its classic scene of old buildings on the opposite side of its curving riverbank.

The suburbs on the other side of the town were aesthetically dull, but before long, we were turning off onto a little lane running along the west bank of the muddy River Nene, with the A17 crossing at Sutton Bridge ahead of us, and a power station on the opposite bank.

Sutton Bridge was an unpretentious little village and after fuelling up on 'Yuk', we were ready to find our first lighthouses at the mouth of the river, which was about three miles further north.

There was a lighthouse on each bank:

Guy's Head lighthouse on the west bank, and the less creatively named East lighthouse on the...well, I suppose that's obvious really!

Both were built in 1829, ready for use in 1831. They were never lit. The original intention was for them to form a grand entrance to the port, which a BT worker told us had collapsed in the mid-nineteenth century. Whether he meant collapsed financially, or literally that it had sunk into the water, I've no idea.

The east light once housed the famous naturalist, Sir Peter Scott, who now has a walk named after him along the Wash to King's Lynn. The west light's claim to fame is that it was once a customs and excise post.

Both buildings are white in colour, with an octagonal top and a chimney pot. They are fairly modest in scale and height, and were kept at least thirty feet away from us by 'foot and mouth' restrictions. This point was reiterated to us by a farmer who was in the process of putting up prohibition signs.

The BT man seemed quite interested in our mission, and when we said that we were from the Ashford area, he informed us that he had relatives there.

Times have changed:

It was not long ago that you could travel anywhere north of London or west of Brighton and be met with the response, "Ashford - where's that?"

Now it seems, everybody has either lived there at some point, or knows somebody else who has lived in the up-and-coming Kentish town.

We drove the six mile round trip from the west light to the east via Sutton Bridge. It would have been a matter of a mere hundred yards if Hyundai Accent's could swim, but then, not even DeLoreans can do that!

There were boats being loaded with sand as we drove along the bank, proving that the area's status as a port isn't completely redundant.

Apparently, the coast was thirty miles further inland during Roman times. Straight channels like this one were dug in the mid-seventeenth century to drain the area, under the order of the Duke of Bedford; hence, a number of the channels being named after him.

With rising sea levels and climate change ever in the news, I would feel a little uneasy living in a reclaimed area such as this, on those violent October nights that are now becoming as much an annual autumn event as Halloween and Guy Fawkes night.

There are those that say that cutting emissions would harm the economy. But do hurricanes, floods, droughts and tornadoes not have precisely that effect?

I am firmly in the 'prevention is better than cure' camp on this issue, particularly as there *is* no cure, except perhaps another ice age! I can well envisage the 'Peter Scott Walk' becoming the 'Peter Scott Swim' sometime during my lifetime!

It amazed me that during the autumn of the year 2000, two stories dominated the news; the fuel-tax protests and the horrific floods. Yet, no link was made on any bulletin that the two issues go hand in hand. The problem is that you could tax people to the hilt on fuel, but with public transport receiving so little investment from either government or the companies that own them (companies that seem far more interested in lining their own pockets anyway), we are still not going to see any major change in people's lifestyles, although we may see a major change in the climate!

Then there are those who insist that the whole 'greenhouse' thing is bunkum (usually Americans!). I read an interesting article on the Internet which stated that the whole 'greenhouse effect' theory is a conspiracy to keep the public alarmed and undeveloped countries, undeveloped. This same report stated that global temperatures raised themselves by one degree Fahrenheit in the first half of the twentieth century and haven't increased at all since.

Furthermore, a TV documentary I saw stated that the earth's climate has been unusually stable for the last eight thousand years; this being the very thing that has allowed humanity to develop farming and civilise in the first place. So, are we simply clutching at straws trying to explain natural processes?

There are even two scientists, (and I'll leave you to guess their nationality), who are actually advocating increased CO_2 emissions to offset what they believe to be an approaching ice age.

All this notwithstanding, I still think we are gambling with an unknown quantity. Like the young BMW driver on the Isle of Portland, we are careering round the corner at breakneck pace with no idea what may be round there.

And what's more, the stakes are being raised. With the 260 million USA population refusing to sign up to any environmental protocol, what chance have we of persuading the two and a half *billion* inhabitants of countries like China and India to hold back their development by adopting 'green' policies?

Better learn to swim, I suppose!

Am I depressing you yet?

It could be worse. You could be one of a herd of cows we saw grazing next to the A17 in a narrow strip of land which was basically a mud bath with a haystack in the middle. This sorry sight seemed a sad reflection of the foot and mouth crisis, which had placed a restriction on these poor cows' movements.

Soon we were in King's Lynn. The centre is reached via a narrow archway. We were looking for a library, in the hope of getting some Ordnance Survey maps to aid us with our navigation. This historic town, in spite of the archway, did not fill us with the desire to stop and savour the atmosphere, for all the usual stores and road systems were to be found in abundance here.

Furthermore, the out-of-town warehouses and car show rooms seemed to drag on relentlessly, which surprised me in what I thought was a small country town.

The height of the Norfolk hills was an eye-opener too, with the long climb out of the suburbs and the A149's long descent towards Sandringham. The scenery wasn't what we'd expected of flat Norfolk, comprising of evergreen trees and gorse. It was as if this foliage had been put there just for royalty. Perhaps a past monarch had issued an edict that all royal stately homes must be situated in identical surroundings to give that air of regality. Immediately the servants would set to work planting conifers, trying to recreate Berkshire wherever the King or Queen was likely to go!

We decided to check out Hunstanton - or 'Sunny Hunny' as the

BT man had called it.

It was indeed sunny, and had just the feel you'd expect from a small resort, a little like Burnham-on-Sea.

After several diabolical kerb-mounting attempts at reverse parking which were being watched, to our embarrassment, by half the elderly population sitting on benches enjoying the Spring sunshine, we were ready to savour the general ambience of the place, which was pleasant enough to persuade me to part with some cash and purchase two CDs at a pound each.

I had no idea what was going to be on them, but was strangely intrigued by the description 'instrumentals depicting corporate power performed by small pop groups'.

Little did I realise that I'd just purchased over two hours of 'musak' intended for play at corporate presentations. The kind of functions where pinstripe suited managers would stride confidently to the podium and prepare to tell their employees what a great year the company has had, and paradoxically that next year must be even better;

"We must push our company forward, embracing new technology and forging new pathways to achievement".

Negatively rhetorical mumbles of "Will there be a pay rise?" reverberate through the audience, but not through the CD, which sticks grimly to its motivational task!

I have always believed that it's not so much what is being said at these presentations that instils company loyalty, as the free cans of beer and glasses of Asti Spumanti!

Hunstanton has a short main street and a wide green separating the town from the sea front. We were unable to see the lighthouse from the front and promptly lost each other around a block of toilets on the green. Whatever side of the building I went to, my Dad must have gone to the opposite - the kind of farcical scene you would see in a Laurel and Hardy film!

The lighthouse was about a mile up the road at Old Hunstanton. We viewed it through a stone archway which was the remains of an old thirteenth century chapel dedicated to St Edmund who, legend has it, first landed at Old Hunstanton in the ninth century, aged fourteen. This is the 'St Edmund' from whom Bury St Edmunds takes its name. He became King of East Anglia in the year 841, but was murdered in 870 by the Danes. Guthrum became King of East England and in spite of his associates being responsible for Edmund's brutal demise, he minted coins to honour the man posthumously.

This inter-Viking rivalry was all rather futile, as it was the Saxons who first gained rule over all of England. At this stage though, Alfred the Great was still struggling to extend his rule eastwards from Somerset.

After that historical interlude, I'll slip in some info on the lighthouse, which is white in colour and has a stout, rounded tower, perhaps forty feet high. It is attached to a two-storey house. Built in 1778, redundant since 1921.

Soon we were on our way across North Norfolk on the A149, in search of accommodation.

The road wound its way through numerous small villages with cobblestone buildings. At some of these settlements, the road was just narrow enough to surrender its white lines for a few hundred yards, and in one, traffic flow was constricted sufficiently to merit a 20mph speed limit.

Wells-next-the-Sea had promised to be an ideal place for us to stay. That's if the road signs which routed the place from twenty odd miles away were to be taken as an indication. We were disappointed, and I can confirm this place to be the worst example of rural decline we have encountered anywhere on our countrywide bonanza.

The High Street seemed to consist of a convenience store at one end, and an antiques shop at the other. All the buildings in between seemed to be private houses which still retained large 'shop' windows. This seemed to be the only evidence that the road had ever had the credentials to call itself a 'High Street.' If I've missed any thriving central business district bustling with commerce, I apologise, our visit to Wells was brief!

On to Stiffkey, a smaller place, which is occasionally pronounced 'Stoopney'. Its claim to fame was in the thirties, and concerned the Reverend Harold Davidson who became involved in the London stage scene. He was eventually stripped of the cloth for 'disreputable conduct' and was late for his own defrocking. Things went from bad to worse, as he ended up protesting by making himself a sideshow on Blackpool promenade, sitting naked in a barrel. His turbulent life came to an end when he was mauled by lions whilst squatting in their cage in Skegness. It seemed the lions' appetite for flesh had proven even more devastating for him than his own had reputedly been!

Further along our merry way, the road wound around marshland, with low grassy cliffs. An unusual feature of these North Norfolk villages were the cylindrical church towers, which we almost mistook for lighthouses! Indeed, many of the first coastal beacons were lit at the top of church towers. The parish church in Cromer (the town we would finish at today) once served such a purpose.

Next we encountered Sherringham. A narrow street lined with tightly-packed, old-fashioned buildings curved downhill steeply, with a view to the sea below. The verdict: quaint. There were shops here, but it was expensive for accommodation. This factor, combined with the thought of an evening in front of a big screen surrounded by yelling football fans, propelled us on to Cromer.

Cromer threatened us with accommodation at £42 per person, but we eventually found a nice hotel beside the road we'd travelled in on, which gently descended to the town centre. The damage here: a more comfortable £22 each, although there would be an extra £9 charge if we wanted breakfast. A greasy spoon beckoned!

So, we reclined at the bar and tried the Norfolk ale, which was very fruity in flavour. We chatted to a man from Cambridge about our mission before wandering into the town centre for food. This is when I tried three foodstuffs I'd never tried before - crab, partridge and venison. That was also the order in which I enjoyed them, with the Cromer crab being highly recommended, and venison being a delicacy I am quite happy for the rich to chomp away on at my exclusion!

There was also an unusual new concept on the menu – a 'healthy' kebab!

From my experience, kebabs are something you eat after a flagon of ale at the local boozer. On a cold winter's night, you will often get up the next morning to find that the juices from the meat have spilled out onto your coat, solidifying into a waxy deposit.

Now, logic tells me that eating this isn't particularly healthy, yet, there it was, larger than life in the 'healthy eating' section of the menu!

Some kebab vans now offer a free can of drink with the meal. This is referred to by most of my mates as 'the antidote!' The idea being, that you take the can home and keep it by the bed within arm's reach, so that when you wake up at 3am with the kebab-eater's symptom of 'glue mouth', you reach for drink, pull the ring-pull and blissfully wash away the Araldite-like coating of solidified animal fat from one's palate!

This consumption of liquid then prompts one to rise phoenix-like from the bed to visit the lavatory!

Furthermore, kebab shop staff seem to have a sadistic streak when it comes to the application of chilli sauce! It seems that if you say 'yes' to this fiery addition, you will find your kebab just hot enough that you get a burning sensation. If however, you say 'just a little', they will smother it with so much that the meat, salad and pitta-bread will all have no distinctive flavour except the sensation of filling one's mouth with the contents of a blast furnace!

I once dared a mate to down a small jar of chilli sauce for twenty pounds. Why I would spend such a quantity of money so liberally just to see a valued friend perform such a garish task, I still have no idea. But there we were, on a cold wintry night, asking for the van owner to fill up this quarter-pint receptacle with the aforementioned dressing.

After a reverent pause with the cup in his hand, my mate downed it in one. What followed was a series of shouts, gasps and swear words! The kebab man frantically sliced up a tomato for him to eat as a kind of anaesthetic, I reluctantly handed over the collateral, my mate prepared himself for a day off work and we were informed that this task paled into insignificance compared to some nutters who had asked to do the same with a pint glass of the stuff!

Anyway, in Cromer I had eaten sufficiently and it was back to the hotel for a final pint (that's beer, not chilli), and in the words of Samuel Pepys, 'so to bed'.

Wickham, Woodbridge, Where?

(or 'No room at the inn')

51) CROMER* (5 white flashes every 15 secs)
52) HAPPISBURGH (redundant)
53) GORLESTON-ON-SEA (quayside light)
54) LOWESTOFT* (white flash every 15 secs)
55) SOUTHWOLD* (white/red group flashing 4 times every 20 secs)
56) KESSINGLAND/PAKEFIELD (redundant)
57) ORFORD NESS* (white flash every 5 secs with lower fixed sector light on tower)

A new day dawned and the sky had changed from blue to grey. What's more, the air had changed from fresh to moist. Yes, the weather was back in default mode - drizzle!

We wandered into the town for breakfast in a cafe for a mere £2.50. An elderly lady called Dolly confidently introduced herself to us. While this was going on, I sat stunned by an article in the newspaper concerning a lady who described a £20,000 bonus as 'insultingly low!' OK, the point was that her male colleagues had received a lot more, but the connection of a lump sum of more than the average annual wage with the words 'insultingly low' was too much for me to see beyond!

Cromer definitely has my seal of approval as, upon returning to the car, we discovered that my Dad had left the keys in the door-lock, dangling like a carrot for any light-handed passer-by, while we had single-mindedly been devouring our fried comestibles, meeting cheery octogenarians and imagining what kind of obscene amount of collateral a certain lady's masculine workmates must have received as a bonus.

In any other town we would have found that we'd just sacrificed the car for two plates of bacon and eggs; and would now be looking for stations - first 'police' and then 'railway!'

After an interesting race, where a young man who had definitely not just taken on board a full load of saturated fat decided to run along the pavement trying to keep up with the car, (he did surprisingly well), we set about finding the lighthouse. From an eastern suburb of the town, a footpath discreetly led up some shady steps from the roadway before descending into a valley of heathland. We then clambered up a very steep hill, which gave us the impression that we were not following an authorised path, and viewed the 60-foot octagonal lighthouse, which was constructed at this point, half a mile from the cliff edge in 1833.

Upon the stout tower, which seemed about the same height as Hunstanton, is a balcony surrounding the thin round light compartment. The buildings are white and there is a single storey dwelling beside the tower and a standard detached house to the south. This lighthouse also boasts its own heli-pad.

The original light at Cromer, as I briefly mentioned earlier, was shown from the parish church. Now that's what I call 'spiritual enlightenment!'

So it was back to the car to continue our journey along the Norfolk coast. Small villages appeared at a high regularity. Mundelsey was one of the larger ones and had an almost resort-like feel to it. Later before we reached Bacton, we passed the huge terminal for the North Sea gas - as if there to suddenly remind us that, in spite of the quaintness of the last fifty miles, we were still in the twenty-first century (just!).

Church towers lined up on the horizon as one village followed another. Then between Happisburgh church and the next one, a red and white striped tower could be seen - Happisburgh lighthouse. I have been told that you pronounce this one 'Haysboro' and that asking an East Anglian for directions to Hap-pis-burg is probably like asking a four year old to outline the basic principles of quantum mechanics!

The 'classic' lighthouse tower is reached by one of those stony tracks with grass up the middle, and is tall enough to contain five alternating bands of colour, 110 feet I am informed. There are two private cottages at its base. Some locals informed us of its interesting history. There were originally two lights here built in 1791, but the lower light was removed when it was a mere 92 years old.

More recently, Trinity house wanted to close the upper lighthouse, but the villagers protested and as a result, it is open to the public on Sundays - today was not one of them!

Apparently this lighthouse had been featured on the TV show 'Challenge Aneka'. For those who don't know, this was a programme that featured an energetic lady frantically enlisting the support of various businesses in exchange for a little bit of good publicity in front of a few million people, in order to complete vast charitable works on a microscopic timescale. As a result, the tower was completely repainted, inside and out. Unfortunately, it was a bad choice in paint and a new problem resulted - condensation.

Two months after we visited, Happisburgh hit the headlines again. This time, an African vulture with a wingspan of eight feet had escaped from a zoo. It eventually decided to roost in a 60-foot high pine tree, but this wasn't until it had encircled the lighthouse a good few times. Recapturing the giant bird may have proven difficult - these creatures can soar higher than the average jet aircraft.

So there you have it. Every place has its tale. This place had a pair of wings and a savage beak as well! (Bad pun, sorry).

Next up: Gorleston-on-sea.

The B-road wound its way towards Great Yarmouth passing two types of farms; agricultural and 'wind'. As with most of the wind farms we would see along the East Coast, it didn't seem to be running at its full potential.

A recent plan for a wind farm, not too far from where I live, is really sorting the truly environmentally-minded from those who merely pay lip service to such ideals. After all, why complain about a wind farm intruding on ones view when, thanks to global warming, your whole area is destined to be engulfed by the sea in fifty years time anyway?

To redress the balance, I have been told that a vast area of land would need to be covered with turbines to produce the same output as a single coal/oil power station. Putting my mind to this poser, I remembered that seventy percent of the earth's surface is covered in water – what a vast untapped 'surface' that isn't in anybody's backyard!

Some would doubt the practicality of this 'shot in the dark' idea, but in the past science has always found ingenious ways around such barriers. So instead of genetically engineering featherless chickens and implanting pigs with spinach genes, (both examples are for real, by the way), perhaps the world's great brains could apply their intellect to more pressing issues like climate change before we all end up with weather like California.

No, not California, USA – I mean California, Norfolk! This is the land of chalets and caravans, a kind of transitional zone between rural Norfolk and Great Yarmouth. Today the sky was overcast, but we would be a little further down the coast before the rain set in.

At Great Yarmouth, we crossed the River Yare - the gateway to the broads, and continued into Gorleston, which is where the river meets the sea.

And there between the aptly named 'Lighthouse News' shop and an amusement arcade, rose a chimney-like structure - a brick lighthouse tower discreetly tucked away with its own little 'garden gate'. A speedboat whizzed past both us and the busy industrial area on the other side of the river out to sea. The lighthouse is a few hundred yards in from the river mouth.

The verdict - easy. We were knocking these off quicker than Aneka Rice could build a care home!

And so we crossed the border into Suffolk, and Lowestoft, Britain's most easterly point. We parked along a humble section of the A12, and walked down the stepped cliff towards the sea. Two yellow and black buoys fooled us into thinking we were at the most easterly point. There is another pair of these exactly one nautical mile north.

The cardinal point is actually south of both pairs, and is merely a slight bend in the exposed sea wall. There was a wheel-shaped declaration of this fact embedded into it showing distances to capital cities all around the world. A passing local described it as a 'waste of money' but I found it rather interesting. It still seemed strange to me that when we'd visited mainland Britain's most southerly point - the Lizard, two years ago, there was nothing to indicate its significance at all.

The shores of Britain are like the walls of a castle, and this is one of the points where the sea has declared war. The old sea wall had completely collapsed a few years ago. If the onslaught of the waves causes the pristine new wall to suffer a similar fate, our local passer-by may indeed be right. This project will sadly cease to exist and will have to take its place alongside the dreaded dome in the millennium ignominy list!

The incessant drizzle had now decided to up the ante and began to irritate. We found steps to the 1874 lighthouse which stood atop of the modest cliffs. It has a 52-foot, round, white tower with latticed light compartment approximately 120 feet above sea level. The dwellings on either side looked like normal suburban houses remaining largely hidden by the thin wintry trees.

It was at Lowestoft that the corporation of Trinity House built their first light, in 1609. There have been several pairs of high and low lights here; and it was decided to build the present tower when the high light proved insufficient structurally for the new electric light in 1870. The cost of this construction: £2350.

By the time we had returned to the car we were very damp, and 'damp' at this time of year also means cold. Wiping the mist on the windscreen, we espied a garage. There was only one thing to provide us with solace - 'Yuk!'

Although some maps had indicated the presence of two lighthouses located on quays at Lowestoft harbour, the traffic flow prevented us from parking. However the landlord of a local pub (that's local to me, not local to Lowestoft) has kindly examined these structures for me on a recent visit and my conclusion is that they are merely beacons. Please address complaints to...

Next in line down the coast was Kessingland, but without adequate maps, we wrongly assumed that this one would have to be reached by footpath across a ploughed field. So dire was the weather that we just couldn't face the prospect of heaving our way across sodden clods of earth, with our shoes indistinguishable from the terrain they were trekking over; so we put it on 'hold' and headed for Southwold.

This tower stands proudly above the Victorian terraces surrounding it. Opened in 1890, it was a little reminiscent of the one at Burnham-on-Sea, but more stately and found among quiet little back streets, unhindered by passing traffic. A 102-foot tall, white, rounded structure with small windows at various heights, pristinely gracing this pleasant seascape.

Southwold seemed the kind of place it would be nice to be mayor of, strutting around the place, being a real pillar of the community; in a sort of "Hello Mr Jones, how's your daughters leg?" or "Oi, you two scallywags, keep off the grass" kind of way!

The centre of this little town seemed to be thriving. There were some quite regal looking buildings at the southern end of the town where a lane led down to the mouth of the River Blythe. There were little neatly mowed greens dotted about the place and a lattice-windowed church that was almost cathedral-like.

And I haven't even mentioned Adnams brewery yet, the wares of which we sample later. Well, not so much 'sample' as 'consume voraciously!'

However, there was no time to ponder this idyllic whim any further - we were here on business. The tourist information centre beckoned and a map inside confirmed that there was definitely a lighthouse near Kessingland and that to get to it we would have to navigate the wild, uncharted terrain of a Pontins' holiday camp!

One thing is sure about Southwold - you are never far from a public toilet, which seemed somewhat appropriate for a town with it's own brewery!

So it was back up the A12, with a slight feeling of deja vu. This reminded me, for some reason, of the second in a trilogy of films where a flying Delorean ends up making a return journey to the year 1955. (When will somebody acknowledge those 'Back to the Future' films for the masterpieces they are?). *Our* future was back at Kessingland.

Eventually finding our way into the holiday camp, we headed for the south-east corner, where right in front of the 'gravel and puddles' car-park, stood our destination - Pakefield lighthouse.

With the Union flag waving proudly from the pointed top of this short, white, cylindrical structure, we were welcomed inside - for the first time since Tater Du in Cornwall (lighthouse number seven). Here, 25 months and 49 lighthouses later, we found ourselves climbing the three short flights of slightly curved stairs to the lookout station at the top, where among the charts and theodolyte-looking equipment we found a man willing to furnish us with the following information, proudly announcing "I know more about this one than anybody!"

Built in 1831, it emitted a red light which hasn't been shown since 1864. The building was sold in 1929 for £150 and may have even been used as a bar for holidaymakers in the 1930's. It served as a lookout station in World War II during which nine US bombers were shot down by the Germans overhead. It was thanks to a faulty gyroscope in one of the flying bombs that the structure still stands. The bomb pummelled into the sea in front of it.

In the peaceable sixties, its function was again recreational, with its possible utilisation as a darkroom for the holiday camp photographer. Since 2000, it has been a coastal lookout station.

The cliffs below have a legend attached to them, that being of

'Crazy Mary' whose fisherman husband set out to sea one afternoon and never returned. This rendered her insane with grief and she wandered into the sea to join him. Her ghost allegedly wanders the cliffs wailing for him.

The official statistic is that the light here is 38 feet above sea level, which although the cliffs it stands on are not by any means high, still seems lower than I would have expected.

It always feels so much more satisfying to have been inside like this - an oasis of information in a desert of partly absorbed facts and inspired guesswork! This lighthouse has all the home comforts with a kind of 'chill out' room half way down and a lavatory at the bottom.

Next on the list was Orford Ness, a lonely lighthouse half way down a thirteen mile long spit of shingle.

We headed south to Aldeburgh. Driving right through the town we found this feature of coastal deposition to be reserved for 'boat club members only'. Defying this a little, we parked next to a Martello Tower. For those who are not familiar with these, they are large round structures which permeate the South-East coastline from Aldeburgh to Newhaven in Sussex. They were built in the early nineteenth century as part of our defence strategy against Napoleon and are mostly concentrated along the southern coasts of Kent and East Sussex (an area I am rather familiar with!).

At least three miles away in the stony nothingness stood our Holy Grail. A little way ahead, we could see a gate with a notice on it. We didn't fancy walking all that way just to read a sign stating 'no access due to foot and mouth disease' - after-all, cattle always graze on shingle, don't they? No, we decided to change tack and headed for Orford.

After driving through a forest, which seemed a bit short on trees, and past a flooded field cunningly disguised as a lake for model boats, we reached this stunningly quiet little place. There was a pub in the middle, with a garage-cum-shop, an oysterie and another pub just before the harbour, which was a few hundred yards further down the lane.

An information centre, which was closed, clearly displayed the grim news that no passenger ferries would be running across to the shingle bank for some foreseeable time due to, (wait for it...) foot and mouth disease. Another sign proudly stated the fact that it is the second largest vegetated shingle spit in Europe. It was this vegetation that was the problem, and although I could see no bovine life forms grazing across the water, somebody had obviously thought that it still merited a ban.

So our visit to this red and white striped, tapered lighthouse was merely a glimpse from across the River Alde. Constructed in 1792 by William Wilkins and just a touch shorter than Southwold (almost 100 feet), it is a particularly tenacious tower in that it has survived raids, storms, machine-gun fire and flying bombs. The low light built at the same time met its demise in 1887.

This pair replaced older brick structures, which in turn replaced the original light of 1635 which was built as a result of 32 ships being cast up on the shingle one night in 1627. We would return tomorrow to train the zoom lens on it, but for now we were more concerned with finding some kind of hostelry.

The pub in the middle of Orford could only offer us a double-bedded room. We didn't fancy that, but did fancy a Guinness, thus delaying our search by half an hour – a critical amount of time with dusk falling on this cool April evening.

Out came the maps.

It's no wonder that our multitude of atlases don't agree where there are lighthouses and where there are not - they couldn't even agree on the size of certain towns! In some atlases Wickham Market appeared to be a reasonable sized place, yet on others it made Orford look like a thriving metropolis! On the other hand, Woodbridge was big in all of them, so that's where we headed.

We found it to be a quaint little town, with narrow central streets, where all inns, hotels and accommodating pubs seem to be

a)   of a price where it is necessary to re-mortgage your house for a single night's kip, or

b)   full!

A quote of £95 for a room was enough to send us scuttling away to Wickham Market!

The search began to get tiresome. Wickham Market had a square in the middle which you would expect to be surrounded with pubs, but alas, we encircled it, then headed back out again.

Where now - Ipswich?

No thanks!

In the end we found a nice inn just outside the town called the 'Three Tuns'. Not only was Southwold's own Adnams ale available here; there was also no need to renegotiate our mortgage arrangements!

The traditional 'chill out' ensued, and the relaxed atmosphere of the place allowed this to continue at the bar. The landlord began to chat to us after we'd finished our liver and bacon. We encountered 'Ashford International Syndrome' again when he asked us where we were from. Like our telecommunications expert at the mouth of the River Nene, our proprietor *too* had relatives living near the burgeoning megalopolis.

"Kent sir - everybody knows Kent," wrote Charles Dickens, " - apples, cherries, hops and women". Well, the first part's true anyway!

Ramsgate Reasoning

58/59)   HARWICH (redundant high and low lights)
60/61)   DOVERCOURT (redundant high and low lights)
62)   MARGATE (harbour light)
63)   NORTH FORELAND* (5 red/white flashes every
         20 secs)
64)   RAMSGATE (harbour light)

Due to the continuing restrictions caused by foot and mouth disease, this was to be a three-day excursion, and this third and final day would take us back to our home county of Kent via Essex.

But first, a hearty breakfast and a bemused look over the fence at a car-yard that seemed to deal solely in Citroen 2CVs of varying vintages. This seemed somewhat strange in this most un-Gallic part of rural England.

It was time for our second visit to Orford, for a bit of video footage, which was filmed with the speed and efficiency of a 'smash and grab' raid.

The car stopped, the camcorder came out, the tripod was erected, the zoom lens trained onto the lighthouse, a few minor adjustments to get the perfect shot, and... a camper-van parks right in front of us! In an empty car-park, the driver's choice of space to leave this monstrosity could only be put down to spite!

OK. Take two. More zooming, more adjustments, two pushes of a red button and that's it. Bundle the camera back into the car and hit the road.

The A12 by now had transformed itself into a dual carriageway, but at this stage it was still meek enough to merge into the A14 to bypass Ipswich. My only recollection of Ipswich is that car-park which spirals down like a corkscrew under a large round pool of water. At the age of five, I found this a positively terrifying experience, thinking that our journey up to Norfolk had become a journey to the centre of the earth!

I remember screaming as my Dad drove the car relentlessly deeper and deeper, with my Mum trying to appease me with the words "We're just going round some corners!" I was expecting to be swallowed by a steaming pool of magma at any moment!

Seven years later, we visited again. This time, it just seemed like a very novel way to prevent devoting vast amounts of expensive town centre land to parking. And now, almost thirteen years on again, what was once an essential stopping place on our way to Norfolk, is not even on our list of things to visit. Farewell to Ipswich.

My prized set of replica 1920's cigarette cards, features 'Landguard Lighthouse', a stilted structure on the point of land to the south of Felixtowe, overlooking Harwich Harbour (the outflow of the rivers Orwell and Stour). Our host at last night's inn had no knowledge of this structure, and our maps did not mark it either, so we were confident enough not to be lured from the A14, (which always used to be the A45), until after we'd bridged the River Orwell. Farewell to Felixtowe as well.

We were now headed for Manningtree, crossing the River Stour into Essex, a county renowned for a lot of things, of which being the English county with the longest coastline is generally not amongst. Amazingly, lighthouses are rather scant along this counties' 440-mile nautical frontier.

Say 'Essex' and most people tend to think of boy-racers and promiscuous girls with dodgy accents! The part of Essex we encountered seemed quite the opposite to this personification, providing us with an attractive, winding drive up and down the hills beside the river.

Harwich is not just a ferry port which operates services to the Hook of Holland, which of course accounts for its streamlined A120 approach (reminiscent of Fishguard?), but it is also the location of the Trinity House operations centre which controls most of the remaining working lighthouses in England and Wales. Had we known this at the time, we may have tried to find this pharophillic Mecca. (Pharophillic = of, or concerned with lighthouses!).

Parking in a suburban area of Victorian housing, the upper light could not be missed, its location being beside the road, 150 yards from the sea, which lies beyond a large green. It is a thin, octagonal tower of brownish bricks, with a flight of steps around it leading up to the door – an irresistible urge possessed me to climb these.

It is a substantially tall structure, which also marks the end of the 'Essex Way', a seventy mile long footpath, which begins at Epping.

Beside the sea is the low light. This is a squat, octagonal building with a veranda around the front. It is now a maritime museum. Both were built in 1818, albeit by different architects; and both ceased to operate in 1863, when they were superseded by the next matching pair that we were going to visit, a mile or so down the road, at Dovercourt.

Having negotiated our way past the busy town centre, we parked in this sandy suburb, and the sun smiled upon us as we viewed the two square, stilted structures, reminiscent of the low light at Burnham-on-Sea. They are both made of cast iron, and the one nearest the shore is by far the largest, and has a prohibited stairway which contorts its way up through the legs. Today it was doubling as a climbing frame for a gang of young Essex boys.

Both lights consist of black boxes with a white section above the balcony. The low light was plainer and on a Dinky-toy scale. The tide was in, so its black 'legs' were partly submerged. Both were built due to the movement of Andrews Shoals and both are now redundant, replaced by buoys for that same reason.

Right - 'Yuk!'

Revitalised and not particularly interested in the east and west Trinity House beacons at Maplin Sands, we were now ready to leave sunny Essex for the beautiful county of Kent, crossing the QE2 bridge, being seen by many as the gateway to prosperity. Especially to a multitude of discontented northerners, hoping to relocate in the 'Garden of England'.

We were headed for Margate, and as we traversed the eight-lane conduit of madness known as the A2, 'garden' was not a description that sprang to mind!

The road was at full capacity and the traffic moved at 70mph with the unified determination of a lava-flow, the outer lane being reserved for company BMWs, Mercedes, Audis etc, all containing drivers insistent on maintaining a speed of at least 30mph above the national speed limit!

This widespread contempt for velocity restrictions among the well-monied has led me to the conclusion that many 'fat cats' can be likened to successful middle-aged versions of the omnipresent baseball-cap wearing boy-racer. After all, both social groups have a reputation for being fairly self-absorbed and have a common interest in the pursuit of speed! I hope I have not offended anybody but 'if the cap fits, wear it'.

The high speed traffic mayhem was like nothing we'd seen in the past few days; and as we panoramically descended to bridge the River Medway, a scarred landscape lay before us, the North Downs being ripped open mercilessly – their majestic beauty ravaged into a huge swathe of brown earth.

Of course, I'm talking about the rail link works which I certainly shouldn't object to, being a keen promoter of public transport use. The widening of the M2 was another factor in this ugly sprawl, snaking its way back up the hillside in a tangled weave of bollards and roadworks.

But soon we were in the real Kent. I would say this began around Sittingbourne, with the blue skies and open fields giving us a sense of being able to breathe again. We had left the grip of London and the Medway towns behind and were back to two lanes in each direction again. This was more like the Kent of Charles Dickens.

Soon we were seamlessly cruising down the Thanet Way surrounded by rolling hills, some covered with parallel rows of vines. We then tunnelled under a golf course (this seems a rather expensive way of preserving a business to me), and descended to the marshy flatlands that surround the Isle of Thanet - once a real island, separated from the rest of Kent by the sea. Some locals still maintain this sense of isolation, affectionately referring to it as 'Planet Thanet!'

Then came the reasonably attractive suburbs of Birchington and Westgate, with the A28 reminding us what the original London arterial dual carriageways were like.

Soon we were at the familiar amusement arcade lined seafront. Familiar to the cast of 'Only fools and horses' who had their 'jolly boys outing' here; familiar to Chas and Dave, who were inspired to write a song about the place; and familiar to myself and my chilli-drinking mate who nearly got our heads kicked in by about twenty thugs at the age of twelve!

This incident involved being chased through the streets of Margate by a gang that just seemed to multiply like dividing cells. Luckily there was a train in the station which pulled away at the exact moment we frantically boarded it, leaving the pursuing gang to arrive on the opposite platform and watch helplessly as we waved them 'goodbye'. Well, it was a kind of a wave!

Having set the scene, I must just point out that this is probably not so much a reflection on Margate as a reflection on its two twelve-year-old visitors, who had similar experiences in Folkestone and Hastings, and in Rye became the recipients of a polythene projectile containing an unidentified liquid!

Advancing the clock about thirteen years, you now find me in Margate with my Dad walking past a pub displaying the sign 'Closed Forever' and heading for the concrete pier.

With the gentle sound of waves, seagulls and people on the beach, we approached the tall, thin, concrete tower, which is more like an octagonal obelisk/monument than a lighthouse, and stands on a square platform. Its light compartment is little more than an octagonal lantern on the top.

It was erected in 1954, to replace the original light, which was destroyed by a storm in 1953. This was the last time Planet Thanet was technically an island, when the sea breached coastal defences, turning the ditch/channel that separates the area from the rest of Kent back into a formidable stretch of water.

On the night that January became February, this fateful storm claimed the lives of over three hundred people as it battered the East Coast. 32,000 people were evacuated from their homes and, contrary to popular belief, this proved to be the most devastating British weather event of the twentieth century.

Next on the list was North Foreland light. Situated in a green pocket a few miles further along the coastline, just before the Broadstairs suburbs begin, it stands less than thirty miles from my home, yet I had never seen it before in my life.

There has been a lighthouse on this site since 1499. The first light consisted of an iron basket on the end of a pole, which would be filled with burning wood and pitch, and hoisted up like a seesaw.

The present tower dates back to 1691, making it the oldest tower that is still in use. It originally had an open coal fire in an iron grate at the top. In 1790 two further storeys of brick were added and oil lamps introduced. In 1880, it was renovated. This octagonal, white lighthouse is now 85 feet in height and open to the public, except when we turned up of course!

North Foreland light has been widely touted as being the final English lighthouse to become automated, and hence, the end of an era. However, we would later find an exception on the North-West Coast where a keeper is still employed. North Foreland was merely the last Trinity House light to undergo automation, with the lighthouse keeper figuratively receiving his P45 in November 1998.

The reins were handed, as ever, to the Trinity Operations Control Centre at Harwich. So, yet another case of 'the lights are on but there's nobody home'.

And so to Ramsgate.

We parked above the harbour and descended the walled cliff via a series of steps. As we strolled out along the pier in the cool afternoon sunshine, we observed the large container port to our right; and the bustling fishing boats filling the harbour to our left, whose movements mingled with the sound of the seagulls.

This 50-acre harbour had been created by our hero, John Smeaton (of Eddystone lighthouse fame).

The lighthouse was typical 'quayside' size and appeared to be built of brick-like blocks. It was round, light-beige in colour and had a red top and red door.

When it comes to roads (in fact, when it comes to most things), the 'powers that be' often make strange decisions. Sadly Ramsgate surrendered its status as a passenger ferry port some years ago, but an expensive new bypass which tunnels for almost a mile through the cliff was constructed anyway.

'All is not lost', we thought, 'it's still a quick and easy route straight to the town centre and harbour'.

Well, it would be if they hadn't put an obstruction at the end of it, thus creating a dead-end at vast expense, which is only used by the odd lorry, destined for the container port.

Example number two: on our route home, we used a road called the A256, which seems to shed most of its traffic around the little town of Sandwich. It is only after this point that the road extravagantly becomes a vast dual carriageway, which is generally traffic-free on both sides. Would a single carriageway bypass not have sufficed?

No doubt these two roads have been added to the pantheon of 'recommended motorcycle speed trial routes!'

Anyway, for those who don't know Kent, there is a village called 'Ham' near here, and there is a signpost somewhere in the vicinity that amusingly reads 'Ham, Sandwich'. I think it has been stolen several times, which is understandable - at one point I was the proud owner of two 'station entrance' signs, a 'forty limit' sign (which was huge), and a blue 'cycleway' sign. All found abandoned by the roadside, I hasten to add; apart from one, which I saw in a railway museum and paid £15 for.

Upon moving house, I decided it was time to jettison the products of this transport-orientated kleptomania, and for legal reasons, I now state that I do not condone the theft of signs, bollards, those flashing lights on the tops of bollards, or any transport-related memorabilia.

It is childish and it is silly.

I held on to the cat's eye though!

EAST SUSSEX AND SOUTH KENT

Dungeness Draughts

65/66)   NEWHAVEN (harbour lights)

67)   BELLE TOUT (redundant)

68)   BEACHY HEAD* (2 white flashes every 20 secs)

69)   DUNGENESS OLD (redundant)

70)   DUNGENESS NEW* (1 white flash every 10 secs)

This and the chapter that follows cover two day trips to visit our local lighthouses in East Sussex and South Kent.

As you must be well aware if you started at the beginning and have stoically read on, we have now covered all the lighthouses from Fishguard in South-West Wales to Shoreham in West Sussex, and from the Wash to Ramsgate in Kent.

The illogical nature of this sequencing was caused by the outbreak of foot and mouth disease, which meant that many rural footpaths became prohibited areas at this time. The remaining gap consists of the following: Newhaven (X2), Beachy Head area (X2), Dungeness (X2), Folkestone, Dover (X4) and South Foreland (X2).

So upon hearing that the South Downs Way was partially reopened, on a sunny Saturday morning, we found ourselves en route to Newhaven, a former Channel packet port, which with the advent of the Channel Tunnel, has now fallen out of favour.

Heading south from the town centre along the west bank of the River Ouse, past the entrance to the fort (now a local tourist attraction), we parked beneath the sandstone cliffs, which of course involved parting with a small monetary fee. Then zipping our coats to their maximum capability, we stepped out into the gale force wind to walk the concrete pier.

A narrow covered section, which ran beneath a continuous row of arches to our right along the half mile long pier, afforded us some shelter from the gale force wind. This lengthy pier was constructed in 1891, we assume the cast iron lighthouse, atop a steep upward slope at the end, dates from the same period. This sturdy white lighthouse, with a narrow red strip around the middle like a belt, has a rusted bottom section and was covered with graffiti.

Intrigued as to what kind of hieroglyphs one can expect to find daubed on a lighthouse, we realised that it was about as witty and inventive as any other piece of graffiti you are likely to read; i.e. in large bold letters was what Paul Simon described in song as being a 'single worded poem comprising four letters' - something which Art Garfunkel when introducing the song had once termed the 'old familiar suggestion!'

Somebody else had been a little more prosaic in writing a short poem of which the last line went 'you need an orgy once in a while!'

Out on the end of this breakwater, it was so windy that I had difficulty holding the camera straight to get a shot of the other light on the eastern side of the river mouth. This was a small white box on 'legs' with a lantern on top of it.

From my wildly shaking video-footage of this beacon, it was difficult to establish anything more about it. What's more, this was the closest we would get. For we made several attempts to get to this shorter wooden pier, but ended up getting lost in an industrial area around the redundant Newhaven Marine railway station.

When I say 'redundant', I use the term a little frivolously, for one train per week is shunted down to this Marine station to get around the red tape and expense of officially closing it. So, as we sit packed like sardines on commuter trains, it's good to know that elsewhere they have the luxury of running the things around completely empty. Nice one!

When in doubt, find a corner shop and get some supplies: I had a pie which seemed to be filled with wallpaper paste and was rather devoid of flavour and texture. When I looked at the ingredients, it was no surprise to find that the second on the list, i.e. the second largest ingredient, was water!

Uninspired by all of this, we left Newhaven with a minimum of footage or information, and headed through the short 'green belt' that separates the town from Seaford, beyond which the road descends to a little bridge over the meandering River Cuckmere, before climbing steeply onto the South Downs. We dived off the A259 at the picturesque village of East Dean and headed for Birling Gap.

It was difficult to imagine on this sunny afternoon that some two centuries ago, this area and the nearby Cuckmere haven were the scene of many bloody skirmishes between the revenue 'preventative' men and a large and obdurate group of local smugglers. All manner of valuables; tea, tobacco, French lace and brandy in the main, would have been landed and hauled through the twisty downland lanes to end in many a squire or merchant's home in London.

After the threat of Napoleon disappeared, and with the formation of the coastal blockade, later to become the customs service, control of the area was slowly regained by central government and many local families found they had an Australian arm after the transhipment of their breadwinner to the colonies.

Today, we find that this area is gradually disappearing into the sea.

We had walked the South Downs from Eastbourne over Beachy Head and the adjoining Seven Sisters cliffs to Seaford back in 1991, and it seems that some of the houses that we remember, have now surrendered themselves and the chalk cliff they stood on, to the sea. Indeed the local council is pursuing a plan to demolish a Victorian terrace that now finds itself perched precariously close to the cliff-edge.

We ignored signs that ran along the lines of 'do not go on beach, cliffs liable to collapse, risk of death' and bravely descended the flights of wooden steps to stroll along the bottom of the huge overhanging cliff-face. Knowing that this brilliant-white precipice had a tendency to shed the odd thousand tons of chalk now and again, made the walk more than a little daunting.

We could see neither the Belle Tout lighthouse on the top of the cliff nor our next Holy Grail, Beachy Head light further round at the bottom of the cliff. So we headed back towards the steps, walking on a smooth white shore where cliff-falls had been smoothed over by the sea, and it wasn't until we were back beneath the lower cliffs at Birling Gap that my sense of unease dissipated.

This time, we climbed the grassy path along the top of the cliff, and at the highest point we found the stout, 1831, round tower, which was 45 feet in height and seemed to be made of stone 'bricks'. This tower rose from a three-storey, box-shaped residence – an earlier nineteenth century fortification.

The problem here was that the light, being so high up, was often obscured by mist, so at the turn of the century it was decided to build a new lighthouse at the bottom of the cliff, a few miles further east at Beachy Head.

Surviving its redundancy, the Belle Tout, now a private house, faces a new battle with the edge of the cliff moving ever closer. The lighthouse was moved a short distance from its original site in 2000, and I believe it was literally run at a snail's pace along to its current position on runners. As my grandmother once said (albeit in a different context), "Anything is possible in this enlightened age!"

This remarkable engineering feat will prolong Belle Tout's life span for a few more years. However, the rate of erosion of these cliffs appears to have accelerated, which some put down to the excessive winter rainfall pattern of recent years. With the cracking cliff-edge only a matter of feet away, one can only wonder how long it will be before this Herculean task will have to be repeated.

I was rather disappointed by the lack of information here, expecting a board with a few facts and photos of Britain's first upwardly mobile lighthouse. But no.

We could see the Belle Tout's replacement further along beneath the cliff from this point. This was not close enough for us, so returning to the car, we drove a short way east, then set off on foot to the treacherous cliff-edge.

Holding onto a bent and decidedly unsteady metal post, we leaned over the 600-foot drop to see the 141-foot tall, white tower with a red middle section. Narrowing with height, this tower was built during 1899-1902. A cableway was erected to carry materials down the cliff-face. This included 3660 tons of Cornish granite, which was assembled using dovetails. It stands about 180 yards out from the cliff, just clear of the water at low tide.

It is surprising that in these health and safety conscious days there are no rails or markers along this cliff-edge. People will always like to look over cliffs, especially if there's a lighthouse below. Beachy Head is a well-known spot for suicides; it makes you wonder if all of them are intentional. Certainly in an earlier era, many a preventative officer was known to miss his footing, by fair means or foul along these pathways.

I would expect that by now, the staff in the nearby pub have become adept social workers, always having to keep an eye out for the lonely drinker who may be enjoying a final last pint before leaping to their doom.

This area is also rather tourist-orientated. After several miles without seeing a single house, it is a burden on the eyes to have to travel past coach-parks and all the trappings that go with it. Apart from that, this particular area of the South Downs is unspoilt, green and majestic. If you live in Eastbourne, it would seem a pleasant nearby place to take the dog for a walk. This is ill advised – I am informed that around a hundred dogs fall over these cliffs each year. Not even a vigilant pub landlord can see that one coming.

Around ten miles out to sea from here in an easterly direction is a very modern lighthouse which we had no chance of seeing. It was built in 1971 to replace the Royal Sovereign lightship, which had been stationed there since the early nineteenth century. This 90-foot high tower with its own heli-pad was floated into position in several sections.

Our next light lies forty miles east-north-east.

Following Eastbourne, it is a long suburban crawl to Pevensey Bay. Had William the Conqueror landed here today instead of 1066, he might very well have changed his plan, upon seeing the crawling traffic!

Bexhill proudly declares itself 'the home of British motor racing' and flows seamlessly into Hastings, equally proud of its status as the 'birthplace of television'.

On this sunny spring day, the town looked quite attractive, but the greensand cliffs to the east at Fairlight are yet another area suffering quite badly from coastal erosion.

Further on, historic, but traffic-clogged Rye gives way to the expanses of the Romney Marshes.

The Marsh is a large quarter-circle of flatness from Rye to Hythe, reclaimed from the sea over a period of 1500 years. It is bounded to the north by the Royal Military Canal which was built for defence against Napoleon. Assuming he would make it across the English Channel, we were hoping that his army would be phased by a small inland waterway! If this defensive boundary were marked out by a compass, the fixed centre point would be at Dungeness.

There is nowhere else on earth like Dungeness. For a surreal view of England, visit on a late afternoon in winter. This shingly stub jutting out into the English Channel, forms an almost lunar landscape, with its two lighthouses and two nuclear power stations dominating the skyline. One of these is due for closure in 2006, hence the wind farm proposal that I mentioned a few chapters ago, which I'm sure will be the crux of many a heated debate over the next few years.

So bleak is Dungeness that during the 1987 'hurricane' wind speeds in excess of 125mph were recorded here.

Unusually, the coast here is expanding. The most reliable source I can find states that the shingle is advancing at around seven feet-per-year. So assuming the Channel is 23 miles across, in around 17,500 years' time, we may find ourselves again joined to France. To put this into perspective, the law of averages states that this bank of shingle will be burrowing its way deep into France long before you will be due a win on the national lottery!

Before we get bogged down into other statistical malarkey like telling you that you are more likely to be kicked to death by a horse than die in a plane crash, and then finding bizarre convoluted ways of comparing such outlandish hypotheticals with how far Dungeness will be on its pilgrimage towards France, I will get down to some hard facts instead.

The most recent lighthouse is the fifth to be built at Dungeness. It rises 141 feet above its concrete base and is very slender, like a black and white striped chimney. It is built from rings, only twelve feet in diameter, six inches thick and five feet high. Its light is visible for 27 miles. This 1963 structure replaced lighthouse number four when it became obscured by the newly-constructed power station.

Number four is slightly shorter at 136 feet. It is tapered with a 38-foot base diameter, is currently black in colour and was built in 1904. If you are feeling fit and pay your entrance fee, you may freely climb the 169 steps to the top.

This replaced number three which was built in 1792. Its keepers quarters were built around the 116-foot tower which was removed in 1904. From the top of number four you can clearly see the roundhouse which looks like a giant 'Polo mint', with the hole being where the tower used to be. An old photograph shows it to be a striped creation. Smaller low-level lights and foghorns were added closer to the ever-receding sea towards the end of number three's life span.

Number two was a coal fired light built in 1635 and this replaced the first light of 1615.

The view from the top is noteworthy also. From here you can see the terminus of the Romney, Hythe and Dymchurch railway - thirteen and a half miles of 1' 3" gauge track with purpose-built one-third scale steam engines. It is unique in that the other 10,700 miles of railway track dedicated to the British public is all 4'8½" gauge.

There used to be a standard gauge line to Dungeness too, built in anticipation of a ferry service from the Ness to Boulogne, intended to rival the ports of Folkestone and Dover. You can still see the route of this former branch as a straight line across the shingle becoming the access road to the power station further inland.

Finally, a lot of this area is now a dedicated bird reserve. If you cast your mind back to the reserve at East Usk in Wales, you will see that this has galvanised my point about power stations and nature reserves. So it was with a slight sense of smug self-satisfaction that we made the short journey home to contemplate that thought over a cup of tea.

Dossing round Dover

71)   FOLKESTONE (harbour light)

72-75) DOVER (harbour lights)

76/77) SOUTH FORELAND (upper and lower lights both
         redundant, upper light had a white flash every 20
         secs)

Another sunny Saturday morning in the month of May.

We set off to Folkestone, allegedly Britain's sunniest place which on this day lived up to this epithet, with not a blade of grass stirring in the warm, still air.

The town's most famous export is William Harvey, whose statue is located on the scenic Leas. Born here in 1578, he discovered the circulation of the blood.

Although, as a ferry port, Folkestone used to be rivalled by none except Dover, there are currently no passenger services from the town. The derelict 'harbour' station is a reminder of more prosperous days. Not so long ago, you could arrive from Bolougne and board the Orient Express here for London. Leaving the station, it would bridge the attractive boat-filled harbour before chugging up the steep '1in30' gradient to join the main line; this climb being the steepest section of regular rail network in Britain.

Now the rails are rusted, the canopy is bare and the walls are adorned with statements like "We smoked dope here, 14th Sept XXXX!"

We walked through this rusting shell of a rail terminus, out onto the concrete breakwater, past the multitude of anglers and out to the lighthouse at the end. A metal gate precluded us from walking right round this structure, which appeared to be constructed of sandy-coloured stone blocks and had a white light compartment on top. It is a standard, round quayside light. The harbour was opened in 1904 by a French ambassador and I am assuming that the light dates from the same time.

Looking back inland, we have the white cliffs of Dover to our right; and overlooking the harbour, the Hotel Burstin, which was designed so that the top part of it looks like a ferry when viewed from a distance. We returned to the car-park, enjoying the atmosphere, which was bustling with positivity on this hot and cloudless day. Folkestone had never seemed so pleasant.

And so to Britain's busiest ferry port - Dover.

Completely different in feel to Folkestone, Dover is not a place to linger. It even hides its beach away behind the A20 between its west and eastern docks. The town centre is limited to a basic handful of stores, and the town itself is lineally confined to the Dour river valley by the cliffs and hills, and is overlooked by the authoritative gaze of the twelfth century castle.

On a day like today, it is pleasant to look across a deep-blue English Channel littered with ships and ferries crossing the world's busiest strait of water. Guarding the port are the four harbour lights, all painted brilliant white and reflecting the sun, which was at the height of its strength.

We first chose to view them from Western Heights. Here there is a superb cliff-top view of the gateway to England. Running from south to north the lights are as follows:

1)   Admiralty Pier - the south-west harbour wall, which runs out from the western docks.

2)   The Prince of Wales Pier - a shorter, more tourist-orientated jetty within the harbour walls.

3/4)   Offshore Breakwater - the outer wall of the harbour.

Our chosen viewpoint was situated by the remains of a Napoleonic fort, but we were concerned with much earlier history, for Dover is the site of Britain's two earliest lighthouses; two octagonal 'pharos' built by the Romans from stone.

The word comes from the ancient lighthouse off Alexandria in Egypt. This was a megalith, 460 feet in height and one of the seven wonders of the ancient world. Constructed in 270BC, this was the most modern of the septet, which were designated by Antipater of Sidon. The lighthouse was destroyed progressively by earthquakes in 400 and 1375AD. (It is also interesting to note that, of the seven wonders, only the oldest still stands, that being the three pyramids of Giza, built from 2580BC onwards).

One of the two pharos' in Dover was built in 46AD. The stone tower was originally eighty feet in height. The remains can be seen today beside the Saxon church of St Mary in Castre, within the grounds of Dover Castle. It was even used as a bell tower at one point.

However, the first British lighthouse was built in 43AD. Its site is now within the Napoleonic 'drop redoubt'. The stone foundations are all that remains of this tower. We set about the formidable task of finding these from several angles.

A wire fence greeted our first attempt, stopping us from falling about thirty feet into the grassy moat of the redoubt.

So we tried another angle. This time we found a footpath leading up a flight of steps away from the road and around the top of the moat. This gave us views right across the town to the castle and the 46AD pharos, and even enabled us to view Dover Priory station aerially, but still no access to the redoubt.

Returning to the road, we found a grassy path leading to the moat. As we merrily tramped along it, I almost stepped on an adder sunning itself on the pathway. This made me shudder a little as it hissed and recoiled upon itself. My Dad, oblivious to the reptilian danger had just one thing on his mind - getting into the redoubt, which is a huge brick fortress. Its long straight walls towered above us.

Having admired the Doverite graffiti and asked two young lads how to get inside it, consequently curtailing their (probably illicit) smoking activities for a few moments, we found a gash in the side of the wall about four feet high and just wide enough to climb through.

Plunged into darkness, with just a few glimmers of light coming through the small, square gaps in the brickwork (presumably just large enough to fire a gun out of), we stumbled about on the stony floor before finding a stairway with a small shaft of sunlight at the top, beckoning us towards it. With a triumphant shout of "The stairway to heaven" from my father, we edged forward.

The stairway was pitch-black and treacherously covered with stones. My Dad had conveniently left his spectacles indoors and had only a pair of ophthalmic sunglasses on his person. This gave him the options of:

    a)   not wearing them and having poor myopic vision albeit dark, or

    b)   wearing them and being able to see perfectly in total darkness!

He opted for the latter.

After much 'should we, shouldn't we?' I stalked off up the stairway with a slightly increased heartbeat induced by the element of darkness and danger, leaving my Dad to flail about blindly behind me!

At the top - a grassy plateau with the odd protruding bit of brick roof to walk about on. When my father had joined me, having climbed his 'stairway to heaven', we found a large lump of stone with brickwork embedded into it covered by a metal cage. There were bits of stone in the ground next to it too, and a fine view overlooking the harbour. Putting two and two together and coming up with ninety-six, we presumed that this was the spot, especially as my Dad was now going on about 'feeling the vibes!'

If we were right, this was known as the 'Breden Stone'. When the lighthouse fell into ruins, it became a place of execution for criminals who had been given a refuge in the church before being released outside the town wall. If they were seen within the town again, they were hurled to their death from this stone, and got to take in 500 feet of breathtaking scenery before finding themselves scattered across it!

From 1668-1892, this stone was used for the ceremonial installation of the 'Chief Warden of the Cinque Ports'. The other Cinque Ports were Hastings, Romney, Hythe and Sandwich, together with the 'limbs' of Rye and Winchelsea. These ports had been commissioned to defend the South Coast from the twelfth to fourteenth centuries.

Acting as an unofficial Navy, their influence at the King's court was very powerful, until through a series of natural disasters like rivers changing course, silting of harbours and a demand for larger ships, their influence waned. Today it is largely ceremonial.

A lot of history had taken place here. Yet this site is clearly not officially open to the public and we were faced with a nausea-inducive descent down a pitch-black stairway, and a trek along a serpent-ridden path back to the car. No wonder the public were not encouraged!

Admiralty pier forms the outer harbour wall, running for over 4000 feet out from the former Western Docks railway station, now a cruise terminal. Unfortunately, we were a little premature in expecting this long jetty to be restricted to unauthorised members of the public. I have since seen many a fisherman perched upon this concrete structure casting his line into the brine.

So having dismissed the idea of accessing Admiralty pier, and with the offshore breakwater, well, offshore, we assumed that the only lighthouse within our grasp would appear to be the shorter 'Prince of Wales' one.

We parked beside Dover's 'seaside' beach, and walked out along the surprisingly long and busy Prince of Wales pier. At the end of this stood the aptly named 'Lighthouse Cafe' which seemed the perfect place to alleviate our thirst by speedily downing some 'Yuk'!

Beyond the cafe was a metal fence (we were beginning to get used to these by now), and beyond that, the lighthouse, which is considerably smaller than the 'lighthouse on stilts' at the end of Admiralty pier and the light at the south-west end of the offshore breakwater. (The other offshore light is similar in size to this 'Prince of Wales' one and is some distance from the north-east end of the breakwater).

The Prince of Wales pier light is, in fact, remarkably similar to the quayside light at Folkestone, being round and made of blocks, except here it has been painted completely white.

Looking northwards from the pier, the white cliffs towered over the eastern passenger port, which is on an 'apron' of land beneath them, with the main A2 road spiralling its way up out of it. The fields on top of the cliffs were bright yellow with rape seed, and about three miles further along them stood a white structure, our next focus of attention - South Foreland lighthouse.

A few miles north of Dover lies St Margaret's-at-Cliffe, a well-endowed village with several pubs and a range of amenities. To the south of the village is a network of parallel-running stony tracks amidst bushy heathland – a good test of any vehicle's suspension.

At the far end of this area lies the lighthouse. There are actually two lighthouses at South Foreland, 385 yards apart. The upper light dates back to 1843 and was designed by James Walker, while the lower light, now a redundant feature of a private dwelling, was built in 1846. Both replaced a series of earlier structures.

We were just in time to catch the final guided tour of the day in the National Trust owned upper light, which has a white, square tower, except that it looks as if the vertices, (that means corners!), have been filed off; and if I may stretch your geometric mental agility further, behind the lighthouse is a walled quarter-circle containing the living quarters.

This lighthouse has a lot of history, originally lit by the oil of sperm whales, it soon became noticed that the whale population was seriously declining, so the fuel was then switched to rape seed oil. It later became the first lighthouse to use an electric generator - initially a short-lived experiment from 1858-1859.

Another first is that it was also the site of the first radio transmission made by Marconi to communicate with ships out on the treacherous Goodwin Sands. These sandbanks, alternatively covered and uncovered by the tide, became a veritable ship's graveyard, hence the work of the lighthouses was backed up by several lightships which had to be moved because of the shifting nature of the sandbank.

After climbing the fairly modest stature of this 69-foot high tower, we received a demonstration of the optic revolving on its bed of mercury. The light used to have a range of 26 miles and was taken out of use in 1988. Upon descending again, we received a mild reprimand for making our own video footage (although the tour guide seemed quite content to star in our movie!).

The quest to view the lower light was less satisfying. It is situated within the grounds of a private house and is closer to the cliff edge. Although we risked a rather rapid encounter with the beach, (around 300 feet below), by wandering around on the unfenced grassy cliff-top, our best view had been at the end of the drive, where the top of the 49-foot tower of the low light looked like a stone castle turret poking above the trees, with the empty frame of a light compartment on top of it.

Our short snippet of camera footage is not the lower light's only encounter with celluloid, as it provided the location for the 1967 vehicle for Oliver Reed and Flora Robson, 'The Sheltered Room'.

Final point worth noting: North Foreland, South Foreland (upper) and Dungeness were all used in the Second World War for transmissions with the aim of jamming German radar installations along the North Coast of France.

And so, we reach a turning point in our mission, with 77 lighthouses under our belts, (which means either a very large pair of trousers or a metaphor indicating a modicum of success!). If you were to draw a straight line across the country from Grimsby to Aberystwyth, we have now covered every mainland lighthouse beneath it. Well, except for Avonmouth (jobsworth), Orford Ness (foot and mouth), St

Ives (lazy-itis) and the more Easterly one at Newhaven (assessed as a beacon).

On second thoughts perhaps we should give up now!

But no! We didn't throw ourselves off of the cliff edge, but headed for Dymchurch. This is a seaside village half way between Folkestone and Dungeness, with all the usual rides, candy floss, whelk stalls, 'shops selling gifts with no practical value' and 'slots in which to dispose of your money', that you would expect in such a place.

Here we found a pub where our well-earned Guinness went down almost as smoothly and quickly as those pints did in Hayle, after that epic day walking the Cornish coast path to Tater Du.

It was in a similar spirit of reverie that we perused my recently purchased set of 1920's cigarette cards depicting fifty British lighthouses. We recognised many, but there were still many for us to see.

It feels like the halfway point in our challenge, and as we sat in the car waiting to go into the pub, it was fitting that the soothing classical music on the radio should be the bittersweet music from a well-known beer advert. It had been a memorable day. There would be many more memories to come.

Let's drink to that!

'HUMBERSIDE'

Withernsea Wonders

78) OUSEFLEET (riverbank light)

This, the second half of the book begins with another gripe; for the rest of our story takes place in what we in the South collectively refer to as 'The North'.

The North is an area, which as yet seems largely unaffected by the issue that I am about to thrust at you. So if you will excuse me for once again turning this tome on pharophilia into a platform for more personal views, here goes.

Eight percent of British citizens live in 'the countryside' or should I state that they merely sleep in the countryside? For rural England is fast becoming a museum, i.e. it looks very nice in passing but all the exhibits are lifeless remnants of a bygone age!

Yes, I bemoan the decline of the Great British rural community. Fair enough, there are still clubs, organisations and events in most villages; but when it comes to shopping we are generally about as community-minded as a rotweiler that has been hit on the back of the head with a cricket bat! - Content to stand by while our shopkeepers languish somewhere near the point of bankruptcy; yet should anybody dare to brand a small community with adjectives like 'sleepy' or 'listless', these supermarket shoppers will immediately spring to the defence of their moribund abode.

"Why this sudden outburst of preachiness?" you ask.

Well, it just seems odd to me that whenever foxhunting is threatened there is a stampede, yet I have lived in the country all my life and have never even seen a hunt. Therefore it seems odd to me that when the very fabric of rural life (i.e. trade) is being slowly unwoven, nobody bats an eyelid (or indeed the back of a rotweiler's head!).

As you may have now worked out, it was at this point in time that several services in my own much-beloved village were under threat; some have since been expunged forever.

In the North though, you can be justly proud. Your villages have filling stations, fish and chip shops and even banks. I think that's worth spending an extra fiver a week for, don't you? What's more, because you aren't constantly tearing to the supermarket, (where you can buy just about everything from a packet of crisps to a nuclear warhead!), your roads aren't full of drivers who view breaking speeding regulations as a God-given right!

Having vented my spleen sufficiently for at least five minutes, you find us heading for Humberside. Please don't write to me stating that 'Humberside' ceased to be an administrative region some years ago, I know. I merely use the term to mean the area either side of the Humber. Some of it is Lincolnshire, some of it is Yorkshire, there are 'easts' and 'norths' all over the place and I get confused!

We chose to use the 'Great North Road' as our axis away from London. I was amused to notice how the southern part of the A1 mercilessly ploughs its way through a number of villages and small towns like Sandy. It seemed strange to see houses and even shops opening their doors more or less straight onto this arterial dual carriageway. Then all of a sudden it 'freaks out' into a dead straight eight-lane superhighway, which doesn't fill me with confidence in the Government's 'green' credentials.

"We want to encourage people out of their cars and onto public transport", I seem to remember being the gist of things. Well, a brand new section of the A1(M) which is almost as wide as it is long should really get people onto the trains, shouldn't it?

We turned off at Newark onto the Foss Way - Britain's longest Roman road, running 218 miles from Exeter to Lincoln. (The other long one is Watling Street running 215 miles from Dover to Wroxeter - now just a small village near Shrewsbury).

Lincoln cathedral is a positively stunning sight, crowning the hillside and dominating the town with its splendour. Next, came another Roman road, the A15 or Ermine Street. This particular stretch towards the Humber is often quoted as the longest straight section of road in Britain, but I can honestly say that, like the information, it is not *completely* straight. Having ignored the deviation around an airfield, there were still slight curves all along the route. Perhaps, deviations in the road's course of only fractions of a degree, but in my book 'straight' should mean 'straight!'

Soon we were in familiar 'lighthouse territory', i.e. flat ground similar to the approach to the Wash. Unfortunately, thoughts of rural decline back at home popped into my mind again as we drove through Crowle, which wasn't a huge village, yet it seemed to sell everything, even petrol!

We soon found ourselves crossing the flatlands on progressively smaller and smaller lanes to Ousefleet - a tiny village just south of the raised riverbank. I am being careful here, for this was the River Ouse - the Humber is merely the name that is given to the river after the Trent from the south, joins it.

After the Severn and Thames (which includes the Isis and Churn), this Trent/Humber combination forms Britain's third longest river, with the Aire/Ouse/Humber being fourth.

Incidentally, near here is the area to which the Ordnance Survey allocates its blankest grid square on any map.

It was not immediately apparent to us as to the best way to approach the river, but we decided a straight course was the best. Savage dogs yelped viciously at us as we flippantly strolled across what seemed like an extended lawn from somebody's house - and we hadn't even hit it over the head with a cricket bat - how very uncommunity-like!

Standing on the bank was our first lighthouse – a grubby-looking, white structure, round in shape with a balcony. Very similar to the standard 'quayside' ones.

A little further eastwards along the river, our library of atlases showed another lighthouse in the middle of the estuary where the various waterways meet. This would be just opposite the tiny hamlet of Faxfleet.

We tried to view this from a bird sanctuary, but a very friendly man with a fine North Country accent explained that all we would see would be reeds, and that we would basically require a crane to see over them. Furthermore, he had lived there thirty years and had never been aware of a lighthouse, just a series of red lights placed on poles at regular intervals along both sides of the river. If there was anything to see, we would be better off viewing it from the other side.

Apparently in Roman times, there was a dry route across the river at Whitton Sands. In early 2002, a herd of cows were possessed by an urge to cross in the same manner. Not renowned for their waterborne properties these cows ended up having to be airlifted to safety. They must have been mad!

More sensibly, we headed for Goole and crossed via the Boothferry Bridge. We followed a B-road which clearly used to be the main road to Hull before the M62 was built. This motorway leaps over the river by means of one of the least stylish bridges in the country.

Back on lanes again, we crossed the railway line, which is widely quoted as the longest straight section of track in the country, completely undeviated for eighteen miles from Hull to Selby. People are very direct up here, you see.

We parked up, climbed onto the levee, observed the 'Footpath Closed due to Foot and Mouth Disease' sign and stared zombie-like out across the rushes. Where was it? Foolishly, we left the area without a conclusive 'yes' or 'no' which meant we would find ourselves back here again the following day, for we were well on our way to Hull when we remembered the friendly ornithologist describing a wooden platform at Faxfleet where boats could moor up and ignominious lighthouse explorers could survey the grey waters of the Ouse!

Heading for Hull, we passed the majestic Humber Bridge, which until the late nineties was the longest suspension bridge in the world. Its hyperbolic status has since been superseded by the Akashi Strait Bridge in Japan and the Great Belt/East Bridge in Denmark.

With the impending Izmit Bay Bridge in Turkey and a two mile long bridge connecting Sicily to mainland Italy, the Humber's estimable position seems destined to fade.

Hull, correct title - Kingston upon Hull, (the Hull is actually a small river which flows into the Humber from the north), is a seafaring place which happens to be the hometown of the band, the Housemartins, who later metamorphosed into the Beautiful South. I begin to understand how the band got the inspiration for its name - compared to this, the South must seem very beautiful indeed! For we drove past endless warehouses and huge chimneys to the east of the city.

But hang on a minute, here I am knocking large urban areas whilst being disgruntled about 'country life' gradually becoming an oxymoron.

Heading out across Holderness, we came to the happy medium - Withernsea. It is these unpretentious little towns that have impressed us most on our travels. There have been a long line of them; Fowey, Burnham-on-Sea, Hunstanton and Southwold all spring to mind.

The next thing to hit us would be the outstanding value. Having become used to bed and breakfast places in East Anglia that require you to take out a 25-year loan to spend one night there, we almost laughed at being offered a room in a guest-house, including breakfast for a mere sixteen pounds each!

This is a town that is proud of its lighthouse too, the 127-foot high, white, octagonal tower which narrows with height from its seemingly massive base, is visible for a good few miles as you approach the town. It looms proudly over the terraced streets below.

Soon we were in our natural habitat of boozing establishments, with a refreshing pint and some of the worst karaoke performances I have ever heard. It seemed that being tone-deaf was the only requirement for taking part - mere drunkenness would not be sufficient!

In the South, I find that the early part of any karaoke evening is when all the real professionals perform whole repertoires whilst sounding exactly like Dolly Parton or Kenny Rogers. This formidable professionalism then delays any of the regular punters from taking part until at least 10pm when both performer and listener are considerably drunk enough not to give a monkey's how it sounds! The difference is that up here, people just get on with it, and to hell with the consequences - the reason being, there won't be any - it's just a bit of fun.

It would be another four months until my Dad would submit himself to such vocal abandon in Whitley Bay.

The background chatter was in good wholesome Yorkshire accents and, like almost anywhere else in the UK, it was peppered with the frequent use of a four letter word, except that up here it rhymes with 'book' instead of 'buck!'

Next culture shock: A starter and two good quality meals for £10.35. Equation to convert to southern prices: Multiply by two and add a few quid for good measure.

Then came our first game of pool since that drinking marathon in Hayle. How bizarre that on all these trips, we had been to pubs with pool tables on those first three consecutive nights in Cornwall and had not so much as looked at the game on any of these trips since. No wonder we played so badly!

My only criticism on this second pub we frequented in Withernsea was their insistence of playing '190 beats-per-minute' techno and aimlessly aggressive 'new era' heavy metal at high volumes, when the clientele here looked far more likely to be into Frank Sinatra, or indeed Dolly Parton/Kenny Rogers karaoke soundalikes!

Next came the conversational bit. I'll give you a multiple choice question on the subject matter. Was it:

a)   knitting
b)   pheasant plucking
c)   rural decline, or
d)   advanced principles of geometry?

I suppose that was a little like one of the easier driving 'theory' test questions really, where you are asked to choose from one correct answer and three ludicrous ones!

And so it was back to our guesthouse for a good healthy dose of 'Newsnight'.

I often find that watching this programme is purely voyeuristic, with Jeremy Paxman repeating his questions dalek-like at politicians with more 'spin' than the average fairground ride and more U-turns than a mountain pass!

If you want your answer to be like the A15 or Hull to Selby rail line (i.e. straight), stick to questions of no real political importance, e.g. jam making, ancient Greece, knitting, pheasant plucking, advanced principles of...

Bright lights at Bridlington

79/80)   SPURN HEAD (disused high light - formerly 1½ secs flash every twenty secs, and remains of low light)

81)   WITHERNSEA (redundant)

82-84)   PAULL (riverbank lights - all redundant)

85)   FLAMBOROUGH HEAD OLD (disused)

86)   FLAMBOROUGH HEAD NEW* (4 white flashes every 15 secs)

'Comforting' was the word my father had used to describe the view from Withernsea seafront last night. To our north we could see the characteristic four flashes of Flamborough Head lighthouse and to our south we wrongly assumed that we could see Spurn Head lighthouse. In actual fact, it was the lightship that has replaced it, stationed just off Spurn Head.

Today we would check out both areas and of course the magnificent structure in Withernsea itself, but first we were given an ultimatum concerning our desire to spend a second night here. We would have to either vacate our room for one without en-suite facilities, or leave! There was no mention of any reduction in price, so we took the second option.

We had almost two hours to fritter away before Withernsea lighthouse opened its doors to the public and as we had now fully explored the town, we decided to pay a fleeting visit to Spurn Head.

We had seen the castle-like entrance to what used to be Withernsea pier until a boat ran into it in 1885. We had seen the new sea wall which was built after a huge storm destroyed the old one in 1993. We had even seen all we wanted to of the exterior of the lighthouse, which is reputedly the furthest from the sea, built so far inland because of continuous coastal erosion. And where do you think the eroded material was slowly relocating?

Why, Spurn Head of course!

Hurst Spit, Orford Ness, Dungeness and now the tip of Holderness; we were growing accustomed to large quantities of sand or shingle bolshily jutting out into the sea. Spurn is a three mile long spit of sand where the Humber meets the sea.

We passed the large Easington gas terminal to reach it and were soon heading down the concrete toll road to the point. This road was built during World War II. Previously the only access was via a railway built in World War I. We noticed occasional remnants of the rails embedded in the concrete road.

There are several points where the road has clearly altered its course, this is where the sandbank has collapsed. In spite of this, Spurn Head is growing, but only at a rate of two feet a year; a tortoise-like pace compared to Dungeness.

But what of the lighthouse? The 120-foot, 1895-built upper light is very similar to lighthouse no.4 at Dungeness. Thinning with height, it is black with a white centre section. There used to be two fixed lights on this tower as well as the revolving light.

This Thomas Matthews' lighthouse followed its predecessors into redundancy in 1985. These were the high and low lights built in 1776, noteworthy because they were constructed by that legend, John Smeaton, and apart from Eddystone these were the only other lighthouses he built.

Just to the south of Mr Matthews' tower you can trace the round brick foundations of an earlier lighthouse in the dune-like sand.

To the west of the peninsular you can observe the tower of Smeaton's lower light on the beach. This is now a dirty white tower with a stumpy black section on top where the light compartment would have been.

Whilst looking at the information board which seemed a little incongruous with its facts, we were startled by a river pilot's vehicle which came roaring past with a sense of paramount urgency. The pilot's job is to board any vessel greater than sixty metres in length that wishes to enter the Humber estuary. This is in the interest of safety, which clearly isn't viewed as such a priority when it comes to land-based transportation!

Having gleaned about all we could from this area, we returned to Withernsea; and as we approached its stately lighthouse down a long, straight, Victorian avenue, 'Classic FM' came up trumps again by playing what sounded like a Brahms' Hungarian dance, which whipped itself up to a frenetic pace with all the pomposity it could muster as we neared the familiar and formidable octagonal, white tower.

We paid our money and climbed the vertigo-inducive spiral

staircase which was lined with flags, to the top. We were told that it had one more step than the similar sized tower at Spurn Head and was built at around the same time. (Withernsea=1894).

In the base are two museums; the RNLI and coastguard museum and the Kay Kendal museum.

The late Kay Kendal was an actress who famously starred in the film 'Genevieve'. She was raised in Withernsea and as well as being related to Captain Cook, was also the cousin of somebody we saw taking a party of school children round.

One of the two volunteers running the attraction had recently moved here from London. He told us that he found it too quiet here and that he missed the M25. This seemed a bizarre thing to say to me - a statement akin to "I miss having toothache" or "Mornings are too dull without bills to read!"

We pointed out that we live near Kent's own mini-London, and I suspect our host has since been scanning the property pages for houses in Ashford! And at that, we headed back towards the Humber and the village of Paull, after first stowing away our certificates that we had been given for climbing to the top.

About half a mile before we reached the village of Paull were two lighthouses. They stood on the riverbank about a hundred yards apart. They both had 'domed' tops, the left one being red and standing on 'stilts' and the right one, a standard 'quayside' light, i.e. small, round and white. (Sounds like a description of Ronnie Corbett!).

Both were rendered inaccessible to us as the only access was down a 'foot and mouth' prohibited farm-track. However, this visit was not to be completely barren of information. A notice on a telegraph pole informed us that both lighthouses were due to be moved 350 yards westwards.

Due to rising sea levels, 5000 acres of land here would be allowed to flood, with better sea defences being built further inland. Sailors were concerned about a resulting drop in the river level, but with proof of global warming and rising seas steadily amassing, they will soon have the world as their oyster - there will be water, water everywhere!

The fact that these structures were being moved gave us hope that lighthouses are beginning to be recognised as buildings worth preserving. So this pair will join Belle Tout's exclusive club for upwardly mobile lighthouses. Who knows, maybe somebody has even stumbled upon the very first one we visited at Fowey and has since cleared the undergrowth, gave it a new coat of paint and designated it a listed building!

I think not.

The third one at Paull was in the middle of the village, clumsily 'stuck' onto the end of row of houses. With its balcony at roof-level, its light compartment is just higher than the chimney pots. There are two windows in the white 'tower' and it too has a domed top. The structure is 'vintage' 1836, and just overlooks the Humber from behind the sea wall.

Passing through Hull a second time, we felt like we'd been 'to Hull and back!' We were now heading for that tranquil void known as 'Faxfleet' to try again for the missing lighthouse.

Faxfleet can barely be described even as a hamlet. The only sound to be heard was the wind rushing through the tall reeds. I counted a mere two dwellings; so if the average household contains 2.4 people, I estimate the population here to be 4.8! As I've never seen 0.8 of a person, we'll call that five. Still that's only three less people than were aboard Noah's ark!

We soon came to another Hamlet called 'Blacktoft Sands', which even boasted a pub. Our thirst for both beer and information led us inside. We drank our pints in the beer garden which was the bank of the River Ouse and obtaining our clearest view so far of the waters, we concluded that the concrete stump perhaps a mile and a half downstream, is all that remains of the lighthouse. Upon this stands a white beacon.

Returning our glasses to the bar and ourselves to the car, it was time to head for the lighthouse Mecca of Flamborough Head.

The B-road to Beverley, which was the county town of the former Humberside, covered unspoilt rolling hills before descending to the quaint little town with its cathedral-like church.

The A165 to Bridlington has two guises: if the road is quiet, it is a genuine 60mph road; if it is busy, it is one of those painfully slow crawls that make you feel like you are a disc in the backbone of a lethargic serpent!

To the north of Bridlington lies Flamborough Head, which can be held responsible for cementing my Father's idea for this whole exercise. Back in 1993, whilst visiting this area, a few years after a previous family holiday near Portland Bill, my Mother glibly commented that we were working our way round the lighthouses of Britain.

I was reading Tom Vernon's book, 'Fat man on a Roman road' at the time, so my Mother suggested a snappy working title of 'Thin man up a lighthouse!' Little did I know that almost six years later, my Dad would resurrect this idea as a serious project after his enforced early retirement. I wanted to see Cornwall; he wanted to see lighthouses, and thus we became lured into this whole murky world of Smeatonesque towers, mercury-bedded optics and scavaging about in a haze of beer and 'Yuk' for facts, figures and 'pharos'.

Upon reaching the chalk headland you will see one of Britain's oldest remaining lighthouse towers, built by Sir John Clayton in 1674, this 79-foot, white, octagonal monolith is very rugged and has a door and three windows vertically above it. Its width is unchanging from bottom to top.

Its success was limited due to its distance from the sea, thus Samuel Wyatt built the 1806 one that we were about to visit. The substantial round, white tower musters a height of almost 90 feet and has a collection of two-storey buildings at its base. Here we were given a guided tour, which taught us a lot about how most lighthouses operate.

The light shines continually with the flash sequence determined by the revolving optic lens. As it revolves on its bed of mercury some sections of glass refract the light upwards to create the gaps between flashes. If the bulb fails, there is another positioned next to it which will kick into action. If this fails, there are fixed lights, which run on batteries around the outside of the tower.

The light itself is switched on and off by a sensor, which detects when it is getting light or dark.

We learn!

So after a successful day's lighthousing, we retreated to Bridlington and found a very busy pub to begin the proceedings.

My Dad, being a keen enthusiast of real ale, found the rather nondescript brew on offer a little dull. This was resolved by purchasing a pint of Guinness, drinking half and creating a cocktail with the remains of each pint. It sounds disgusting, but it was actually rather nice!

Next we found a guesthouse, and what followed was 'panic' followed by 'revelation'.

The 'panic' involved the disappearance of the car keys. Visions of parting with the greater part of a ton in cash for 250 miles of 'clickety-clack' and announcements beginning with "We apologise..." came into my mind, with the prized red hatchback left locked and marooned in Bridlington.

After much searching, my Dad found the keys in a pocket he never uses, supposedly. A sense of calm returned, and it was time for the languorous, half-attentive, TV-watching period before the search for food. Thus came the 'revelation'.

Michael Palin was purveying a radical new form of thinking - that the automobile doesn't have to be the central tenet of human existence. You may have noticed that I have a penchant for environmentally-friendly transport and local shopping, so you will understand that, in spite of my enjoyment of being on the road, this was like music to my ears. At last a celebrated member of the Monty Python team, has come out of the closet in support of such things.

Of course you are thinking 'the ministry of silly walks was a better idea', but this programme concluded with a snapshot around Britain's major city centres revealing that they all have one thing in common - rows of metal boxes containing angry people, glued motionlessly together. Like Mr Palin, I am unconvinced by these adverts for 'cars so comfortable that you will be glad to sit in a jam!'

Train delays are equally frustrating I admit, especially when the whole network seems to grind to a complete halt whenever a leaf, twig or other deciduous matter hits the rails. You'd think they would have got it right by now – autumn happens every year after all, so there's no a great element of surprise to contend with!

But when things are running smoothly, how nice it is to be gently lulled to sleep by the rhythmic motion, blissfully unaware as the miles scurry past, then quietly awakened as the carriage slows to pull into your station. Yet when I tell people that I actually 'choose' to travel by train they generally look at me as if I've just landed from Andromeda! I find that talking to people on trains is a little like talking to smokers, in that nearly all of them intend to give it up.

Alternatively, there's cycling. There's nothing more satisfying than narrowly whizzing past scores of stationary vehicles knowing that you are achieving this entirely under your own steam. Of course the down side is that you are twelve times more likely to die in the process. Still, as Mr Palin himself sang, 'Always look on the bright side of life!'

Time to hit the town.

First, half a pint in a bar, which specialised in loud music and video games, seemingly aimed at a market of about a quarter of our combined ages (and I was only 26!). We decamped to an empty restaurant next door:

"Are we too late for food?"

"No, not at all" came the reply. But after a deep-fried seafood starter and a microwaved lasagne which cost considerably more than last night's almost 'cordon bleu' offering, the young waitress stood with the door open, eager to usher us out!

Feeling about as welcome as a town crier in a library, we downed our beer so fast that it brought a rising feeling to the oesophagus, and before we could say 'thanks' for our hurried meal, the door was slammed shut and locked behind us!

Exiled to the street, we tried to find a more old-mannish establishment where we could quietly review the day's perambulations. We wandered down to the seafront and there, at the end of the concrete pier, was a flashing lantern on chunky, white lamp-post - a missing lighthouse perhaps? Hardly, but it is used as a navigational aid for Bridlington harbour mouth. Meanwhile, the characteristic four flashes of Flamborough Head shone seductively across the ripples as the sun set modestly.

But what of the nightlife in Bridlington?

Well, if you like 'techno' it's great!

If you enjoy having your ears blasted with 180 beats-per-minute 'thumping', with a ridiculously fast jumble of notes over the top of it, it's excellent! This inane music was pulsating from virtually every amusement arcade and trendy drinking bar in town.

So we returned, unenticed by these remnants of mid-nineties rave culture, to our room to watch another entertaining verbal dogfight on 'Newsnight' and then try to sleep.

What my Dad must have heard was a non-stop rustling of bed clothes, interspersed with sighs growing in volume and aggression, as sheets were hauled across the plastic cover on the bed in a vain attempt to create a sleepable covered surface on what was basically a shelf positioned at an acute angle. This culminated with a loud exclamation of "This bed is just ridiculous!"

A groan of acknowledgement was emitted from my Dad's bed and, after several complete remakes of my own bed, I abandoned the idea of being comfortable and slept on top of the tangled weave of covers.

Why can't guesthouse beds be more like railway carriages?

Industrial Immingham

87-89) KILLINGHOLME (two red flashing lights, one redundant light)

Another day, another breakfast, another debate on TV (today's was on paganism), and out to the car for a large portion of A165.

At Beverley, we encountered the most bizarre 'bypass by stealth' which utilises everything form 'trunk road' to 'unclassified lane' in order to keep through traffic away form the town centre. It was a little like the drunken man's walk around a lamp-post, zigzagging in and out repeatedly until a bang on the head serves as an abrupt reminder of the direction you *should* be going!

Soon we were crossing the Humber Bridge and were heading for Immingham where our final set of lighthouses on this particular leg is located.

The A160 leads terminally towards the forest of chimneys and industrial structures which sprout triffid-like from the flatness, like a scene from a sci-fi film set in the year 2250. It's hard to imagine that within my meagre life-span this area has been transformed from farmland to this.

Parking along a straight, wide, 'made for lorries' road, we sauntered off up a public footpath, which seemed to disappear amidst a network of huge pipes. Surrounded by anti-trespass warnings and fearing that if we were caught we would be made to sit in the guardroom and be subjected to the third degree, we thought we'd try a different approach.

We headed to the port of Immingham, and when the road had reached a dead-end, we consulted some workmen who kindly showed us how to remove a bollard, exhorting to us that it must always be replaced. This allowed us to continue on four wheels along a concrete sea wall now heading southward behind all the heavy industry. This seemed like the kind of place that you would not find many tourists!

The concrete platform was like something that had been designed by robots, with no curves but straight sections with the occasional thirty-degree change in direction.

All three lighthouses here have domed tops and balconies around the light section. The first one we encountered was the redundant one, which is attached to a private house. It is very similar to the one in the middle of Paull, except more run-down and dirty. Like Paull, it dates from 1836.

The other two emit a red flash in unison, which I would imagine appear one above the other if a sailor is on course to enter the River Humber. The taller one lays back from the road and is pink in colour, whilst the shorter roadside one is a very grubby white. This pair, owned by Associated British Ports, are known as the Killingholme lights.

After a brief glance at the tangled weave of pipes that allow massive oil tankers to discharge their valuable cargo to land, it was time to head back to pastures green. And that was that.

The A46 provided us with a smashing view as we came off the Wolds at Caistor. What's more, approaching Lincoln from the north is completely pain-free, as one minute you are still above the city's bypass, the next you are right in the centre by the towering cathedral. However upon descending the hill, you are faced with mile after mile of incessantly dragging suburbs, which clearly weren't there when the Romans built this road, for this is the beginning (or end) of the Foss Way.

It is interesting to note that the Romans managed to build their roads so straight by using beacons on the tops of hills and then lining them all up. Of course, you would usually only be able to see one in front of you and one behind. This meant that the lining up procedure was almost as time-consuming as building the actual roads, with many adjustments inevitably necessary.

The achievements of the Romans are nothing short of amazing, especially considering that everything they built was constructed manually. From aqueducts to tunnels for mining, to drainage systems, to farming equipment and so on. The only other period of ingenuity that comes near in my mind, is that of the railway building achievements of the Victorians.

And so to the A1.

The weather changed as we headed southward, from dull and overcast, to sunny and hot. Suddenly, whilst shedding a jacket, I realised why so many people desire to live in the South. Of course - the sunshine!

The jumper came off somewhere near Cambridge.

THE NORTH-EAST

Whitby Wiles

90) SCARBOROUGH (harbour light)

The clock moves forward a few months, and we find another potential World conflict on the horizon.

Heeding Basil Fawlty's comely advice, "Don't mention the war", I shall cut to the chase. The chase being our 320-mile journey to Scarborough - the beginning of a five-day marathon that would take us right up to the Scottish border.

Journeys of this epic scale are an unavoidable hazard of these last few trips, and as ever, once we'd covered the eight miles to the motorway we could settle down for six hours of tedium!

Six hours of following slow-moving vehicles, then finally mustering up the courage to overtake, only to find they have just discovered that their throttle can be pushed down another three inches, leaving you a little humiliated in the outside lane!

Six hours of articulated lorries pulling out in front of you because the lorry in front is doing 65mph when they want to be doing 65½. Then, realising that they are approaching a steady incline, which the other lorry is better equipped for, the two lorries travel side by side until reaching the summit when the whole procedure can begin again. Of course while this is going on, you have a sports car driver behind you with a fanatical desire to drive two pencil-lengths from your bumper whilst testing his horn and headlights!

Six hours of blue signs, white lines and white knuckles! But the thing is - motorways are the only way to get anywhere quickly. After all, thirty years ago, most people would have considered this to be a two-day journey.

Of course, a previous Prime Minister in a moment of enlightenment tried to make it quicker still by creating 'the cones hotline!' This noble idea meant that whenever your journey was slowed by speed limits and lane closures with no clear evidence of any work taking place, you could ring this number, and within minutes somebody would be dispatched to investigate and hopefully remove the offending orange plastic bollards.

Unfortunately, five little words from workmen could result in the whole thing falling flat on its face; those words being 'We're on a tea-break!'

Having clipped the Sherwood forest, we were soon in the industrial North, with the chimneys at Ferrybridge nestling together like an eight-pack of beer cans, with their plumes of white smoke rising vertically in unison which, from a distance, appeared like a huge oblong of gas which puffed out into a massive mushroom cloud at the top.

Further north, the A1 decided to re-enact its Cambridgeshire grandeur, by doubling in width for the M1 to feed back in, as if to celebrate their reunion - their first since London.

Soon we were seamlessly traversing the A64, which beyond York is far more interesting, with the Yorkshire Wolds to our right, and the moors to our left. After Malton, the road passes through a number of villages, all with ample provisions. Before long, one is entering Scarborough.

The sun was shining, the breeze was negligible and the air felt positively warm. The area around the harbour could easily have been 'St Ives' with amusement arcades. This part of the town has preserved its traditional seaside-resort feel well, whereas many other resorts seem to have slid into decline.

I was tempted by the stalls selling cockles, prawns and whelks, unlike my Dad who described eating whelks as "Chewing a piece of gristle with sand in!" In the end, we settled for a hot-dog.

The lighthouse was the most impressive harbour light we'd seen, being a large, round, white tower, with four windows vertically above each other and a balconied light compartment on top. It is joined to a flat-roofed, oblong, two-storey building, and its beam has a range of nine miles.

First light here: 1806. Second storey built: 1850.

In 1914 a German shell sliced through the tower which was rebuilt in 1931. It is situated at the end of 'Vincent's' pier which has a footbridge, built in 2000, allowing vessels to enter 'through' it into the harbour which is bounded by the longer east pier.

A Norman castle stands on top of the headland that divides the town into two bays. As we drove through the quieter north bay, still reeling from the shock of a minimum parking fee of three pounds, we noticed that work was being done to protect the headland from erosion.

After Scarborough, the road climbs up onto the moors, snaking its undulous way to Whitby.

In my opinion, the best way to approach Whitby is by train, particularly if you have just been on the steam train through the moors from Pickering. The bus-like diesel train enters the fishing town in the Esk Valley, providing views of the older houses which creep up the sides of the valley in terraces, overlooked by the thirteenth century abbey ruins. By road, you are subjected to the usual industrial estates and bland suburbs that could be anywhere.

Weird salesmanship abounds in Whitby.

Firstly we tried a hotel which stated a price of 'eighteen pounds per person', but upon enquiring, we found that it was actually £27 each. That's a total of eighteen pounds extra - or six parking tickets in Scarborough! I smell a rat as soon as I encounter the phrase 'prices from...' as in 100% of cases, this minimum price is never offered.

Things worked the opposite way in the next hotel where we were offered two rooms for the price of one.

Being from the cynical South, we could not understand the logic of this from a business point of view, especially as shortly after we'd accepted this deal, a potential customer who telephoned the hotel was told "We are fully booked now, and I'm afraid you will find that everywhere else in Whitby is absolutely stacked out!"

We were in a separate building from the main hotel and were astonished to find that between us we had the use of two toilets, two showers, six beds, eight cups and eighteen towels. I was tempted to make full use of this decadence by setting an alarm clock to ring accordingly to wake me twice during the night to change beds, and both times have a quick shower using a different towel to dry each limb. That leaves me one towel to mop up any spillages from my four cups of tea!

Whilst resting from the long journey and sleepily wondering if I'd selected the most comfortable bed, I was aroused abruptly by an ear-splitting siren. Like the other residents, I found myself ponderously stepping out into the corridor, wondering whether it was just a drill, a signal for us to swap beds(!) or merely a fault we should ignore. (The last option being a little difficult as I could envisage my ears bleeding if it went on much longer!).

It soon became apparent that water leaking through the ceiling into a light fitting had created an electrical fault; and much as I'd have liked to imagined Basil Fawlty rushing around maniacally shouting at Manuel (the Spanish waiter who had just set himself alight) "It's not fire, it's only drill", it really wasn't that dramatic.

We decided to allow the mayhem to sort itself out while we checked out the town. We settled on a pub which seemed to have an Irish theme. I tried two local specialities: lobster tails (a little like scampi), and cask John Smith's (which real ale drinkers will find considerably superior to the pressurised variety).

The next inn that we discovered had a vast number of beer mats adorning the bar and walls. There was live music from a young folk trio, which seemed to go down very well. I get the feeling that people actually listen to live music up here, rather than using it, as we tend to in the South, as a background wall of sound.

The great thing about Whitby is the variety of drinking establishments on offer; you can literally fall out of one pub and into another, totally different. So our final pint was in a quieter establishment with old hits on the TV being punctuated by the sound of colliding pool balls.

A sign we'd seen earlier proclaimed 'If you lose all your inns, drown your empty selves for they are the heart of England'. Perhaps if we in the South heeded such warnings, we would find there is less to be cynical about.

Value at Peterlee

91/92)   WHITBY PIERS (redundant harbour lights:
          west - green, east - red)
93)   WHITBY HIGH/SALTWICK BAY* (white/red
          isophase every 10 secs)
94)   SOUTH GARE (redundant harbour light)
95/96)   HARTLEPOOL HEADLAND/HEUGH

Unfortunately, our surfeit of beds did not also apply to breakfast, but in the town we found a coffee bar which offered a choice of four: American, English, Continental or Mediterranean. Looking to build our fat reserves for what promised to be a hectic day's walking, we chose the English variety, and were rewarded with a hearty breakfast containing black pudding and another regional speciality - pork and chive sausages.

The gentleman serving us had a prominent American accent, and furthermore, the two TV screens were both issuing forth a steady diet of 'CNN news' being broadcast live from the States. Naturally this consisted entirely of the latest developments in the 'war on terror.'

After glancing at the door marked 'Restrooms' (that's transatlantic for toilets!), we put two and two together and made eleven, postulating that CNN's intention could be to drum up support, much as in the past when mobs of 'press-gangers' tried to achieve this end. Glancing at the scattering of nonchalant customers, it would be likely to suffer a similar lack of popularity.

It was almost a case of having to check we were still in deepest Yorkshire. Yesterday in Scarborough, we had heard such authentic Yorkshire dialect at "Coom on 'n' carry ya's cort" being spoken to a young boy who had abandoned his jacket. Today we had yet to hear a local accent.

"Time f'rous to hit t't piggin' roard!"

That we did.

Whitby has two piers, one on either side of the mouth of the Esk. There are lighthouses on each one, and both of the jetties have stilted extensions with a beacon at the end; the west one is painted green and the east, red. This river mouth is famed as the point of arrival to Britain for Bram Stoker's Dracula.

We parked up, and walked past a tramp fast asleep on a bench, to the west pier lighthouse, which is by far the taller of the two. Built in 1831, its brownish, chimney-like tower is grooved like a Roman column and stands some seventy feet high. The lantern at the top is white, and the base is square in shape.

On the side, a plaque quotes 'Mightier than the thunders of many waters, mightier than the waves of the sea, the Lord on high is mighty'. Inscribed underneath are the words 'God is always greater than all of our troubles'.

This was our first sectarian lighthouse! And I must admit, against the troubled background of the time at which we visited, this information seemed far more appropriate than the crude daubings we'd found on the only other prosaic lighthouse we had come across, at Newhaven.

The light on the east pier is a more humble affair. The similarities are the grey/brown colour and the white octagonal lantern. This is a standard pier light akin to Folkestone or Ramsgate, built of large blocks and far more modest in height than the west pier lighthouse. It is also around twenty-four years younger – built in 1855. We reached this by crossing the bridge over the River Esk and driving through the narrow cobbled streets of the old town. We parked and then descended a steep footpath to the wide jetty. More fortification work against the encroaching North Sea appears to have been recently carried out here.

Looking back up the river, the town was no longer mellowing in autumn sunshine but cowering beneath clouds, perhaps being fuelled by the on-going fish-smoking activities!

Leaving Whitby, past the ruins of the thirteenth century abbey, we headed a short distance south to try to locate the lighthouse overlooking Saltwick Bay.

Known as Whitby high light, the only thing stopping us from reaching it was that old chestnut 'foot and mouth disease'. The drive was prohibited to all except those on business, and we didn't fancy our chances at convincing an angry farmer that looking at lighthouses was a viable enterprise! So we parked up in a caravan site to the south of the abbey and set about walking a mile and a half of the Cleveland way. This section of the path, popular with ramblers, had recently been closed due to cliff-falls.

The footpath followed the edge of the grassy cliff-top; and about two hundred yards before the present lighthouse, we encountered the white, single-storey foghorn building, which ran parallel to the cliff edge. Having again raided the Trinity House website for info, it appears that this was also once a lighthouse, being the more northerly of a set of two, showing fixed lights over the treacherous Whitby rocks.

Its more southerly compatriot however, survived this culling, and was altered in 1890 to display a more efficient light. It too consists of a long bungalow terrace, and is slightly further up the hillside/cliff than the foghorn building. It has a neatly-groomed lawn in front which, like its collection of garden gnomes, seems to be gradually disappearing over the cliff-edge. The round light compartment sits on top of the dwellings and is the centrepiece of the row. This is a vintage 1858 James Walker lighthouse, 42 feet in stature. The light itself is around 240 feet above sea level.

As we walked the footpath behind the lighthouse, accompanied by the approaching drone of a grass-strimmer, its current tenant welcomed us into the grounds. He informed us in a fine Teeside accent that the light was still in use. He and his lady had been tenants of many lighthouses and this was his latest temporary residence. The council worker, eager to clear the path, which had only recently reopened, was now strimming away behind us, and the conversation became somewhat lost in the irritating monotone whine.

Reciprocating the twelve furlongs of walk back to the car, I felt an insatiable desire rise within me - that being the addictive need for thirst-quenching 'Yuk'.

But horror! Before we knew it, we were the other side of Whitby in the shopless void of the North Yorkshire moors, being pursued by a flotilla of large cars which overtook us one by one with a business-like arrogance.

We were keeping an eye on the weather, which had been threateningly glum, but as the road briefly became a dual carriageway and descended steeply before Loftus, sunshine and blue skies were in evidence. It was as if we'd pushed the bad weather further north, challenging the elements like a modern day King Canute. And winning!

We then turned off, heading for the coast via the long suburbs of

Redcar. Parking on the western edge of the town, we quickly found a small shop, and within the downing of some metric measure of pink moo-juice which equated to just under a pint, we had not only recovered ourselves from the last walk, but were now ready for the mammoth walk out to South Gare light, at the eastern side of the mouth of the River Tees.

This was to be an epic.

Redcar basked in cool sunshine, a wide sandy beach curved infinitely away, and a white speck reflected the brightness about three and a half miles in the distance. Between us and the Tees was a huge grey foreboding cloud, like an impenetrable band of gloom, seeming to be a result of the relentless discharge from the heavy industry going on beneath it.

Scientifically speaking this is due to the particles of dust in the smoke that provide a surface area on which water vapour can condense. Unscientifically speaking, this was a pain in the butt!

This sense of impending bleakness was further enhanced by two words painted in bold, white letters on a concrete block sticking out of the sand, 'Beware - Perverts!'

Trying to push disturbing scenes from the film 'Deliverance' from my mind, we fixed our eyes on the distant harbour light and began walking in a dead straight line towards it, ignoring the contours of the coastline, which was bounded by dunes.

'If the Romans ever had to do this walk', I thought, 'this is how they would have done it'. This linear approach to things gave it a purposeful sense of destiny and what's more, we weren't getting rained upon either.

As the miles lolloped by, we saw a long line of ocean-going vessels queued up, patiently waiting to enter the estuary. First in line was a supertanker which drifted in slowly, behind the lighthouse, behind the quay and behind the moving vehicles.

Behind the *what*? What was this - a mirage? Our hearts sank at the thought of being committed to walking a seven mile round trip that could actually have been driven.

Climbing over the dunes, our worst fears were confirmed. There was a lane which headed back towards the industrial area, (still shrouded in gloom), and all the way back to Redcar. It is at times like this that certain authors may interject a little Anglo-Saxon into their works, but as we were about to commit trespass, I shall continue in Puritan format.

Having walked around 280 chains, (I love those old fashioned imperial measurements that nobody uses anymore!), a 'chain' would be about the only thing that could possibly prevent us from going out onto the jetty. A 'Strictly No Admittance' sign, or indeed a 'Trespassers Will Be Prosecuted' sign simply would not be enough to deter us. Besides which, the gate was open anyway.

We found our way down to the slippery lower level of the huge concrete jetty to discover that we were not alone, but among 'fishermen friends'.

I hate to say this but the lighthouse was fairly unremarkable, being a standard quayside structure - a round, white tower, built of cast iron and rusting at its base. It has a balcony around the light compartment and was built in 1884. It is also redundant, having been replaced by the beacon next to it.

Walking back, the church in Redcar was the focal point this time for our direct Romanesque military-style walking, looking down only to avoid stepping on heaps of decaying seaweed which flies buzzed around. Our mental focus was as direct as our visual focus - we needed 'Yuk.'

Leaving the continuous unbroken roar of the sea behind, we returned to the exact same shop, purchased the same drinks as the first time, tore off the foil tops with the same vigour, and drank.

With energy levels replenished, we were ready to negotiate our way through Middlesborough, encountering the beginning of the A66 - the English equivalent of route 66. Like its US counterpart, it is an east/west route across the country. Unlike its US counterpart, there is no song about it, but ours *is* still a major trunk route, whereas the more famous 'route 66' has been superseded by the 'interstate'.

The junction with the A19 was like a dietician's spaghetti junction with our chosen strand leading us nearer to Hartlepool.

Hartlepool hit the headlines in spring 2002, when a wily candidate for 'mayor' exploited an interesting piece of folklore to great success; this being the tale of the Hartlepool monkey, which during the Napoleonic wars was discovered roaming on the beach. Believing that this ill-fated creature was a French spy (these people didn't get out much), the primate was promptly arrested and hanged in the town square! There is now even a folk song about this legend.

Modern day Hartlepudlians are far more discerning though, after all collectively, they are the ninth happiest in the country about where they live. (This result was announced during the week that we visited).

It seems an up-and-coming place. Modern developments around the harbour area have changed the layout to such an extent that we found it difficult to navigate our way to the Heugh, or Headland.

There are two lighthouses here. The easterly one is white in colour and very similar to the quayside type, being a round, white, simple tower. It is surrounded by a wall and shares its compound with a white 'block' building and a mast. The first lighthouse here dates back to 1847, and was demolished in 1915 so that the lighthouse battery guns could be fired out to sea. The lantern was sited at a tower on the town hall until the present lighthouse was completed in 1926.

The other lighthouse on the headland faces south and is known locally as 'the red light'. It is actually a white weatherboard box with two thin, red, horizontal stripes. It is sited at the end of a short jetty, and above its square balcony a blade rotates in the wind like a propeller.

Its light varies in colour depending from which angle a vessel is approaching, red one side, green the other, and white if ships are dead on course.

The headland seemed a very quiet spot, and the seagulls called as they enjoyed the late afternoon sunshine, which lent a slight glow to the late nineteenth/early twentieth century houses along the shore. Hardly what you'd expect a 'red light' district to be like!

With today's quota of lighthouses achieved, we headed northwards through Blackhall Colliery which seemed a stereotypical northern place with its grim terraces along the road. Without any questions asked, we decided to find somewhere to stay in Peterlee.

We found a hotel which looked as though it dated from the sixties, with plenty of big glass panels. It was the kind of design that was often used for pub/clubs on housing estates that were built in this period. Initially attracted by the price, we reclined at the bar that served anything you liked as long as it was a popular brand of Australian lager!

To be fair, the place was in a period of transition, and the bar was being run down ready for relocation elsewhere in the building. Still, this lack of choice would serve as a good preparation for my Dad who would be off on holiday to Australia a couple of months later - I understand they like it there!

After a meal we decided to venture outside in search of a bar that served more than one beer. We were stunned that in a town of around twenty-five thousand people, we could only find one other place to drink in the town centre.

This public house was also built in the 'square' 1960's style and had the snappy title 'VFM'. Upon asking the barman what this stood for, he replied simply, "Value for money". A quick glance at the bar prices meant that it was not necessary to start quoting the trade descriptions act!

The High Street was very unusual too; feeling like the kind of small shopping centre that you often find in other similar-sized towns. It consisted of a mall of shops, which opened into a dead-end square at the bottom where there was an upper balcony. It made no attempt to aesthetically disguise its concrete construction.

Collating this information in our lager-soaked minds, we were a little slow in reaching the conclusion that we were spending the night in a 'new town'. The town was built to house workers from the nearby mine (now closed). It was established in 1948, and named after Peter Lee (1864-1935), a local man who had mined since the age of ten and had later became President of the International Federation of Miners. Of the twenty-eight officially recognised new towns, Peterlee is the smallest, except for one in Wales, which is appropriately named 'Newtown' (although the name was changed from 'Cadewain' in the medieval period, long before its status officially matched this epithet in 1967).

It became apparent that most of the nightlife had now been flung out onto industrial estates at the edge of town. People here generally used buses or taxis to get about, and at the time that we visited, you could buy a small terraced house for a mere £12,000, that's about a quarter, or even a fifth of the price of a similar dwelling down south. - The price people will pay to live where there's a choice of beers!

Having spoken to a few of the locals and observed the frequent usage of the word 'champion', it was time to retire; and our room had an added feature to it - it doubled as a sauna! With the heating system throwing out even more hot air than your average politician, the room soon became saturated with warmth. Waking up sweating in the middle of the night was perhaps the second part of my Father's preparation for Australia.

What we wouldn't have done for a flagon of Aussie lager now!

'Wet' in Whitley Bay

97)   SEAHAM
98)   SUNDERLAND (north pier light)
99)   CLIFF PARK/ROKER (relocated south pier light)
100)   SOUTER POINT (formerly red flash every 5 secs with lower sector light)
101)   SOUTH SHIELDS PIER
102)   GROYNE LIGHTHOUSE (South Shields)
103-105) NORTH SHIELDS (various redundant)
106)   TYNEMOUTH (pier light)

The Wednesday morning started off low-key. Little did we know the day would end on a high note, albeit off-key!

As soon as we awoke, our first priority was to fling wide the window and allow the hot, stuffy atmosphere in the room to dissipate. As cool, moist, fresh air infused slowly, the continual hiss of puddles being displaced by tyres suggested to us that today would not be easy or indeed, pleasant. After all, we had an unprecedented ten lights to view.

Breakfast was in a basement with plenty of large windows, through which to view the green, bushy surroundings and the steady drizzle dripping through the leaves and branches. Here the sound was the unchanging low-level roar of the rain; a sound quite cosy to listen to when in bed, altogether different from the end of a draughty pier.

It was time to leave Peterlee. Like King Canute who, we are told, believed he could hold back the waves by standing on the shore, we too had failed in pushing the wet weather northwards and would likewise be met with a watery defeat!

A few miles further up the A19 we found our turning for Seaham, a small seaside town with a fairly busy little port. The poet, Lord Byron spent some time here and described the coast as being 'dreary' - thanks to the merciless conspiring of the elements, we would be forced to depart with the same conclusion.

Leaving the warm cocoon of the car, we strolled to the port entrance battling to keep the umbrella from turning itself inside out in the wind, whilst trying to walk in such a fashion that a larger proportion of both of us could be sheltered by it. We were not successful at either.

We *may* have been able to casually saunter past the little security hut, but we decided to do things by the book (knowing how seriously these port officials take their work), and stepped inside to ask permission to proceed. The response was one of prohibition. Having said that we just wanted to view the lighthouse, we were taken about as seriously as somebody who says that the railway is their preferred form of transport. I could see that the gentleman was expecting Jeremy Beadle or Noel Edmonds or anybody else who has made a television career out of making people look foolish, to step out from behind us with a microphone at any moment.

The draconian regulations were not confined to the port either. Having defiantly told the guard that we would just go and view it from a different vantage-point, we discovered that the grassy area between the road and the low cliff-edge was not dedicated for public use.

So the closest we got to this round, fairly substantial, tapered, white tower with two black stripes was a view through a metal fence from around a third of a mile away. It opened in 1843.

Returning to the comforting womb of the automobile, the noisy blower chased away the mist from the windscreen as we mused on the fact that being warm and wet is far nicer than being cold and wet!

Driving today would be a battle against condensation, just as walking would be a battle against pneumonia, hypothermia or any other nasty experience associated with feeling like a drowned sewer rat!

Continuing northward, we soon found ourselves in the suburbs of Sunderland, with the road metamorphosing into a multi-lane one-way system (as they invariably do in the centre of large conurbations).

Having crossed the River Wear, we turned off of the main drag and descended to the sea. We found ourselves in a modern, red-bricked, red-roofed residential area of coastal development similar to that around Hartlepool Headland. A wide, curving pier ran out into the North Sea ominously for about half a mile. As with the two other long piers we would walk today, this one is closed to the public in extreme weather. A hardy fisherman returning with his rod advised us to walk on the right-hand side, so we would not find ourselves washed overboard by crashing waves.

Once we were beyond the lockable gates, we kept our heads well down and the umbrella in front of us until we reached the end. The round structure was thinner at the top, gently curving outwards to a wider base (a little like Smeaton's Eddystone tower, now at Plymouth Hoe).

Its external blocks are a pinky-red colour and look a little like brickwork. There are also a few greyish-white bands. A glance through the window reveals a brick reinforcement layer. Originally built in 1802, this lighthouse was moved and relocated at the current end of the pier after it was lengthened in 1841. Again, we returned to the car saturated. It was a very short drive to the next one but just long enough to get as comfortable as you can get in sodden clothes.

Cliff Park lighthouse is sited in the suburb of Roker, on a green between the main road and the low cliff-edge. It is a smooth, round, white tower some fifty feet in height, built of wrought iron. A plaque on its side gives us a glimpse of its past, being originally built in 1856 and situated on Sunderland's south pier, the other side of the Wear. It was dismantled and reconstructed here in 1983 to allow harbour improvements to take place.

Roker is a fairly spacious suburb of Victorian looking semi's, perhaps one of the more salubrious parts of the Tyne and Wear conurbations.

Onward and upward.

Next, Souter Point (rhymes with 'hooter'). This lighthouse is situated in a green cliff-top area, which acts as a breathing space between Whitburn (north of Roker) and South Shields. It was not always so; this was originally the site of the mining village of Marsden, which was flattened to the ground when the coal mine shut. It was the shipping of this coal that made the abundance of lights in this area necessary.

This point has not always been known as 'Souter' either - it was originally called Lizard Point, but underwent the lighthouse equivalent of 'deed poll' taking the name of the point a mile south where its construction had originally been proposed. This was to avoid confusion with Lizard Point in Cornwall.

The tower is 76 feet in height and was designed by James Douglass, a luminary name in lighthouse construction with such achievements as Smalls Rock (South Wales), Wolf Rock (near Land's End) and most notably, the present Eddystone light under his belt.

He constructed this white tower with red stripe and red top in 1871. Behind it is a symmetrical two-storey terrace, and there is a separate block-shaped foghorn building in front of it. The lighthouse keeper used to receive tuppence-an-hour 'noise benefit' for living in close proximity to this.

Being our one hundredth lighthouse, it was fitting that this was a National Trust owned property where we could enjoy a guided tour and some respite from the drizzle. Amazingly this was only the seventh lighthouse we had actually got to go inside.

As our tour-guide climbed the spiral staircase, eager to rush this tour through before a visiting school party arrived, he found himself a little out of breath. This did not phase his rapid-fire approach however, he simply spoke on the 'in' breaths as well!

The lens, which revolves on mercury, is bio-trioptic which means it has three faces and is double the height (like two lenses, one on top of the other). A prism reflects some of the light down the tower to a fixed lower lens whose light is used for navigation, appearing different in colour depending on your position at sea. Our guide also explained how radio waves are transmitted in a way that uses this same principle. This lighthouse was also the first to use an alternating current.

In the base several reconstructed rooms could be seen, showing us how the interior of an old lighthouse keeper's cottage would have been. An interesting poster on a wall displayed a kind of 'hierarchy' of classic lighthouses. From a distance it looked like a city skyline, but the skyscrapers here were scale outlines of various structures with the huge block-like Roman 'pharos' dominating the skyline at 460 feet high. Also among the tallest were Douglass' Eddystone light, La Corunna (the oldest fully working lighthouse in the world, built by the Romans in Galicia, Spain over 1800 years ago) and the familiar outline of the modern, pencil-like lighthouse at Dungeness.

With our brains saturated with information, our tour guide ended his fast-paced discourse and hurried in to begin again for the benefit of the schoolchildren. An adrenaline charged tour-guide combined with a crowd of hyperactive school-kids should just about have filled the place with enough hot air for it to lift off the ground and take off like a rocket!

Having wandered about on the green with our tools of photographic and videographic reproduction, oblivious to the curtain of damp drizzle that continued to enshroud everything, we were again thoroughly moist by the time we got back to the car.

Our next point of tribulation was at South Shields. It was an easy glide into the town and we left the car by an area of parkland and wandered to the seafront. We took a short cut to the pier, via a fun fair and over some mountainous heaps of sand. This pier looked even longer than the one at Sunderland, curving first one way and then the other for getting on for a mile, out to the round, grey, stumpy lighthouse which was topped with a red light compartment. Again, there were rail tracks running the pier's length.

We were at the mouth of the Tyne (which is the UK's seventeenth longest river), and across its tidal entrance stood a taller lighthouse perched on the end of another long pier which we would find ourselves trekking along later. These piers and lights were originally designed by James Walker in the 1850's.

I wouldn't have fancied being tossed about on a boat in today's blustery conditions. Then again, the windswept fishermen that passed us were probably thinking the same about being on the end of a freezing cold pier looking at lighthouses! But after a two mile walk we had become oblivious to the weather.

The other lighthouse at South Shields was level with the coastline on a short jetty. Getting as close as we could to it, we parked by a large hotel. We were little amused by the self-satisfied glances from the patrons as they paused over their lunches to watch two drowned rats skulking by!

The light is a red, octagonal box on stilts, which dates from 1880. Its balconied, octagonal light compartment is painted white on the seaward-facing side. I climbed the metal stairway up through the legs to the entrance, where a sign proudly displays its name - Groyne Lighthouse.

During the short walk back to the car we were intrigued by a collection of large 'weeble' type things fixed to the ground in a seemingly random formation in an open space. For those born after 1980, 'weebles' were weighted, round-bottomed toys, which looked like fat, legless, inch-high, little people that would always finish right-way-up whether you pushed them, turned them on their heads or threw them twenty feet across the room.

These granite-looking, two-foot high replicas seemed to have been arranged to make it look as though they were in conversation with one another. They were probably complaining about the weather! Then again, why should it bother them? After all, they were 'legless' and had hearts of stone!

Driving towards the Tyne Tunnel, we encountered about fifteen roundabouts in rapid succession. The Tyne Tunnel itself is about a mile long and single carriageway.

From across the river we had seen two large, square buildings. These were the upper and lower lights of North Shields. As yet, we did not know if they were lighthouses or not, so we stopped at a pub close by to extract some information. Fortunately for us, the barman actually lived in the aptly named 'Trinity' buildings, so by hook or by crook we had found a historically important lighthouse centre.

The enjoyment of our excellent locally-brewed ale was only slightly marred by the attentions of a locally-born dog, which noisily reminded us that we were impinging on his territory.

Stepping outside and allowing our eyes to get adjusted to the daylight again, we leaned over the wall along the road, and below us, in the dock area beside the river was the square lower light of 1808. This had six storeys with arch-shaped windows in a vertical line in each of the four faces. On top was a square light compartment surrounded by a balcony. You could describe this wide, off-white/cream-coloured building fairly accurately as an early-nineteenth century skyscraper.

Its counterpart, also built in 1808 was a short stroll along the road from us. This upper light is very similar but on a smaller scale, with only four storeys between the square balconied light compartment and the ground. Attached to this tower is a small house. Unlike the lower light, it has been treated to a new coat of white paint.

A matter of yards to the east is the light it replaced. Also one of a pair, this building dates from 1727. It is again a white, square building, and is now at the end of a terrace of houses. This time there is no balcony and the windows are square.

These pairs served the usual navigational purpose, where if one light appears directly above the other, you are on course for a safe entry. The replacements in 1808 were necessary because of a moving sandbank in the river. The very first light here was the low light of 1540.

Before we moved on, we savoured the fact that from this vantage-point, we could see an astonishing six lighthouses.

One of them was to be our final lighthouse for today, situated at the end of a long pier on the north side of the river. We had seen it clearly from the long pier in South Shields but now it was time to visit properly. A short drive found us parking near the ruins of the eleventh century priory and fourteenth century castle.

A footpath curved down to the straight pier, which was built on two levels. We walked the upper level; the lower level to our right had the usual rail tracks along it. As we neared the round, white topped, grey brick-pattern lighthouse, seagulls swarmed as if it were a scene from a Hitchcock movie. The wall to our left had been jam-packed with the birds, which as we moved closer, took to the air, one group after another, until the sky in front of us was an indistinguishable jumble of gliding wings.

We circled the tall tower as the gulls circled us. An inscription declared that the 3060-foot long pier was built in 1909. This was after a storm had damaged the original pier.

* * * * *

You could probably write a whole chapter on our night in Whitley Bay. It was only by chance that we stayed here, having driven up as far as Seaton and then deciding that we had passed all the accommodation, we retraced our steps.

After the inhospitable day we had endured, it seemed ironic that in a town where hotels and guesthouses are two-a-penny, we should pick the one that was so fastidiously economical with the heating. And had no towels.

It was peace and quiet that we were after and this seemed a reasonably priced little hotel in a secluded back-street. Peaceful it was; as I sat there on the bed shivering in my coat, my attempts at reading were certainly undisturbed by any noise from boilers, heaters or radiators!

Still, mustn't grumble, I would soon warm up with a large stir-fry in a pub that felt very much like one of those chain pubs. This establishment seemed to have got it right, finding a niche market, that market being for people who do not view perforated eardrums as being a necessary consequence of a night out! For as dusk fell, this quiet seaside town began to transform itself into a raver's Mecca. The various watering holes all vied for our attention by blasting ear-splitting disco music out of open windows into the street. The resulting mish-mash of conflicting rhythms sounded like a tribal call to war.

It worked; the streets were humming with sixteen-year-old girls in microscopic skirts and eighteen-year-old lads with a keen interest in 'sixteen-year-old girls in microscopic skirts', all eager to get past the smartly-dressed, bulldog-faced bouncers standing guard at the doors,

The effect of this prestigious demonstration of aural assault on us was the opposite. Wishing to defer the decision on where to drink next, I suggested that we go and have a look at the local 'Metro' station.

Impressed by the efficiency of the trains and the cleanliness of the station, we headed for the lesser of two evils – a pub with 'big screen football'. Both of us had preferred watching the trains!

My Dad's master-plan was to return to the bar in our hotel for a few quiet drinks in a low-key atmosphere. Of course this wasn't what we got; our road was now a mini Las Vegas, with hotels brightly illuminated. Some silver, some red, all noisy! As we wandered back a car was relentlessly driving round pulling a trailer supporting a huge billboard advertising, of all things, a 'wet T-shirt' competition!

What was this – some sort of sick joke? We had spent most of the day drenched to the bone in a lighthouse enthusiast's purgatory and there was this outlandishly sized sign seemingly rubbing our noses in it! Had the competition taken place a few hours earlier, we could have donated a wet jumper, a wet coat, wet trousers...

And there in the middle of all this madness was our little hotel, barely noticeable had it not been for the noise emanating from within.

This was Whitley Bay on a Thursday night, and it appeared that, like it or not, we were going to have to enter into the spirit of things. So preparing ourselves for a heaving party atmosphere, we ventured in to find...

...the barmaid, one drinker, the karaoke bloke and his wife!

The drinker soon left!

Summing up his audience, the music changed from the latest

ambient-techno-rave-hiphop-triphop-hardcore-house-garage-pigsty-barn music to the Beach Boys! This was to be a karaoke night for two – our own private performance. You will understand the irony we saw when our compere began to sing 'I write the songs that the whole world sings!'

To cap it all, I glanced out of the window, and what should go gliding past, but a huge billboard advertising a wet T-shirt competition. Glancing around the empty room, I began to notice that the walls were adorned with 'artistic' semi-pornographic photographs. If you've ever seen any of the early episodes of the TV comedy programme 'The league of gentlemen', you will understand that we were beginning to draw comparisons with Royston Vasey! More beer was in order.

Several pints later, it was time to show our gratitude for this gentleman who had been singing his heart out to two people and 'X' amount of cubic feet open space. My Dad rose to grab the microphone, I ran upstairs to grab the video camera, a car advertising a 'wet T-shirt competition' passed outside for about the eighth time and the opening chords of the Animals' 'House of the rising sun' began to chime out of the speakers. This was my Dad's party piece, as massacred at my eighteenth birthday and again five and a half years later when we got the encore at my sister's eighteenth!

This was the most harrowing version ever. It didn't help that my Dad stuck rigidly to a key which wasn't the one that the backing track was in. The fact that he began singing some of the lines several bars into the verse was a minus point too. However, the 'piece de resistance' was the way that his voice wobbled and broke over some of the strained high notes.

Still, the overall result was legendary. My Dad insisted that the 'slightly less than professional' sound was purely because it wasn't the real Animals playing the backing. He then instructed the 'entertainer' to pick out any Bob Dylan song for me. I suppose that in this surreal atmosphere, it was fitting that the only one he could find was 'Everybody must get stoned!' (Correct title: 'Rainy day women no's 12 and 35' – perhaps also appropriate after today!).

As the lights went up and the equipment was hurried back into carry-cases for the night, a certain vehicle passed for the umpteenth time, and I began to wonder if the so-called competition would have been as well-attended as the karaoke night was. Time to investigate.

161

We took it in turns to ask the young barmaid rapid-fire questions about Whitley Bay, and it became apparent that a national pub chain had just opened its latest venue in the old fire station. Ever the optimist, she was convinced that, given time, the punters would return for the simple fact that there would be no music at the old fire station, let alone hypoallergenic techno!

For this is what they like here; low music equals low trade, and no music equals no trade.

Oh yes, and they like 'wet T-shirt' competitions too!

Bonhomie at Berwick

107)   ST MARY'S/BAIT ISLAND (redundant)
108)   BLYTH PIER (harbour light)
109)   COQUET ISLAND* (red/white flash 3 times
          every 30 secs)
110/111) AMBLE (harbour lights)
112)   SEAHOUSES (harbour light)
113)   BAMBURGH* (occulting white/red/green
          flash twice every 15 secs)
114)   BERWICK-UPON-TWEED (pier light)

The variability of the British climate never ceases to amaze. We found it as difficult to forecast as it was to predict where we would be staying at the end of each day. The morning was crisp, clear and sunny, and Northumberland beckoned us. This county was the birthplace of the venerable Bede, who wrote the first history of the English people, completed 731 AD.

Our first lighthouse today was a mere five minutes up the road. St Mary's light is on Bait Island, which is linked to the land at low tide by a stone causeway. We parked in an area of green parkland known as 'Curry's Point'. The name originates from John Curry, who was hanged in chains at this point for the murder of a landlord.

The lighthouse which was completed in 1898 is pure white and very tall. From a distance, it looks as if it is pointing to the sky. Closer examination proves that it is not pointed, but has a small dome on top of a larger one above the light compartment, which sits upon its tapered shaft. I have been informed that its height is a whopping 126 feet.

The round wall, which reinforces the island it stands upon is also white in colour, and there is a light keeper's house here too, built to the usual design. We were unable to get a guided tour as the information centre was staffed but closed.

After circumnavigating the island and managing to lose each other on land the size of an allotment, we finally met at the steps that leave the island.

Next up: Blyth.

A mere five minutes further up the road, we found a suitable place on the sea wall above the sandy beach from which to view the lighthouse, which is situated on the end of the pier. Standing on the concrete sea wall above the beach, I set up the tripod and zoomed in on the round, stumpy lighthouse, which again appeared to point to the sky due to its 'dome upon dome' roof. It sat on a round concrete cylinder at the end of the pier, which had vertical struts like a row of soldiers on parade. Along its length were a series of electricity-generating wind propellers.

The beginning of this pier is actually to the north of the town across the River Blyth. Our error was to completely bypass the town (due to our preconceptions that its nature was mostly industrial, being a former ship-building town). Not only did we miss our turning, having to do a U-turn at Newbiggin-by-the-Sea, but we also missed a lighthouse!

It wasn't until I glanced at my AA book of British towns that I realised that there is another lighthouse behind a row of houses near the quayside. Unfortunately this 'glance' was several months later and three hundred miles south, in the comfort of my own bedroom. We would have to return.

Trying to gain access to the pier was also a dead loss. Signs warned that trespassers would be hung, drawn and quartered, so we parked by the railway sidings which ran into the industrial plant, viewed the wind farm, ate an extra strong mint and headed off back up the lane past the massive industrial buildings, back to the dual carriageway A189.

We streaked past Ashington, noticing the ubiquitous red-roofed modern housing. The same styles that have sprung up on the outskirts of every medium-sized town from Weston-Super-Mare to now, here in Northumberland. Perhaps the North and South will eventually blend into the same nondescript formality.

Above Newbiggin, you could say that we were beyond the 'grip' of the Tyne and Wear conurbations. All that stood between us and Scotland were unpretentious misty Northumberland hillocks and small distant coastal towns and villages.

It is interesting to note that Newcastle is level with the western end of the Scottish border (it is also roughly the end of Hadrian's 74½ mile long wall). The eastern end of the border is some sixty-odd miles further north.

This whole area to the north seems to have a distinct air of calm about it. It's as if once you get beyond Newbiggin, the hustle and bustle no longer matters. Before we reached Amble, we detoured to the coast to get a good view of the 72-foot lighthouse on Coquet Island from the dunes.

About a mile across the water stood this chunky, square, sandstone tower, the top half of which was painted white. Upon this stands the round light compartment.

Completed in 1841, this was built upon the remains of a fourteenth/fifteenth century monastery, originally housing a group of Benedictine monks. The keeper's house next to the tower stands where the former chapel was. The first lighthouse keeper here was William Darling, the elder brother of Grace, of whose heroism you will shortly be reading.

Amble, a mile or so up the road from this point seems a very peaceful little town. We parked by a fish and chip shop and walked alongside the River Coquet with a wide green to our right.

At the entrance to this river are two jetties – one each side. At the end of the more northerly one is a small, white, square based structure, which resembles an elongated pyramid on stilts.

The pier on the south side is vertically strutted, and has a 'no access' sign which clearly doesn't apply if you have a fishing rod. Upon it stands a red and white striped mini-lighthouse on a wide cylindrical base. It looks a little like a perpendicular stick of seaside rock.

You could best describe this as a Dinky-toy scale version of Happisburgh lighthouse. My Dad described both of them as beacons and left somewhat unimpressed.

As we left the town thinking we had seen it all, we discovered a bustling High Street but our schedule was too intensive to stop.

Pressing on up this coastline, our next port of call was twenty odd miles further north at Seahouses. We were now, surprisingly, as far north as the Isle of Arran. The sky had become a little hazy, but Seahouses seemed a cheerful little place with a quaint harbour area that could easily have been in Cornwall. The growth of the harbour here is largely due to herring fishing.

At the end of the stone jetty stood the white hexagonal tower. It was a fairly mundane looking structure adorned with a large notice displaying the harbour speed limit of three knots. There was a large mast attached to the lighthouse, which rose well above the top. Upon this was a lofty weathervane.

A single door, a red buoyancy aid and a yellow litter bin added a splash of colour to this, at a guess, 25-foot high tower.

We weighed up the pros and cons of boarding a tour-boat here for the Farne islands, which are between two and five miles out to sea. From this vessel, we would be able to view both the Inner Farne lighthouse and the more famous red and white striped Longstone lighthouse, which used to be the home of Grace Darling.

This lady saved nine storm-tossed sailors in 1838 by rowing out with her father (the lighthouse keeper), in treacherous conditions to the rocks where these survivors of the shipwrecked 'Forfarshire' steamer were clinging for their lives.

Her heroism is noteworthy because, although local fishermen had declared it too dangerous to attempt a rescue, it was Grace who persuaded her father to undertake the mission.

Unlike amazing Grace, we decided against a boat trip, not for fear of a similar experience but for fear of a slight reduction in wallet weight! Besides, we had a tight schedule, so we continued forth to Bamburgh.

The whole of this long north-east coastline from Whitby to the borders seems to be littered with ruins of ancient abbeys and monasteries. Around the seventh and eighth centuries, this was indeed a hotbed of early religious thought and learning. Many of these learned souls were subsequently elevated to sainthood.

St Oswald (d.642), a pious king of Northumberland supposedly had his right hand kept at Bamburgh and his head with St Cuthbert's remains, now at Durham. (St Cuthbert incidentally died at his hermitage on the Farne islands 687AD).

But we were not in search of missing body parts, and the imposing view of Bamburgh Castle upon its mound seemed to fill the windscreen as we approached. Today's impressive sight of the fortifications is, to some extent, a historical sham. The early Saxon fort was sacked by the marauding Danes, and the later Norman castle was allowed to fall into ruin after capture by Yorkist, Edward IV in 1463. The stately pile we view today is thanks to massive expenditure on renovation by a Victorian arms manufacturer during the 1890's.

Having found the little lane to the lighthouse, our minds turned to more mundane matters like parking. We were soon ambling along the rugged coastline, glancing back occasionally to notice the fine white spray breaking on the rocks. The castle, now a mile behind us was shrouded serenely in a light hazy mist.

The Trinity House maintained light is unusual in design, for it is a white, rectangular block with a green door and two circular windows above it, which looked a little like two eyes and a mouth. This structure, less than 30 feet in height was built in 1910. The round light compartment on top is painted black, and the whole building is surrounded by a stone wall. On the rugged rocks in front of it is painted a white deer. Why? I have no i-deer.

Oh dear!

It was a short drive to the A1, which by this stage had been tamed into a single carriageway. We wanted to quickly visit the Holy Island of Lindisfarne. There is a road onto the island, which is flooded at high tide. In the middle of the channel is a clearly marked area where it is safe to remain if you become stranded by the tide. The down side to getting stranded is that it will involve several hours of sitting motionless with nothing to look at but water.

The island itself was famously home to the missionary bishop, St Cuthbert. The old Benedictine priory is now a public attraction, as is the castle. The tide was in, so unfortunately our visit was to contain no such religious dimension, and our thoughts turned to knocking off our final lighthouse on this day's foray, and searching for vittles and a warm roof.

Had we have been able to cross to Holy Island we may have noticed two Trinity House lights: Guile Point East – a stone obelisk which overlooks Holy Island harbour from a peninsular on the Northumberland Coast; and Heugh Hill light - a skeletal frame tower. However, both these descriptions and the Ordnance Survey map give the impression that these are merely beacons, and thus the lighthouse hunters are vindicated!

Berwick-upon-Tweed is England's most northerly town. This town has changed hands between the English and the Scots fourteen times. The last of these was in 1482. I even heard that the Scottish tourist board had recently put in a bid to buy the place back. The shopkeepers clearly still like to hedge their bets anyway, diplomatically displaying both the flags of St George and St Andrew all the way down the street. I suppose, being less than three miles from the Scottish border, it is not wise to alienate half your market.

The accents are different here too. We are now way beyond the Geordie 'You can have a fishy on a little dishy/when de boot cooms in' accent here - this is almost 'Donald where's your troosers' country!

Of course, not wishing to offend half of *my* market, I would like to point out that we noticed a pub advertising a 'West Country' evening, which I'd imagine involves dressing up in old fashioned shepherds smocks, with a blade of grass in between one's teeth, taking the Mick out of the zoider-drinking people of Zummerzet and Dorzet. Who knows, you may even get to hear the Wurzels at such an event. Perhaps I should have looked for that album here instead of Taunton!

Before any such frivolity could take place, it was time to check out England's most northerly lighthouse.

We parked beside the River Tweed, with a fine view of the three bridges that cross it. Most impressive is the rail bridge with 28 tall arches built by Robert Stephenson. The other two are the original arched road bridge and its replacement, a more modern construction.

Also worth noting architecturally is the wall around the town, which was originally medieval and has been extensively rebuilt over the years. This central part of the town is north of the Tweed.

To the east, you can drive along the narrow riverbank wall, which is completely unfenced. Fortunately we didn't have to pass any other vehicles.

On this quiet periphery of the town, a long stone/concrete pier runs out to sea. To the north of this breakwater, a series of poles protrude from the water. An affable elderly gentleman informed us that in days gone by, these were used by local people who tethered nets and lines from them, returning later to extract whatever 'catch' they may have made.

The pier deviates to enclose a wide haven at the river mouth. At the end stands the round harbour light. It is white bodied, with a red bottom section and a red cone shaped top. It is of the usual 'quayside' dimensions and it dates from the 1820's.

This seemed another pivotal moment in the mission, having covered the entire English East Coast. All that remained for us to do now was North-West England and North Wales. We were on the home straight.

So we gazed out into the expanse of the North Sea for a few minutes, emulating the peaceful empty area before us, clearing our minds to impart a feeling of quiet satisfaction.

Being so close to the Scottish border, it seemed fitting that we should take a trip out of the town just to cross it.

The A1, rather peculiarly, becomes a dual carriageway again above Berwick, as if to make some kind of civil engineering statement along the lines of "We have dual carriageways in Scotland too - just not as many of them!" As soon as the border is crossed though, it humbly reverts to its 'muzzled' single carriageway status.

There are lay-bys on both sides of the road at the border, but it seems that the entrance to Scotland is much more prestigious. Here, you have a pristine area with both a sign and a large stone proclaiming triumphantly that you are in the land of the thistle.

We drove the purpose-built loop over the road, which enables English visitors who had done what we'd just done to do a U-turn. We then passed the bedraggled lay-by into England. Here, the stone had been graffitied and there was a burnt out litter bin, with the items that should have been inside it strewn across the tarmac!

But then I thought, 'This is not so much a poor reflection on the English as on the Scots'. After all, why would we want to vandalise our own sign? Unless, of course, these juveniles were trying to make some sort of tongue-in-cheek post-modernist statement about the state of the country.

Much, as I realise that yobbery is one of the few areas where England can still teach a lot to other nations, I couldn't help but bring to mind a barbaric Scottish folk song which goes along the lines of 'They'll hang you up and slit your throat/and pick your carcass clean/ if they smell the blood of an Englishman/in the cave o' Sonny Bean!' Apologies if I've misquoted slightly, but I think you'll see that while we are concerned that younger generations may be listening to violently aggressive rock music, our ancestors were getting drunk and singing debauched lyrics like that!

Which brings me neatly to our final resting-place today - the bar.

We had a meal in a northern outpost of a certain chain-pub before returning to the inn we were staying for a lengthy and slightly surreal drinking session.

The locals were very friendly, both young and old. One young lad who had never been further south than Newcastle was trying to arrange a trip to a night-club about twenty miles away. Then, whilst talking to some of the older gentlemen, we realised that most people up here think we are all filthy-rich in the South.

From the corner of the room a self-made millionaire piped up, declaring that he had worked his way up from poverty to his alleged affluence. Now in the South, the much-touted 'classless' society doesn't seem to have permeated to this degree. After all, here we have either a millionaire or an inventive storyteller freely mixing with the proletariat. To socialise with such a wealthy person back home, would require having an annual salary the size of the gross domestic product of a small country!

We seem more than a little obsessed with money, right down to the fourteen-year-old conditioned into sweating over exams, to get the university places, to get the high-powered jobs, so that they can get a bigger car, a bigger house and bigger debts than their classmates. If you dare suggest that there may be other important factors in life apart from money, most people will begin thumbing through the 'Yellow Pages' to try and find a nice secure home for you with padded rooms!

Just then, three or four basset hounds ran energetically into the room. Scampering around the floor with wagging tails. The debate was adjourned.

The millionaire asked my Dad for a light. Presumably, he would not deign to be seen purchasing a box of matches! Or is that the secret of amassing a fortune? In contrast, we boldly asked the landlady for another round of drinks. It was a lock-in.

*****

A new day dawned and as we looked out of the window to greet the morning, we noticed two empty beer kegs had appeared overnight in the alley below.

Just as the mass of parking tickets which had been multiplying on the car windscreen were all that remained of our week, so these kegs appeared to be all that remained after our night in Berwick.

Large quantities of beer had ensured that we were able to sleep through the noisy water tank's night-time rumblings.

After breakfast, we drove slowly and regally along Berwick's main street and it was as if the bagpipe player on the roadside was playing us a fanfare as we left the town.

A last look at the historic wall, a sudden turn left, and we were heading for the A1.

The road was misty. It would be inappropriate to call it a 'Scotch mist'. We had a seven-hour journey ahead of us. Places we had always thought of as being 'far north' were now 'way down south'. In a few hours time they'd all be north again!

SOME LOOSE ENDS
AND THE NORTH-WEST

Utterly Orford!
(or 'Orford revisited')

By the powers of deduction, you may have realised that a couple more trips should see us through to completing our jaunt around England and Wales.

Our next foray was to occur in April 2002. In the meantime I was to visit Italy and my father, Australia.

As I savoured the view of the canals of Venice, lighthouses couldn't have been further from my mind, yet upon reaching the top of a bell-tower, it was as though an automatic homing device had taken control of my video camera, and I found myself zooming in on a tall white structure across the water!

My Dad's experience was even more pronounced. Having traversed half the earth's circumference for a three-month sabbatical down-under, it seems that his priorities were not Sydney and its eponymous bridge and opera house, nor the rust-coloured megalith of Ayer's Rock. From his photographs it would appear that viewing as many lighthouses as possible along the South Aussie coast was far higher on the agenda!

Back in good old Blighty, it was time to tie up a few loose ends.

With the 'foot and mouth' epidemic now laid to rest, we at last had the all clear to visit Orford Ness in Suffolk. Bemused at why a bovine disease had perturbed us from accessing this isolated shingle bank without any cow, pig, goat or llama in evidence, we discovered that summer grazing in previous years was the cause for restriction.

Within a couple of hours of leaving home, we once again found ourselves at the quiet waterfront of Orford. Purchasing our tickets from the National Trust office, we climbed aboard our ferry, (a small wooden boat with engine), to traverse the short stretch of water onto the spit.

Due to its bleak nature, you are counted and briefed before you are let loose in this wilderness, and recounted as you return. Thus any poor souls left straggling about somewhere on this stony expanse after the last boat has departed, can be herded up and safely dispatched to the mainland.

There are numerous buildings scattered about this area and in some, nuggets of information about the spit's military past can be gleaned. For scientists were once stationed here for research, which eventually led to radar (pre-1940), and atomic bomb sightings and trajectory recordings (post-1953).

With its days as a testing site now well over and its purchase by the National Trust in 1993, the area is now a birdwatcher's paradise, and there are numerous endangered plant species here including sea-peas.

It seems that the only info-shed that we didn't find was the one on the lighthouse - we were in fine form once again! The sun teased us as our hands grew increasingly numb from the bitter wind, and upon reaching the round, white tower, which in its setting seemed huge, we had to wait several minutes for clouds to pass in order for there to be optimum light for the all-essential camera footage.

From its wide base, the structure narrows with its 100-foot height. It has two red bands and a lattice-windowed light compartment. With a couple of small keepers buildings nearby, it is surrounded by a circle of markers, like white painted milestones all engraved with 'TH 1925'. Many visitors have mistaken these for gravestones, although the idea of finding half a dozen or more people with the initials 'TH', all of whom died in the same year, and burying them around a lighthouse seems a little incredulous to me!

No, 1925 was the year that Trinity House took control of the site, and the circle marks out the area of land they now own. The lighthouse is far older than this, and we were told that it has been around since the 1790's. It was once accompanied by a wooden low light, which was rendered invalid by a storm in the 1880's.

Further up the Ness a large, low-rise block dominates the horizon. Apparently this is the transmission centre for the BBC World Service, chosen because it is a convenient location for broadcasting to Western Europe. Perhaps one day the airwaves will be transmitting nightly readings from this book. Although that might prove 'a light too far' for this increasingly inscrutable corporation!

Reaching the A14 via Tunstall and Wickham Market, we glimpsed inquisitively at rural Suffolk. It seemed that around here it is compulsory for every place to end with the suffix 'market'.

Both this road, and the relentlessness of the A1 prompted me into a couple of short cat-naps as we continued ever northwards. Our bed for the night was to be in a 'Travel Tavern' type place on a roundabout near Retford. I shall use this particular term to avoid evoking any brand names, whilst acknowledging that its linguistic creation was as a boarding-house for jinxed chat-show host Alan Partridge in the TV comedy series.

Our stay was very comfortable, which was just as well as we'd already pre-booked our second night in such an establishment near Carlisle.

But what of Retford?

What indeed? I cannot say that anything particularly struck us about the place, which has a pedestrianised High Street and a market square at the centre. We found a hotel on the outskirts to be the most suitable place to nourish ourselves. As I tucked into a succulent piece of steak, I noticed how much more enjoyable a meal is without the impending deadline that one encounters when eating with a group of mates, who seem to treat the event as though it's some kind of Olympic sport!

Having completed their meals at breakneck speed, I am usually left with half a platefull, which then becomes a chore to eat because basically the meal is now over.

Still, with my Dad the opposite is true, and once I had cleared my plate, I was able to notice the inappropriately-dressed people around us, while he polished off the last remnants of his lamb chop.

For here we were, resplendent in wax jackets and several jumpers, while one of our fellow diners was attired in little more than a bra! Such immunity from the cold would have been nice out at Orford today.

Finishing in another restaurant/bar closer to our night's stopover, we tried the local brew from Retford's Broadstone brewery. The 'Fletchers' ale proved to be a fine, full-bodied bitter which lulled us into a relaxed state of mind.

Returning to our 'Travel Tavern', we secretly wished for an appearance of Alan Partridge to liven up the proceedings with his sledgehammer tactlessness, but all we got was exactly what we'd expected - a good night's kip!

Hadrian's Heap

(or 'Blyth Revisited')

115) BLYTH – BATH TERRACE (disused)

We awoke to the American dream.

Here we were, conveniently located on a roundabout surrounded by filling stations and eateries. We had a number of breakfast options at our disposal but were lured by the 'golden arches' of a ubiquitous fast-food outlet. The vacant space in my wallet was also a clinching factor!

But is this transatlantic dream really a nightmare from which it is too late to wake? For, like the US, in Britain we no longer have amenities where people live, but clustered around major road junctions like bees round a honeypot.

All is well and good until you find yourself involved in some form of outdoor pursuit such as hiking, biking or walking to remote lighthouses. In need of light refreshment, it is common to proceed to the nearest village to find that the closest shop is now six miles away. Then, when at last you arrive there gasping and panting, and soaked either by sweat or rain, you are greeted with the news that the shop is only open on Tuesdays and Thursdays between 10am and 1pm, due to competition from the nearest supermarket which is eleven miles away along a busy dual carriageway!

Speaking of which, as we began our journey bound for the North-East, which entailed us enduring a hefty portion of the A1, we passed numerous cyclists racing; not in the safety of the gap at the side of the road bounded by the continuous white line, but out in the main carriageway.

This seemed like utter madness, but on second thoughts during a recent bike ride along this supposed sanctuary section of our own A2070 road, I inadvertently cycled into a road sign, which caused the front wheel to lock and me to be catapulted over the handlebars for a close examination of the tarmac! Abandoning my bike in the hedge, I was then forced to walk the remaining three miles home, all the time wishing that the trains ran at midnight or that taxis were cheaper!

The A1 is sufficiently curvaceous to maintain a modicum of interest until just beyond the turning for York, where it presents you with a bland laborious slog across North Yorkshire. My Dad informs me that in Australia, where the distances are much greater, curves have been added to the dead straight roads in order to prevent drivers falling asleep at the wheel. Thinking back to the A15 North of Lincoln, (allegedly Britain's longest straight section of road), perhaps the Romans had already come up with this idea some millennia before the advent of the motorcar!

As we neared Durham, the fuel-tank was perilously low, so due to some perverse reasoning that we would support local business, having just passed a filling station on the A1 which was well-signed in advance, we made a detour into this historic city with its castle and cathedral, (which houses the bones of the Venerable Bede), dominating the skyline. The place seemed attractive from all angles, but reinforcing my earlier point about amenities in the UK, the one thing that we were looking for eluded us.

We passed two of the 'closed forever' variety of the lesser-spotted filling station (now the most common species), and nearing Chester-le-Street and the point at which the horizontal nature of the needle on the dial becomes a little discomforting, our fears were allayed. Once we'd filled up, petrol stations began to appear with even greater regularity than cold-calling telephone sales enquiries at mealtimes!

We were soon beyond the Tyne metropolis and back in the familiar area of Blyth – the town we had callously bypassed seven months ago to our detriment.

Our ancient AA guide was spot-on, as behind a Victorian terrace, a round tower of white-painted brick (which was not too dissimilar from the rugged old lighthouse at Flamborough Head), overlooked the fenced-off port area.

Adorned with small windows and crosses in the slightly grubby brickwork, it appears that the top half has been added or renovated at some point due to its smoother external surface.

My Dad came up with a convoluted theory that this metal-looking top half was added as a water storage tower, the evidence being that one of the houses in the terrace in front was clearly marked 'Bath House'. Meanwhile, I was beside the lifeboat station trying to get another shot of the pier lighthouse at the end of the line of wind turbines.

With our loose ends now tied up, it was time to head for Carlisle and the start of this leg of the mission 'proper'. Having had our fill of major trunk routes today, we decided to take in Hadrian's wall.

Glancing at a map, it would appear that one would be able to view this ancient Roman defensive boundary adequately whilst driving along the B6318. Yet this is not the case, and if like my Dad, you have a certain reluctance to leave the car in bad weather, I suggest you save yourself the aggro and use the A69.

It wasn't until after we'd covered at least twenty miles that we noticed a crumbling relic running parallel in the field to our right. It is of a similar appearance to the dry stone walls, which run in grey lines along the roadsides and across the fields all around this area. Hadrian's wall is considerably wider though – in places, perhaps four feet.

Driving a little further, the wall promptly disappeared into the grass as quickly as it had appeared.

As the terrain grew hillier, I was sure that the wall was now undulating its way across the rugged landscape, capping the hills to the north of us. I suggested that we take a right turn to investigate, but on this now damp and drizzly day, my Dad emphatically stated "It's rubbish" and drove ever westward, muttering under his breath about 'Hadrian's heap!'

He did concede that the sheep seem to like climbing on it, nevertheless, I was not used to hearing World Heritage sites being likened to refuse in this way, and became ever more determined to take in all I could of this intermittent pile of old rocks! My Dad eventually relented, and I was rewarded with a few hundred yards stroll beside it west of Greenhead. I'm sure I would have continued, had it not abruptly ended with a death-defying drop into a valley.

Unlike the Great Wall of China, Hadrian's wall cannot be seen from space, but it did successfully withhold the Picts for a while. Repelled further north, the Antonine wall was then built from the Firth of Forth to the Clyde to restrict their movements even more, but with little success.

Our evening's movements were restricted by the siting of our next 'Travel Tavern', with the city centre being around five miles away, and the nearest pub appearing to have died a lonely death. So after food and a single pint in a national chain in Carlisle's quiet city centre (which we had lapped three times in a blind search for both this venue and parking), we returned to our lodgings.

A short note on Carlisle is perhaps necessary here, as it is the western equivalent of Berwick-upon-Tweed. In spite of being around six times larger, it shares a remarkably similar history, having changed hands many times between the English and the Scots, before the English claimed it once and for all, comparatively lately in 1745.

Having consumed the least amount of beer ever, it was as if the graffiti, which ran for about a hundred yards along some boarding, had influenced us. It consisted of the simple phrase 'Buy Less, Work Less' - an unpopulist philosophy that has possibly not occurred to most in this wealth and status-obsessed era. Then again, perhaps lack of work was to blame for the fact that somebody's chief form of entertainment is daubing slogans on walls in the first place!

We had spent quite enough time looking at walls today. Tomorrow we would get back to what we were here for – lighthouses.

Apologies to World Heritage.

Beaten in Barrow

(or 'Time and Tide wait for no man')

116)   SILLOTH NORTH
117)   LEES SCAR LIGHTHOUSE
118)   MARYPORT (redundant harbour light)
119-121) WHITEHAVEN (harbour lights)
122)   ST BEES HEAD* (2 white flashes every 20 secs)
123/124) MILLOM/HODBARROW MINE
          (disused)
125)   WALNEY ISLAND

As I lay in my makeshift bed, I lifted the curtain to glance at the Border sky, which was a mottled mixture of grey and blue. By the time we had visited the 'golden arches' for another cost-effective American breakfast, there was not a cloud in sight. It seems that a visit to XXXX really does brighten your day!

Beyond Carlisle, heading south-west to Silloth, the fairly flat agricultural landscape was green and easy on the eyes. To our left, in the distance, loomed the grey apparition of the Cumbrian Mountains, (which contain Scafell Pike – the highest mountain in England), and ahead of us across the blue water of Solway Firth rose the tall hills of Dumfriesshire.

We approached Silloth along a seafront lane from the more northerly hamlet of Skinburness. The homes that lined the road seemed to be in a very privileged position, with a short green in front between the road and the Firth, which on this cool sunny day was like a millpond, with the majestic hills of Scotland behind.

It was on this green that our first lighthouse stood, a tall, wooden construction painted white. It consists of a black topped, octagonal light compartment, on four legs with some reinforcing cross-struts. This square based creation was a bright and cheery sight sewn among the daffodils.

Silloth used to be the port for Carlisle and I have information that there has been a lighthouse at Silloth Point since 1841. The only other lighthouse that *we* found though, is sited on the beach to the south of this quiet little town. This meant a short walk for us from the car, which we parked to the south of the inlet that serviced the old flour mill.

Here we faced a previously unencounterd hazard - flying golf balls! The route of our footpath was marked out across the course by two parallel white lines. Crossing the dunes, we found ourselves upon the wide sandy beach.

The epithet 'Lees Scar lighthouse' is hardly deserving of this 'beacon' which consists of a light on a square platform atop of four poles rising from the shore. They seem to be anchored by four blocks, one at each corner of the square base. Yet most of our maps showed this as a lighthouse rather than a beacon.

The beaches around the North-West are notorious for their fast moving tides, which have often left people stranded due to the speed the sea encroaches upon the gently sloping shore. Morecambe bay in Lancashire has actually claimed the lives of folk out exploring the vast sandy expanse. The tide has come in at such a rate that they have become isolated by channels of water; or worse still a mist has rolled in, making negotiation of a dry route back to the shore nigh on impossible.

I felt a little like a news reporter dashing into a war zone for that ultimate bit of video-footage and dashing back out again to safety; for this structure stood on an area of stones, which were as dry as Silloth's cobbled main street as I walked out, yet after a few minutes water was bubbling over them from both sides at a gain of several inches-per-second. I ignored my Father's increasingly terse shouts of "Come on!" as the situation became a little like the Red Sea after Moses had led the Israelites out of slavery, with the waters closing in on the pursuing Egyptians.

With the all-important ten seconds of camera footage, I sprinted back across what was now a shallow channel of water, which given the state of my shoes, now several months past their expiry date, meant wet feet for a substantial part of the day. By the time I was back at the shore, still slightly out of breath, this so-called lighthouse appeared to be rising out of the middle of the sea.

It was unfortunate for me that I had recently lost my only decent pair of shoes a week before. What had started out as a gentle cycle ride eventually turned into a mudbath as I opted for a little off-roading on a byway. Over a mile into its route, it became a quagmire, some ten inches deep, which sucked off my steel toecapped boots, leaving me to face a twelve mile bike ride home unshod!

Needless to say, a letter was written to the district council responsible for dedicating this trail of sludge as a byway, stating that this fitted the term 'byway' about as much as Lees Scar deserved the epithet 'lighthouse!'

Because this luminary nearly cost me my life, or at least another pair of shoes, it is even more tempting to disqualify it, but I am feeling lenient so 'lighthouse number 117' it is.

The three ports of Cumbria, (Maryport, Washington and Whitehaven) were planned and set out during the eighteenth century, mainly to export coal to fuel-deficient Ireland from the now defunct local seams. This trade has ceased and although fishing is still of some importance, to our untrained eyes, each has gone its seperate way; Maryport, the smallest, to tourism, Workington to retail parks and distribution, and Whitehaven to both, plus modern industry, chemicals and nuclear fuel reprocessing at nearby Sellafield.

The fifteen mile drive down the coast to Maryport was pleasant as we followed a thin line between green fields and sandy beaches, slowly approaching the low hills beyond quaint Allonby.

Maryport demanded closer examination; our maps showed no lighthouses here, but since when have they been right? We headed for the harbour, which was filled with fishing boats, behind which the light-grey houses crept gently up the slopes around the town.

There has been a light here since 1796. This one was converted to acetylene in 1946. The quayside structure we saw was a thin, white tower with a black lantern on top; thicker than the lamp-post-like beacon at Bridlington and rising from a square, white podium, which in turn rests on a brick block. The quay appears to have been extended, as a hundred yards or so further out, at the very end, there is a white beacon – obviously its replacement. The Trinity House website describes this as an aluminium tower built in 1996 and connected to mains electricity.

We were not tempted to wander out however. Enough damage had already been done, as I disturbed a couple in a passionate embrace when filming behind the redundant lighthouse. The pair shuffled a little further around the back. Not wishing to add a love scene to our movie, *we* shuffled off to Workington.

'Work' seems about right for this place, for its industry is of prime importance. Railway lines ostracise the town from its port, which once thronged with coal and steel shipping. Much of this area has now been redeveloped with DIY superstores and fast food outlets. Beyond this peripheral trade zone, we could see that there were only beacons to be seen along the dockside, so we continued our merry way to Whitehaven.

Whitehaven was once the second port only to London, transporting coal from local mines, which extended for several miles under the sea. It is perhaps a more attractive town than neighbouring Workington, save for the grid-like, gridlocked one-way system around its centre.

We parked on a grassy hillock overlooking the harbour, which appeared to be the site of four lighthouses. I am only going to count three of these structures though, as one of them is merely a redundant watchtower. This tall cylinder of grey/beige stone blocks dates from 1736 and is situated on a spur running across the harbour from the south quayside. A far more modern lookout centre has now replaced it – no way could you mistake *this* for a lighthouse!

A similar grey cylinder is sited behind several buildings on another shorter spur a little further out. This has a rusty balcony and is clearly an old lighthouse. The light at the very end of the south pier is the tallest of the four towers, being a round, tapered, white structure, with the very bottom painted red, and a balcony around its elongated light compartment. Its partner in crime is on the other side of the harbour at the end of the north pier. This is a squat, white cylinder which looks exactly like the 'castle' piece in a game of chess, (apart from the red line around the bottom and the rusty balcony half way up). Although, if the bottom half of my chess pieces were this rusty-yellow colour, I would give them a darn good wash!

A gentleman in my local told me an anecdote from his childhood about this tower. He and his mates used to fish off of the balcony here, and during one of these adventures a storm arose which meant that they were confined to this tower by the huge waves for the whole night. A frightening experience I would imagine, for any child. I think, given a choice, I would opt for my childhood tribulation of being chased around Margate by thugs!

As we left Whitehaven, we climbed steeply to the village of

Sandwith (which I am told is pronounced 'Sannoth'), a couple of miles to the south. We were seeking access to the Trinity House light of St Bees Head, and although we found a paved road, a sign stated that it was strictly for the use of lighthouse officials only. Changing tack, we continued southwards and parked up a dead-end at the top of a steep, narrow hill by some houses.

The mile and a half walk to the lighthouse began on a muddy track with grass along the middle. We eventually reached the paved road, which rendered my Dad breathless, climbing steeply to the brow of the hill that gave us breathtaking views as we looked back to the Cumbrian Mountains. No such effort was required for the disabled chariot that passed us on our way back as its occupant slowly but determinedly tackled the long climb. I wondered cynically what would happen if the battery ran out of juice in such an isolated spot. Then again, it seemed that we would more likely run out of steam first!

The lane briefly became a gravel track to meander around the back of a farm, before leading us up another climb to the 55-foot light, which was textbook 'Trinity House'. For this was a white, round tower with balcony and lattice-windowed light compartment, standing proudly in front of its long 'bungalow' keepers cottage row; all in perfect symmetry with a green line around the bottom.

The surrounding garden was immaculate, the grass having recently been mowed, with attractive bench seats on its perimeter. This set us wondering as to *who* were the beneficiaries of this tranquil scene, as the light is unmanned and visitors are clearly not encouraged!

The original light here was built in 1718, but was destroyed by fire in 1822. St Bees was the last coal-fired light in Britain, and the new structure cost just £2322 to construct. My Dad, like the old lighthouse, felt a little burnt-out and decided not to accompany me as I wandered down the steep, grassy slope to try to establish the nature of a separate white building located on the cliff-edge. The lattice on the front indicated that it was the foghorn.

Returning to the car, we were now faced with a long drive to Millom; so we stopped in the village of St Bees for a quick refuel of calories, startling the owner of a small store who clearly wasn't expecting to sell a lot of 'Yuk' on this quiet Monday afternoon!

We took a meandering A595 past Sellafield nuclear power station (formerly known as Seascale) along the edge of the mountains, with camera poised, as ever, to capture any view of interest but always seeming to be switched on too late when the scene becomes obscured by a car or a wall, etc.

Millom is a small town, and a right turn took us straight out to the disused Hodbarrow iron mine, which closed in 1968. This area now comprises of brushy heathland and is popular with walkers. This area is isolated from the sea by a lagoon, which is bounded by a semicircular outer barrier.

There are two lighthouses here. The first stands atop a grassy mound overlooking the lagoon. It is a cylinder, a little like the watchtower at Whitehaven. It is built from smallish yellow/brown stones and has the skeletal remains of a balcony. It is now open at the top, which looks a little like a concrete balaclava with a hole where the light would have been. The remains of the spiral staircase can be seen through the metal gate barring any access.

The other lighthouse is also cylindrical, but made of iron. It is now completely rusted and has an empty lattice compartment, and a rusty 'hat' on top. Slightly more remains of the balcony of this second light, but again only a fool would wish to be standing on it. The structure stands in the middle of the outer barrier, which was completed in 1905, so one would assume that it dates from the same time.

The car's suspension creaked and groaned as we dodged the potholes on the unmade stony tracks around this quarry-like site. Never quite sure of the legality of driving here, we were reassured by the other vehicle following us. As I looked in the wing mirror, it felt like one of those chase sequences from an American movie, but in slow motion. The state of the car was now a far cry from that first trip down to Cornwall - these missions were killing it!

Our final lighthouse for today was at the southernmost tip of Walney Island - a twelve mile long strip of land reached via a bridge from Barrow-in-Furness - a large port town, which used to be in Lancashire, although marooned from the rest of the county by Morecambe Bay.

Due to the meandering nature of this coastline, the journey to this town, where nuclear submarines were once built, took us almost an hour, in spite of being less than ten miles as the crow flies. The route took us via 'The Green' and 'The Hill' (not the most imaginative village names I have ever come across), and numerous places ending with 'in-Furness'. The pace quickens dramatically for the last six miles into Barrow, (which my Uncle from Lancashire always pronounces 'Barra'), as a new A590 bypasses the town's suburbs taking us straight to the port.

As the road rounds the large industrial buildings here, one becomes immersed in the American dream once again. Like Workington, they have chosen to redevelop their industrial coastal area with DIY and 'fast food' outlets.

Crossing the bridge onto the island and heading south, it isn't long before the road becomes another suspension-battering gravel track - cue creaks and groans. To our left was nothing but quicksand. Back on the mainland, our Ordnance Survey map shows a number of byways crossing inlets around the edge of Morecambe Bay. Extreme caution is advised in this area as stated before - these are byways where you could stand to lose much more than just your shoes!

It was time that was marching relentlessly against us now; for the road terminated about a mile and a half from the tall, white lighthouse. Its location is at the far end of a nature reserve that closes at 7pm; it was now gone six. Tempting though it was to drive defiantly onward, (a prohibited means of reaching the lighthouse), I think the disturbance to the 32,000 sea-birds that occupy the dunes here would have attracted the attention of the warden who may have then locked the gate early on the two miscreants, leaving them at the mercy of some 1600-score hungry beaks!

No, we would have to return tomorrow. Unfortunately this would add a hundred miles of driving to our already tight schedule, as we had already booked ourselves in for the night at my Uncle's house in Over Kellett, a small but attractive village near the pleasant little town of Carnforth - just the other side of Morecambe Bay. However, the A590 made light work of this marathon journey, skirting the southern edge of the Lake District.

In hindsight, I think this is a dangerous road, with its disjointed stretches of dual carriageway that tease the motorist, especially when stuck behind heavy lorries; consequently drivers tend to behave like 'caged animals released' each time the road widens out. These short stretches allow barely enough time to pass these slow-moving dinosaurs before one has to stamp heavily on the brakes for the next single carriageway section. It seems that around here, indicators are used as an optional extra and speed limits are viewed as an option!

Of course the ubiquitous 'white van man' rules the roost, and although I often drive one of these vehicles myself, it makes you wonder if the majority of these vans are running around empty in order to maximise speed. Mine certainly isn't – the company would never allow it!

Parking behind my Uncle's impeccably driven 'light-coloured' vehicle for conveying the tools of his trade, we began our evening with a welcome cup of tea before heading to the local pub, which had a good atmosphere in spite of being very quiet – it was Monday after all.

With my cousin and her husband joining the three of us, I was cajoled into a few light games of pool. Feeling enriched by my three successive victories, my Dad promptly redressed the balance, showing my pool playing skills to be as erratic as the drivers we had done battle with earlier. At closing time, we wandered up the hill and I wandered up the wooden hill to Bedfordshire. We had amply made up for last night's lack of ale.

What's more, we had survived flying golf balls, rising tides and the A590. Phew!

Fleetwood Flashers

126)   MORECAMBE (pier light)
127/128) HEYSHAM
129)   GLASSON (redundant)
130)   PLOVER SCAR

The sun's rays shone in an oblong shaft of brightness across the kitchen, living room and garden at my Uncle's house as I arose the following morning. As I made myself a cup of tea with my Dad still upstairs and my Uncle already at work, I observed the cheery sound of the birds from the sunny conservatory.

We were in no hurry for breakfast, so collating our thoughts, we decided to head straight back to Barrow.

This mellow spring morning of bright blues and greens was abruptly grabbed by the neck and shaken as we encountered road rage of the 'white van' kind on the A590 once again. We were ready for breakfast now!

Parking within a sensible walking distance of a small cafe was a problem. We wanted food, fast; but all we could find was 'fast food'. After much searching we found the 'Last resort coffee shop' in Barrow, or should this be simply 'the last coffee shop in Barrow'?

It was an arty kind of establishment, which I would expect to be popular with many a student. Having a cup of expensive coffee in front of you makes homework/study far more palatable! This meant that greasy fry-ups were out of the question, but we did get a 'healthy' breakfast resplendent with swirling Cumberland sausage. We were now ready to face the swirling sea-birds of Walney.

Back at the nature reserve, we found it to be a pleasant morning's walking, and compared to the temperatures we'd endured at Orford a few days ago, it felt positively tropical! A series of designated routes led us past an oyster farm and up over the grassy dunes in this haven for wildlife.

As we tramped along, following the waymarkers, the deafening squawk of what seemed like thousands of gulls taking to the sky filled the air. It was a Hitchcock-esque scene as their shadows criss-crossed menacingly on the ground as far as the eye could see.

As we neared the lighthouse things became much more tranquil.

Expecting a little chastisement for not registering the 'No Access to the Public' sign, we boldly approached a gentleman working on the white wall around the slim, white, octagonal lighthouse, which measures 60 feet to the railings around the light compartment and 76 feet to the top. Beside the tower is the two-storey keeper's house.

This working light is owned by Lancaster port. It is also the home of England's only resident lighthouse keeper. This man had perhaps the rarest job in Britain - a career option that we had been led to believe no longer existed.

So the aspiring child who replies 'lighthouse keeper' when asked what he would like to be when he grows up should not be belittled and told 'not to be so silly' because the job *does* exist. It's just that there may be an extremely long wait for a vacancy!

The first Walney Island lighthouse was constructed in 1790 and burnt down. The present monolithic tower dates from 1803. If you look north-east from this point, about a mile out in Morecambe bay you will notice a castle – Piel Castle. Not a bad moat, eh?

Passing through Barrow for the fourth time, we decided to check the coastline to the east of the town for any erroneous lighthouses, taking a road that bumped its way over hillocks beside the sea and through small villages like Bardsea, rejoining the A590 at Ulverston. Deja vu or what?

We were Morecambe-bound now. Famous for becoming the adoptive surname of one half of a well-known seventies comedy duo, everything about this place says 'resort'. Leaving the M6 at Carnforth, we approached the town from the northern fringes around a long, sweeping, sandy bay, lined with hotels.

This colourful place was bustling on this fine sunny day. My father drained the last few fluid ounces of 'Yuk' from his bottle, whilst a rousing piece of classical music reached its conclusion on the radio and his son mischievously videoed this to humorous effect. With a sudden burst of energy, we left the vehicle and casually strolled out onto the pier.

The pier was built in 1853 as a railway terminus serving Irish and Scottish ferries. The lighthouse stands barely a matter of feet in front of the single-storey 'City of Lancaster Heritage Building' upon which a plaque displays this information, and is the same grey/stone colour. It is built of blocks and is octagonal with a balconied light compartment, which is painted white. I can only guess its height as being around twenty-five feet. Its location is about half-way along the pier, which is now purely devoted to leisure.

Heysham to the south of the town is the complete opposite. The place perhaps optimistically describes itself as 'Heysham Village' but to us it felt more like a less salubrious suburb of Morecambe; it's got a nuclear power station for goodness sake! By the way, I am told that you pronounce it 'Eesham' – at least that's how my Uncle pronounced it as we resided at the bar last night.

It is near this power station that our next two lighthouses are located. Understandably, we were unable to drive into the complex. For once, I was quite relieved at this, especially as I live within fifteen miles of Dungeness nuclear power station, and therefore like to be reassured that these places are secure.

Similarly, as the trains that carry the used uranium cores away for processing pass through my village once a week, it was reassuring to know that when a lorry hit one of these sealed units on a return journey from Sellafield at a level crossing, the unit remained exactly that - sealed!

Speaking of Sellafield, we were there yesterday weren't we?

A narrow channel of water (surprisingly popular with fishermen) separates the power station from the town to the north, so we viewed the fairly short, round lighthouse from across the water. Its shaft is red and the balcony around the lattice light compartment appears to be reinforced with a high 'fence'. The top is a white dome adorned with a weathervane.

We had already passed the other light once, for it is to be found perhaps a quarter of a mile further north beside the sea wall. This structure seems much older, and is similar to the inland one at Hodbarrow as well as some of the ones we saw at Whitehaven. It is a round cylinder of uneven sized bricks/blocks. This one has what looks like a thin, light-coloured stone, surrounded by a guard rail on its flat top.

At the end of the rocks jutting a few yards into the sea from its base, there appears to be the bottom of a former tower. There was no time to stop and ponder though; we were parked illegally on an unorthodox concrete road with officious-looking industrial buildings to our right. Next up was Glasson; a most unusual village situated on the River Lune - the river that flows through Lancaster.

Negotiating Lancaster's clogged streets took up a considerable slice of our time. Its roads were chock-a-block, right from the out-of-town shopping zone on the flat plains that separate the city from Morecambe/Heysham, to its historic centre that surrounds the comparatively modern cathedral, which was constructed in 1859 - that's six years after Morecambe pier was built.

It is difficult to imagine today, but two hundred years earlier, it was not the roads that were clogged, but the banks of the River Lune; for at the time, Lancaster dockside was busier than the port of Liverpool, hence the reason for the many crumbling redundant lights situate in their lonely splendour on the silted estuary.

The enigma of Glasson lies around six miles south of the city. As one approaches on the B-road beside a former trackbed converted into footpath to one's right, it seems a pleasant little community with plenty of green areas and a placid river inlet. But as one crosses the bridge, it becomes apparent that the rails once served a hive of industry, which can only be reached by ascending out of the hamlet and descending again on a wider, modern road. One is then transported into the contrasting world of the humming bandsaw and clunking hammer - a dusty industrial estate.

At the far end of this we found a sailing club, where we boldly asked a middle-aged gentleman if he would allow us to enter his property to view the lighthouse. His helpful response took us by surprise, and it became apparent that we were speaking to an ex-keeper of such isolated stations as Wolf Rock and Plymouth Sound. We were invited to step out onto an unguarded wooden platform used for mooring small boats, but we weren't quite far enough round to glimpse our sought-after structure.

Within minutes we found ourselves walking down the side of his house and descending an almost vertical bank on our behinds in a cloud of dust! We rounded the point on a bank of hard earth being careful not to slip on the seaweed. We were soon back in the hard hat area. The workmen ignored our blatant disregard for health and safety policy, and allowed us to freely gaze upon the fittingly bizarre lighthouse across the small inlet.

This tiny oblong building had a bright-red door, and looked more like one of those small, white churches that you'd expect to see in the US Bible belt. The light was located in the pointed, square 'steeple' at one end of the sloping roof. There was something like a chimney pot at the opposite end.

Before we walked full-circle back to the car, we stopped between two piles of wooden planks to view the Glasson we had first encountered - quiet and quaint with small shops and a 'picture postcard' riverside scene. I have never encountered such a small place with two distinct halves like this; Glasson must be one of the few places where there are actually more jobs than people!

There is also a surfeit of lighthouses for this short stretch of the Lune, as just a couple of miles south is another one – Plover Scar. This is reached by a circuitous route along narrow lanes, which seem to change direction completely every hundred yards or so. The flat agricultural land is protected from the sea by a raised levee. The lane ends abruptly beside 'Lighthouse Cottage'. The only of evidence of a lighthouse *here* though, is on our ever out of date maps. No, our luminary is a few furlongs south and a few chains out to sea.

I keep sneaking these old-fashioned imperial measurements into the proceedings merely because I like them! A lot of my info about the lighthouses has been given to me in metres, but I have doggedly stuck to good old feet (although I am fluent in metric also). This is my tribute to those defiant souls who have found themselves in 'nick' for daring to trade in such offensive terms as pounds and ounces, feet and inches - those rogue market traders who inherently know that it is easier to work in units of ten rather than 16 or 12, but flex their mental agility daily in the name of freedom. Right on!

There has even been a case of somebody travelling the highways and byways of the South-East amending 'illegal' road signs that have prematurely adopted metric units. Terms like '100 metres' have been crossed out and replaced with the words '100 yards' daubed underneath. Of course this is incorrect - 100 metres is actually nearer 110 yards. Arrest that man!

My favourite of all is the 'rod, pole or perch'. Why just come up with a term for a completely illogical quantity like 5½ yards, when you can give it three different names to boot? In actual fact, this was the length of stick used to control oxen in medieval times, when standing behind a plough. Chain, furlong and acre are also derived from the same period.

Several generations ago children had to not only recite all these scales in the classroom but calculate with them also. Try getting kids to learn their 'five and a half times table' these days! And who said we were dumbing down?

Speaking of which, when I encounter signs stating 'Danger - Quicksand' it generally doesn't seem too great an idea to test its validity; but as we strolled along the grassy levee, a foolhardy couple decided to walk out towards the lighthouse with their canine friend. This was not in a tentative 'let's try our best to evade a certain death' kind of way, but involved boldly jogging so that each footstep pounded a little harder, tempting fate even further.

I did not want to helplessly witness anything nasty from the shore, but in this case it seems that a little local knowledge goes a long way, for they remained above the surface as we stared out at the white structure in the sea from this peaceful spot, with just the hum of a distant tractor permeating above the sound of birdsong and the insects in the long grass.

The waves have rendered the bottom of the squat cylinder, black through to rusty-brown. On top is a thinner, similar cylinder and on top of this the light compartment, thinner still and topped with a pointed dome and weathervane. The other side of the wide Lune Estuary is Sunderland Point, a few miles south of Heysham.

Our goal for the night was now Blackpool, and the main road towards Poulton-le-Fylde was very slow-moving, with plenty of sudden complete changes in direction, as it traversed the flat farmland. The intense schedule began to take its toll again, luring me into a state of premature comatose, drifting off in the car.

However, Classic FM came to the rescue by playing a piece that even its composer had described as being 'very noisy' and 'with no artistic merit'. No, this was not the latest 'flash in the pan' DJ describing his most recent 'Ibiza' anthem; we were talking Tchaikovsky and the 1812 Overture.

This piece was written many years later in 1880, to commemorate Napoleon's retreat from Moscow, thus stirring up Russian feelings of pride at the Moscow Exhibition. I was soon wide awake again!

Once we had negotiated our way out of the mile-long traffic jam going into Blackpool, we were able to head for the coast and start looking at guesthouses. Today's period of deliberation was mercifully brief, and before long, we were chilling out in a large hazy bar room with a well-earned Guinness, observing the down-to-earth clientele as trams passed in the bright sunshine outside.

I had been to Blackpool once before and had forgotten this pleasant feature of the town. The tramlines run all the way to neighbouring Fleetwood (around six miles to the north), sometimes along the promenade beside the road, sometimes in a separate section between two carriageways and sometimes along the roads themselves. Fleetwood was where we were headed on this cool evening, for a value meal and a sampling of the local brews.

Night fell as we filled ourselves, and it was now time to look at the lights. No, not the Blackpool lights – the Fleetwood flashers!

There were two lighthouses here; one tall and a hundred yards or so inland, one short and sited just above the sands. Both are working and line up one above the other when viewed from the north by vessels entering the Wyre Channel.

As we gazed out to sea, a plethora of different coloured lights marked the route of this channel through the wet sands, which when the tide is out, extend for several miles out to the Wyre light, which used to be a proper lighthouse until it burned down shortly after World War II.

Its successor is little more than a beacon, a fact which made it easy for us to resist any urge to pad about on a wet beach, up to our necks in quicksand, in total darkness and hence, in a blind funk to find it!

The two Fleetwood lighthouses winked with a pale-orange tinge to their lights, while the mellow-green marker-lights twinkled on the black, velvet beach. We would return tomorrow to soak up the ambience in daylight.

We couldn't merely return to our hotel without first checking out downtown Blackpool, where the brightly lit amusement arcades and hotels seem to provide a backup spectacle for when the illuminations are switched off (which accounts for most of the year).

The tower was shrouded in darkness except for a few pilot lights at the top. It crept upon us like a ghost, appearing for a few moments while we were beneath it, before disappearing back into the night. Although built as a scale replica of Mr Eiffel's 985-foot Parisian structure, it is barely over half-size towering to a modest 518 feet.

Having given up competing with France, Blackpool has turned its attention to the US, vying to become the Las Vegas of the UK. If gambling regulations are relaxed sufficiently, this good old-fashioned northern 'pie and mash' resort could transform itself into an all-night casino para-dice. (Apologies!).

Our final pint in the hotel bar was really just a token gesture. We were exhausted from two hectic days, and with no local characters to stimulate our weary minds, we sat zombie-like in front of a TV screen showing the BBC's latest 'great new drama'. Enough said!

For relaxation, our room had a spa-bath. Now this particular model seemed sadistically designed to achieve the opposite, as one fumbles around with various switches, most of which seem to exist purely for decoration, trying to get the thing to emit bubbles.

Next came a brief encounter with a trouser press. More success here, except that in my tired state I'd folded the creases incorrectly and had it not been for a rescue bid from my Dad, I would have woken up next morning to a pair of slacks that looked like a road atlas!

Trouser lines / tram lines / white lines / bright lights / Wyre lights / night night!

Shropshire 'Views'

They certainly know how to cook a Great British breakfast in Blackpool - today's was a fry-up I thoroughly enjoyed. What's more, we discovered that we had spent the night in the former seaside residence of the family who originally owned the Cherry Blossom shoe polish business.

Polishing off our sustenance, it was time to venture out to the car and begin another day's preambles. The sun shone enthusiastically and as we drove up to Fleetwood we had a fun race with a tram (they're actually not that difficult to beat!).

The high light at Fleetwood is at the centre of a road junction with terraced houses along the four axes that radiate away. This structure consists of a column-like tower, which is round and of some considerable height. The light compartment is similarly svelte if not a little elongated, with a neat hat-like top. The base is a square block plinth.

Built of large blocks, this tower is a light-brown colour, as is the low light overlooking the beach to the north of it.

The low light is a square structure with a white-painted, square balcony around its round light compartment, which is similarly slender to that of its inland sibling. The short tower stands upon a square veranda, which shelters the benches below. There are two columns along each side, giving this 1841 addition to the coastline a slight look of ancient Rome! One assumes that both towers date from the same period.

A plaque commemorated Sir Peter Hesketh-Fleetwood who founded the town and port in 1836, and the architect Decimus Burton who designed both the town and this lower light. There's even a Roman feel to his name, isn't there?

Gazing out to sea, we watched the 'European Leader' ship pass the Wyre light, which stands on the edge of the quicksand, at the mouth of the River Wyre. In daylight it could be identified as a beacon-like light on four pole-like legs – not too dissimilar from the Lees Scar lighthouse at Silloth. We have decided to include it in our listing because our maps tended to think of it as a lighthouse, its importance still relevant, marking out this busy shipping channel. I'm sure the original structure, which burned down after the Second World War would have fitted our definition of a lighthouse more. An elderly gentleman in a disabled chariot told us of this fateful night with vivid clarity.

Before we leave Fleetwood, I should briefly mention 'Fisherman's Friend'. This fiery lozenge is produced in Fleetwood, and was originally designed to provide some warmth for the windswept sailor on the high seas. I always like that line in the Paul Simon song, Duncan, 'My Father was a fisherman, my Mother was a fisherman's friend!' Knowing that the transatlantic songwriter spent some time in England before he made it big with Art Garfunkel, one suspects the pun is intentional.

It was now time for us to head for an area renowned for producing similarly great songwriters – Merseyside; and our first light on the banks of this river was in a setting, which was hardly what we expected from this locale at all.

The light occupies a space on the north bank of the river, some twelve miles upstream from its outflow into the Irish Sea. It is a little to the south of Hale village – actually in Cheshire.

The journey here was rather bland, both heading for, and on the M58/M6/M62. Upon reaching the Mersey, anybody with reasonably good eyesight cannot help but notice the forest of chimneys to the east at Widnes and industrial Runcorn across the water. Hale itself is a quaint little haven though, even boasting some thatched cottages.

As for the lighthouse, it is a tall, round tower, built of 'bricks' and painted white. It has a balconied light compartment, and has become a little grubby with age. Nevertheless, its substantial height enables it to stand proudly above the private house, the grounds of which it now shares.

A public footpath runs along the riverbank, which at this stage is lined with open fields. This path is reached via a short walk from the car-park at the bottom of the lane from Hale. It was here that we tried our best not to disturb a relaxing trucker with a loud blast from our car radio as we left.

Time to enter the metropolis.

Liverpool has a reputation for consisting largely of run-down Victorian terraces; yet the route we cut through the city seemed no different from a drive through any other large conurbation. As we entered the suburbs, we passed the recently renamed 'John Lennon' airport (one such songwriting genius as hinted at just now). This can be contrasted with JFK airport in New York, after all both were cultural icons and victims of tragically accurate assassinations.

Soon we were at the city's frenetic centre, passing the 295-foot twin towers of the Royal Liver Building, which dates from 1910. It was somewhere in the dock area to the north of this that our next structure was alleged to be.

Although not appearing on the Ordnance Survey map, we thought we'd better make a concerted effort to locate it, due to its appearance in one of our many atlases. Of course this was rendered nigh on impossible; for dock areas, as we well know, are always pretty stringent when it comes to security.

To make matters worse, the well-defined, (at least on our maps), Waterloo Road ended abruptly at a metal fence. Turning about and then following its designated main road successor, we parked and peered through the mesh at nothing more than a gigantic building site and storage area. We assume that the lighthouse, like the road, had finally met its 'Waterloo'.

Having driven up and down the road, we parked and walked to the tall wire fence we had just rode alongside, for a closer look, but all that could be seen were lorries and the usual industrial-looking buildings one finds in these areas.

We figured that the best chance of viewing this light, if it existed, was from across the water at New Brighton.

We didn't 'ferry across the Mersey' (pronounce this 'marezee' if you please) as Gerry Marsden so plaintively advocated - we opted for the tunnel.

For those who don't regard Gerry and the Pacemakers as a particularly important group, it is worth remembering that until the mid-eighties, they were the only group ever to have their first three singles go to number one in the UK charts. This feat should not be diminished by today's bands, which seem to storm straight in at number one with every new release. This is not so much a reflection of artistic creativity as the power of modern marketing.

And what about Elvis, smashing the Beatles' record of seventeen number ones by going one further in June 2002, twenty-five years after his presumed death? Perhaps the ultimate triumph of American music over that of the UK? I hope not. There must be light at the end of the tunnel soon.

But which one? After getting cemented into the flow of the hurtling city centre traffic, we just went round in circles until we at last found ourselves entering something that resembled a hole in the ground! We were actually in the more modern of the two Mersey tunnels - the Kingsway Tunnel, which is 1½ miles long and opened in 1971. As we entered, we wondered if it would be a wide dual carriageway 'box' all the way through, but soon the carriageways parted and we dived into the round westbound tunnel.

The older tunnel is the Queensway Tunnel. At two miles long it is still the longest road tunnel in the country, but when it was opened in 1934, it was the *world's* longest underwater tunnel. As with the bridges, our achievements have gradually slipped down the league table, although the Channel Tunnel has bolstered our civil engineering prowess somewhat. Perhaps one day, we'll catch up with the French and get our rail link open too!

We found the Wirral to be a complete contrast to Liverpool. New Brighton, which sits on the north-east tip of the peninsular, lives up to its name as being a small seaside resort. A picture on the promenade shows it to be heaving with holidaymakers in the fifties. Contrast that with the same view today and you will plainly see that, although well kept, it has passed its bustling heyday.

We parked in a reasonably select suburban terraced street, and wandered down to the seafront to gaze back across to the mass of cranes and industry that line the Liverpool shore. In one of the Beatles' songs John Lennon uses the phrase 'cast iron shore' in memory of another section of the Liverpudlian waterfront – however there was no lighthouse to be seen amongst *this* mass of 'heavy' metal.

Knowing that much of the port area was redeveloped not too long ago, we guessed that the alleged structure was removed during the construction works, and thus our minds turned to the lighthouse we could see protruding above Fort Perch Rock. This walled fort was completed in 1830, and is sited at the point where the Mersey runs into the Irish Sea. The tall, round lighthouse was just a hundred yards or so out in the water. It can be reached on foot at low tide.

It is a brilliant-white tower with a red topped light compartment. The hazard that it presides over is obvious, for under the water we could see a series of rocks running out to it. This lighthouse seemed very similar in terms of shape, scale and situation to two others we would visit in North Wales - Point of Ayr and Trwyn Du, yet is reputed to be only 63 feet in height.

There are three lighthouses along the north coast of the Wirral; and the next one we would visit, the middle 'Leasowe' light, was at the time, the most decrepit. An empty dual carriageway punctuated by roundabouts for every left turn led us out of New Brighton, and eventually we turned off into the flat grassland of the North Wirral Coastal Park.

We parked next to a burnt out car with a thousand remnants of its windscreen strewn across the seats, and strolled towards the white-painted brick tower with arched window inlets at various heights and an unusual light compartment, which has square windows and a balcony only at the front half.

The paintwork on this tall, round, tapered tower has peeled, giving it a mottled appearance. However, there were renovation plans at the time of out visit, and it is perhaps now as pristine as New Brighton light. First light here: 1764.

The structure is now utilised as an office for the park ranger, and as we inquisitively stuck our heads round the door to look at the racks of leaflets for public information, we were mercilessly barked at by a large dog that the ranger seemed to be having difficulty keeping behind the office door at the top of the spiral staircase one floor above us. The natural echo added ferocity to the yelps and so discretion reigned over our natural curiosity and we soon found ourselves on our way to Hoylake.

The journey was largely suburban, past parades of small shops and semi-detached homes. The lighthouse here stands in the grounds of a stately looking private house several streets inland from the sea. Also first lit in 1764, this redundant light has an octagonal, brown-bricked tower with an empty lantern on top. The side view is far less impressive, but it is the clearest attainable view of the tower across an area of grassy wasteland.

About a mile offshore to the west of Hoylake, there is a Trinity House light on the small island of Hillbre. This was owned by the Mersey Docks and Harbour Board until 1973. Looking at both the Ordnance Survey map, and the picture on the Trinity House website, there is no disputing that this is merely a beacon, so we spent no further time searching for a viewpoint.

With our quota of lighthouses for this particular trip now reached, it was time to head inland to deepest Shropshire for our final night, with a view, not of lighthouses in this landlocked county, but to visit our relatives.

Overall, the Wirral seemed far less densely populated than I had ever imagined it to be, reminding me a little of some of the quieter parts of the Isle of Thanet in Kent.

The M56 returned us to the land of the chimneys at Ellesmere Port. Unfortunately for us, somewhere behind this jumble was a chimney-like lighthouse that none of our maps had shown. We would not realise this until it was almost too late.

We briefly crossed the Welsh border bypassing Wrexham and heading for Shrewsbury. Shropshire has always been a county that I have found appealing since a visit to my Aunt and Uncle's house in the quaint little town of Clun at the age of nine.

To my mind it seems to be one of the most unspoilt counties in the UK. With the exception of Telford, which boasts over a hundred thousand inhabitants (a new town established in 1963, and named after Thomas Telford the engineer of Ironbridge), the administrative region seems to consist solely of green rolling hills – some in excess of a thousand feet and topped with gorse, and the historic county town of Shrewsbury.

But are my perceptions correct?

Average population density is lower in all of the following English counties:

Cumbria, Northumberland, North Yorkshire, Lincolnshire, Hereford & Worcester and Somerset.

Devon and Cornwall also come close to a place in this premier league of rurality. However Cornwall has no motorways, whereas Shropshire has a fourteen mile section of the M54. Unfortunately for us, this was the other side of Telford, and a motorway was exactly what we needed to get us out of a five mile long jam on the A5 from Oswestry. Always adept at finding alternative routes, I reached for the atlas and guided us into the county town via a series of lanes. The scenery consisted of flat agricultural land, which was a little like some of the more anonymous parts of rural Kent.

The town centre is encircled by a cunningly disguised ring road, which is at times a modern multi-lane affair, and at other times utilises narrow streets lined with historic shops and buildings. I have yet to discover a provincial ring road so bold as our beloved four-lane circuit in Ashford, Kent. Here, even driving instructors tell you that it will be necessary to exceed the speed limit a little in order to keep up with the flow.

As for Shrewsbury, we found it a little expensive to find a bed for the night, so we ventured out on the winding A488 into the area that I regard as being the 'true Shropshire'. An area where rolling hills are permeated with quaint villages and small towns with interesting names like 'Ploxgreen' and 'Bishop's Castle'.

We decided to stop in Minsterley, expecting a rustic atmosphere in a bar full of people all sounding a little like Pam Ayers. What we found, however, was the most intense proliferation of the 'F' word we had experienced anywhere. Ever!

There are many people, (usually mates of mine!), who like to prefix most nouns with this expletive, but here the middle-aged drinkers were pressing the word into overtime, Polyfillering every nook and cranny of the sentence and prefixing every verb, adjective, conjunction, you name it. Even in the middle of words. No XXXX joke!

And it wasn't just the men. The women were using far worse words still, often in their literal context too! No wonder when our evening meal was ready, we were ushered away into an almost sound-proofed annexe with the doors closed firmly behind us so that we could, at last, feel free to comment.

I pointed out that I have often noticed that many youngsters of a milder manner use the words 'like' and 'you know' in a similar way - as a kind of stalling mechanism in the sentence, if you like, see what I mean.

When we emerged from our cocoon, the gritty subject matter hadn't changed, and we were afforded some respite in the pub across the road. What a contrast - the place was empty!

We harpooned the two bar staff into conversation about Minsterley and its bawdy nightlife, but the surrounding silence was just too all-pervasive. We wished them luck and headed back across the road.

By now, things had calmed down, and three fairly old gentlemen now resided at the bar. It reminded me of a cross between an older version of me and my mates at our local 'Woolpack' and 'Last of the summer wine!'

These three 'country boys' were keen to join us in conversation and it was refreshing to hear them catching up on the days farming and discussing the agricultural tasks they faced tomorrow. Something tells me that they do this most nights.

They were interested in our story too; in lighthouses, in Kent, in whatever. As we ended the night with a round of good 'Shropshire' halves, we quizzed them about Minsterley, and in rustic tones they explained that there is a large factory in the village, which produces most of the country's tongue. You're not kidding!

You don't come across this canned offal so much nowadays, but we were assured that the more boisterous 'tongues' here generally belonged to the factory workers.

As for these old sorts, I liked them. I find that one natural trait of these older locals is a genuine pride in their own town or village no matter how mundane it may seem to outsiders. I may possess a little of this attribute myself. This is perhaps as good a reason as any why the effects of changing shopping patterns concern me.

Pride in one's town or village is not like supporting a football team; football supporters are generally as loyal to their team in the lean years as in times of triumph (if this wasn't the case England would have had to give up years ago!). With a town or village, it becomes harder to maintain a sense of pride when many of the reasons to feel good about the place are now confined to reverie.

"We used to have three pubs in Minsterley/a busy High Street in Wells/twelve pubs in Modbury/two filling stations in Hamstreet", you hear people say.

Nowadays, the culture is to run down one's own dwelling place, a kind of 'my town is worse than your town' mentality, 'at least you have X Y and Z, we've got nothing'.

Then in 2002, we were at last given an opportunity to feel good about ourselves; not just about our own communities but about our country as a whole. Flags and bunting lined the streets, both for the World Cup and the Queen's Golden Jubilee. I think it's a shame that they had to come down again!

* * * * *

By morning, *my* tongue had evidently ceased to function properly, as my heaped platter of fried comestibles failed to taste exactly as my brain was telling me it should.

Our journey home included a visit to my Aunt and Uncle that I mentioned earlier. Peacocks called as we wandered around the pleasant garden and savoured the view of gorse-covered hills rolling down to the valley below.

For old times' sake, we came home via Clun, where when purchasing a paper in a newsagent-cum-cafe, we had to pinch ourselves to make sure we had not just walked onto the set of 'Last of the summer wine!'

As we continued towards Kidderminster, we serendipitously stumbled across the highest point in Shropshire - Brown Clee Hill, which peaks at 1790 feet above sea level. Crossing the cattle grid in the road as we ascended was similar to crossing the snowline of a mountain; we were briefly entering the territory of wild-sheep grazing the unkempt hillside.

The view from the road was nothing short of impressive, with the more fertile land undulating in a lush green swathe below us.

Crossing another cattle grid, we returned to less lofty climes. Soon we were on the M42 and everything looked bland until we reached Surrey.

The M25 was having one of its 'choked to capacity' turns, so we thought that it would make a change to divert off at Leatherhead, crossing the green belt to a series of provincial commuter towns namely Reigate, Redhill and Oxted. The trouble was, 25,000 other drivers had had the same idea! Rush hour approached and gridlock ensued, along with a stifling desire just to be home again.

The journey from hell was complete with a snarl-up on the A21 at Tonbridge, making a five hour journey take in excess of seven and a half. You can keep your commuter belt, Shropshire wins hands down!

We had gone from 'summer wine' to just plain 'whine' in a matter of hours. It felt as though we'd been back to a 1950's rural idyll in a time machine and had just returned to modernity with a bump. Of course we knew this wasn't true - not even a DeLorean would be able to reach 88 miles an hour on the M25!

NORTH WALES

Llandudno Locution

138)   POINT OF AYR (redundant)
139)   GREAT ORME/LLANDUDNO (redundant)

You, our most stoical reader, join us now for the celebrated final leg of our grand tour of the English and Welsh Coasts. Or so we thought at the time.

As we inch our way along the coast of North Wales towards the Lleyn peninsular, will things crescendo to a triumphant conclusion, or merely peter out to an undefined end? Who knows?

Our route to this final stretch of coastline was largely experimental, eschewing the M25 for London suburbs and the Blackwall tunnel, and shunning the M1/M6 for cross-country routes like the A14 and A50. We shared an industrial-sized container of ultraviolet 'Yuk' and some Melton Mowbray pork pies in a lay-by in Derbyshire, and beyond Stoke on Trent/Newcastle under Lyme, the digestive process lulled me into a series of short catnaps, leaving my Dad to negotiate his way to Chester via Nantwich with a minimum of assistance.

We passed over the border into Wales, a little before we crossed the road bridge over the River Dee, and were soon in Flint (which the Welsh spell 'Fflint'); a small coastal town, which seemed to consist largely of Victorian terraces, with its very own twin-tower flat-blocks sticking out like a residential sore thumb.

The road ran along the bottom of the hills, which hugged the shoreline as if this were a practice run for the scenic drive I would attempt to video later, where the majestic mountains of Snowdonia meet the sea beyond Conwy.

Our first lighthouse was at Point of Ayr, where the coastline changes direction for the seaside Mecca of Prestatyn and Rhyl. We parked in the small traditional seaside village of Talacre, which was resplendent with amusement arcades, fish and chip shops, caravans and an empty bakery with an emphatic statement in the window, 'Due to idle gossip and malicious rumours by certain people, we would like to make it known that we have no intention of leaving or doing a flit'. Or should that be 'fflit'? Let's hope the idle tongues have stopped wagging and the business is now thriving.

The beach is a wide sandy one and the red topped lighthouse with a 99-foot tall, white, round tower sits stubbornly in the middle of it. In spite of the beach being bounded by dunes, I understand that erosion is at work here.

The first light here was completed in 1777. The present light, which sits on a concrete base and is thus raised above the beach, was completed in 1819. Its light was once seen at distances of up to nineteen miles away. The entrance is reached by a long platform over rocks, which becomes a short metal staircase straight to the door. I would imagine that this enables it to be reached on foot even when it is surrounded by water. It is now as redundant as the lifeboat station, which was once at the end of Station Road.

Back in the car, the magnitude of the hills surprised us as we climbed steeply at Gwespyr with Point of Ayr and its lighthouse now way below us. We navigated our way to the A55 expressway at Abergele via a series of villages we were unable to pronounce, whose names generally included a lot of 'W's and 'Y's. This combined with the ubiquitous use of double 'L's and double 'F's makes any Englishman's attempt at pronunciation sound as though he has a serious phlegm problem!

Furthermore, it becomes extraordinarily difficult to remember these names, even for the short duration from looking in the road atlas to glancing up at the signpost. I have often performed feats of memory in my local pub such as memorising a mate's credit card number and reciting it back to him, with the expiry date, three weeks later to his unease, but I draw the line at Welsh place names!

We decided to settle upon memorising the last five or six letters, then reading the road signs backwards. A limited success!

The A55 emulates an urban motorway as it cuts its way through Colwyn Bay in deep cuttings with a short tunnel. Turning off just before the most impressive section of this expressway, we headed for Llandudno, a popular seaside resort, which is overlooked by the 650-foot rocky outcrop of the Great Orme, in a way not too dissimilar from the Rock of Gibraltar. 360 feet up the far side of this stands a redundant lighthouse.

The sweeping bay to the east is lined with white-fronted hotels, beyond which looms the smaller headland of the Little Orme. Having found suitable lodgings, we decided to knock off the lighthouse.

Great Orme is circumnavigated by a toll-road. A surly gentleman collected our two pound fee in a manner that was a little brusque, if not downright rude. Firstly, when we asked a series of questions, we received the same metered response each time, in a way that merely conveyed 'stupid English!' Finally, when asked about the lighthouse, we were offered two facetious 'Yes Sir's as he fixedly focused his eyes on a sheet of paper (probably blank!).

To be fair, perhaps he had had a long day being asked the same questions by English morons, but I can think of at least one job that would be more testing on the patience:

Every time I pass the toll-gates at the Dartford Bridge/Tunnel, I feel sorry for the poor folk who sit in the booths for hours on end just sticking out their hands and saying 'thank you' when the correct coinage is placed therein. Imagine breathing the fumes of an endless queue of vehicles, all dependent upon you performing the same mind-numbing action. It must seem a little like being a human battery-hen. And that's something else I hope the government has the guts to outlaw as it is discussing doing. At least, unlike the chickens, Dartford toll staff have a choice in the matter!

Our journey was a million miles away from both hellhole egg-producing factories and the M25. The little lane resembled a scenic mountain trail, steadily climbing the rugged protuberance. A stone wall, the same colour as the sandstone cliff ran alongside us.

The lighthouse took some searching for, as it is now a classy guesthouse. The building looks like a small castle, is grey in colour and was erected by the Mersey Docks and Harbour Board in 1862. It is a stately-looking square structure with many chimneys and turreted walls, and at the front is the lamp room, which you can actually stay in if you have the cash. It is unusual in that it sits like a rounded conservatory at ground level.

Wishing to see the interior, my Dad boldly approached the front door and summoned some attention. Rather than explaining that we were lighthouse enthusiasts that wanted to see the lamp room, he meekly asked for a beer, which was met with a look of incredulity! Although unable to purchase any real ale, we did glean the information that the light ceased to operate in 1985. It is now housed in the museum at the top of the Orme (which can be reached by both tramway and cable car).

Luckily for us, the cliff overlooking the guesthouse was fenced off, for the wind, even on this sunny day, was enough to sweep you off your feet. Had we at last found a spot that is even blowier than our own Dungeness?

Back in Llandudno, we found a pub with an urban feel to it. My Dad seemed half-afraid to ask if food was being served. His reticence, he later explained, was due to the mind-numbing 'musak' regularly punctuated by the pistol-crack of a frenetically hit pool ball, followed by the obligatory Anglo-Saxon utterance. This was not conducive to thinking, something that he likes to do a lot!

We eventually fell back on our regular crutch of looking for chain pubs. Yes, the atmosphere can be a little same-ish at times, but you always know what you are going to get.

This was one far from sterile - my Father's face lit up as though he had just fallen through 'the looking glass' (fitting for Llandudno - more later). This alehouse was an imaginative reworking of a former cinema, complete with rows of seats in darkness on the balconies, (not for use by drinkers), offset with tasteful lighting illuminating the white decor and boxes. The area behind where the big screen clearly used to be is now a raised section for family use.

The pub was crowded in a civilised manner, buzzing like a contented hive. Perhaps all redundant cinemas should undergo this conversion, after all, they were built to house a local populace at play.

I bit the bullet and opted for the mixed grill, and I soon felt as though I was munching my way through an entire farmyard, identifying which type of meat I was feasting on with each mouthful. I failed to clear my 'abattoir on a plate', but enjoyed it nonetheless.

Llandudno is not exactly bustling with pubs; I expected to come across far more in a resort town of this nature. I did notice, though, that on the road signs here, Welsh takes priority over English, as if to remind the influx of summer visitors that they are guests in another country; although diplomatically, most of the European flags could be seen flying along the promenade. I even noticed a St George's flag flying proudly outside one house, no doubt for the World Cup. Well, you have to support somebody, don't you?

The temperature seemed to plummet as dusk fell, yet the young girls out for a Saturday night prowl, which just seemed to multiply, were anything but wrapped up warm! It was like Retford all over again.

The buildings were far more ornately-attired than the girls, with almost every shop fronted with awnings, a little like a street scene in those 'Wild West' films. This comparison with this time period is actually not too far off the mark, as much of the town dates from the 'railway building' mania of the 1880's. Prior to this, the area was known at Ormes Bay.

Our evening concluded with a visit to Rhos-on-Sea, a quiet suburban place beyond the Little Orme. Although it afforded us pleasant views across to Colwyn Bay, it seemed a little nondescript, although our perceptions were probably marred by the pub we chose to frequent; for not only was there the loud regimented thud of dance music here, but also a big screen displaying the latest going-ons in a certain house with a lot of cameras in it. Yes, we are talking 'Big Brother'.

Too many people are talking 'Big Brother'.

Far from being George Orwell's frightening vision of 1984, it is the frightening realisation that after seventy years of television history, we have reached the grand plateau of watching ordinary people pick their noses and go to the loo!

It seems to me that when this televisual equivalent of watching paint dry is on, it is impossible to go for a whole night in a pub without somebody bringing up the subject and everybody entering into a discussion as if the candidates are all mates of theirs. I resent the fact that I am forced to become a social outcast for around ten weeks a year merely due to the incessant mulling over of this programme. This renders me unable to contribute to the majority of conversations for almost one fifth of my life!

No matter how many psychologists you get in to make it look like a 'social experiment', the end result is always a group of like-minded people being prodded into acting outrageously by the double-pronged fork of boredom and the hope of a large cash prize. Even when you transplant the idea to a desert island and call it 'Survivor', it still sparks about as much interest in me as a conversation about lino-cutting!

Soon we were back in our hotel, at last reclining on our beds. My Dad turns on the TV to break the silence, expecting the novelty of hearing people speak in Welsh, and what do we find that three of the ten available channels are tuned into?

Big Brother!

Heart Flutters at Holyhead

140)   LLANDDWYN ISLAND (redundant)
141)   SOUTH STACK* (white flash every 10 secs)
142)   GOLEUDYLIGHTHOUSE/HOLYHEAD
       BREAKWATER (harbour light)
143)   SALT ISLAND (harbour light in Holyhead)

A familiar sound was strangely absent in Llandudno. Not a single call from a seagull graced the air. Very strange.

I wonder if a certain Charles Lutwidge Dodgson noticed this back in 1862, for it was here that a little girl visiting the town on holiday inspired him to pen a particularly surreal children's adventure. That little girl's name was 'Alice', and Mr Dodgson adopted the pseudonym 'Lewis Carroll'.

Over a hundred years later, we too thought we were in Wonderland, for as we tucked into a hearty breakfast, we realised that the sun was shining. In Wales!

In fact, not a drop of rain would fall upon us at any time during our visit to the land of the leek, or should I say 'leak!' This dryness meant that a watershed in cinematographic history could take place - the filming of the A55!

I believe I told you about my 'road movies' many chapters ago. This particular stretch of tarmac from Llandudno junction to Llanfairfechan is one of the most interesting you will come across. Even die-hard road-cynics would have to acknowledge the A55's grandeur as it tunnels beneath anything that dares to obstruct its path.

The first of its tunnels takes the route beneath the River Conwy, as it bypasses the town of the same name. Conwy has two claims to fame; a thirteenth century castle built by Edward I from which to preside over the Welsh, and a suspension bridge which was built by Thomas Telford of 'Ironbridge' fame. This is now sandwiched between the more recent road and rail bridges.

The A55 continues unabated, piledriving its way through the massive headland and around the town of Penmaenmawr, before pummelling into another rocky precipice. This dual carriageway masterpiece has even stolen the Britannia Bridge onto Anglesey from the A5, as it now streaks all the way from Chester to Holyhead.

Travelling in the opposite direction, the carriageway follows the twistier route of the old road around the two headlands, with two very short tunnels round one of them. Either way, the road is impressive and I have tried many times to film this journey, only to find that drops of H2O keep making a smeary mess of the windscreen. The height of the hills makes this inevitable though, as clouds forced upwards feel compelled to drop their watery load, especially onto vehicles containing indignant cameramen!

Anglesey is the largest island in Wales. It is larger than the Isle of Man and almost twice the area of the Isle of Wight but with half the population. The Welsh name for this 275 square miles of rurality is 'Ynys Mon'.

Holyhead and its accompanying mountain are actually on a different island - Holy Island, which at 15 square miles is Wales' second largest island. We were heading for the ninth largest island in Wales - Llanddwyn; a meagre 0.12 of a square mile in area and joined to Anglesey by a sand causeway.

So I put down my camera as we turned off at Llanfairpwyllgwyn-'lots of words that only Welsh people and those with few other talents to show off at parties can remember'-gogogoch and headed south.

At 58 letters, most maps and sane people opt for the 20 letter official version of this placename. However 58 letters just isn't enough for some people, so the Fairbourne steam railway (just across the water from Barmouth - where we would end up tomorrow) came up with the 67-letter place name 'Gorsafawddachaidraigddanheddogleddollonpenrhynareurdraethceredigion' in order to outdo Llanfairpwyllgwyngyllgogerych-wyrndrobwllllantysiliogogogoch.

Phew! No wonder we were having difficulty spotting our turnings!

Anglesey is wonderfully unspoilt, but after the majesty of Snowdonia it can seem a little bland, for it was all fairly flat agricultural land until we turned off into the popular Newborough Forest.

Here, rather than paying somebody to insult our intelligence, there is a machine, which silently exhorted us to part with two pounds sterling. After much fumbling, my Dad placed the said coins therein and the obstruction in the road duly collapsed allowing us to proceed, to the relief of the queue that had begun to build up behind. Perhaps our churlish friend at the Great Orme was merely concerned about impending replacement with this friendlier alternative!

We found a car-park in the evergreen forest, and once we had locked the doors and prepared ourselves for an epic walk, we noticed a driver pull up, casually open the gate which we had presumed would be locked, and drive meekly onward. It was too late for us though, we were walking now and that was that.

Soon we were climbing over the dunes at the bottom of the forest and crossing the sandy beach onto the 'island'.

Again a distinct lack of seabirds was in evidence as we walked between the grassy hillocks to the southernmost end of the island where the old lighthouse or 'Twr Mawr' stands.

There appear to be the ruins of an abbey here, alongside both a Celtic cross and the cross of St Dwynwen. This seems symbolic of the coming of Christianity to the Celts (or am I reading too much into it?). For those who require more accurate facts, there are various buildings containing pertinent information scattered about. Today they were all locked. However, we did gather that that the white tower to the south-east of the lighthouse is actually an old boathouse.

The redundant light tower is a chubby, white, tapered structure, which sits upon a rocky outcrop surrounded by a small stone-coloured wall. The door and two upper windows are in the land-facing side, while adjoining the sea-facing side is a small square block. Gazing inquisitively through the broken window, it must have been the kitchen area. I noticed that there were two empty drink bottles on the dusty floor. Whether they had been 'posted' through the window or left by the last workmen to service this redundant light, I don't know.

I decided to inject a little interest into the walk back to the car with a change of route. This circuitous little trail hairpinned its way up and over every hill it could find. This we did not need on what we envisaged would be a fairly hectic day, so we detoured to the shore, upsetting the obligatory courting couple, scrambled over the slippery, grey rocks and made a beeline for the car.

Just as well, as our next lighthouse would present us with 560 steps - 400 down the cliff-face and another 160 to the top. This lighthouse being South Stack, at the far side of the 700-foot Holyhead mountain, which, (and I know I've used this expression before), overlooks the town like the Rock of Gibraltar.

Our route was a picturesque drive beside sandy inlets and over small hills. The white cottages scattered about the gentle green landscape reminded us a little of Cornwall.

We eventually came out onto a deserted A5, which once hummed with Ireland-bound traffic but has now been superseded by, (and I'm not deliberately trying to see how many mentions I can give it in a single chapter), the A55!

The crossing to Holy Island was barely noticeable. We made our stop for supplies in Trearddur Bay, a tourist-orientated seaside village, which struck us by having two general stores virtually opposite each other. The one we went in had Welsh-speaking customers too!

Passing an eerie-looking house perched on top of a rock that would be perfect for making horror films, the lane wound its way over rugged, grey rocks, with the mountainous outcrop omnipresent.

Parking at an info-centre-cum-cafe, we bought our tickets for the tour and wandered a couple of hundred yards up the lane to where the steps began their descent, with an ice cream van conveniently placed at the top.

As we zigzagged down the cliff bounded by stone-coloured walls, which resembled a contorted mini-'Great Wall of China', I clutched my video camera and tripod tightly under my arm. We received knowing glances from numerous birdwatchers. Unlike Llandudno and Llanddwyn Island there *are* birds to watch here.

There is even a camera embedded into the rocks, so that the avine specimens can be zoomed in on and viewed from the lighthouse without disturbance. Of course, these ornithologists had no idea that we were imposters – lighthouse watchers (or 'lighthouse perverts' as one of my mates so eloquently puts it!).

A covered bridge crosses the ravine onto South Stack Island. The Trinity House light sits atop a white, 90-foot tower, which is joined to a long single-storey building pointing back inland. This looks a little like a school canteen, save for the familiar green paint strip around the bottom, resembling an outdoor skirting board.

Although our tour guide was informative, there was little that we didn't already know. When we told him that this was our 141st lighthouse, he seemed duly impressed, but deflated us a little by saying that it's all been done before.

What, all 150-odd? Are you sure?

This lighthouse opened in 1809. Due to the lantern's height above sea-level it became necessary to build a railway down the front of the cliff, so that a lantern could be lowered down when visibility was reduced by fog. In 1859, the Royal Charter steamship sunk here in a storm. Coastwise, 200 vessels were cast ashore and 800 people died, including the lighthouse keeper Jack Jones who was hit on the head by a falling rock.

The fog signal is now located on North Stack, which lies between here and Holyhead. When we had reached the top of the spiral staircase, we were able to view this through the latticed glass. Also noteworthy was the amount of switches and gadgetry, all for just a 150-watt bulb - barely brighter than you would have in your living room. As you will no doubt realise, it is the lens that gives the light its strength.

On our way in, a zealous RSPB representative had drawn our attention to some fledglings up on the cliff, which could be seen on the screen. On our way out, she invited us to join the society, and it was at this point that I had to blow our cover stating that we were here for the lighthouse - the ruse was up!

The closest I get to ornithology is observing the cooing of the wood pigeon as I lay in bed in the morning. It isn't actually that hard to miss when it perches proudly on your chimney pot singing its heart out from dawn till dusk on most sunny days. I do particularly enjoy hearing the dawn chorus as it gets light though - especially if it's summer and I know there's still another three hours before I have to get up!

I recently heard a story concerning some people who had moved to the countryside, only to find that that they were regularly awoken early by the cockerel. Complaints were made to the farmer who owned the offending bird, and as a result the poor creature's life was terminated somewhat prematurely.

To my mind, this is savagery akin to having your neighbour's sports car towed to the crusher because it wakes you up when he leaves for work at 6am. Perhaps the moral here is to be careful what you complain about - occasionally somebody will do something about it!

Note the emphasis on the word 'occasionally'. I have often been moved to pen the odd letter about matters I consider to be slightly more concerning than the vibrations within a farmyard animal's larynx, yet have never once received a response along the lines of 'You've got a good point there; we will look into how we can deal with this issue and act accordingly'.

Unfortunately it's these ludicrous complaints that are taken the most seriously. My Dad has even stayed in a rural hotel, which is threatening to sue a nearby farmer over a cockerel. Apparently, they have got a good case. It all just seems like 'fowl' play to me.

Due to the vast increase in red tape (which is no doubt in place mainly to help bizarre grievances like those of people who don't want to hear birds in the countryside), inaction is now the most desirable option for proper suggestions. A 'thank you for your opinions' letter is generally sent in the hope that I will never darken their in-tray again! Any further correspondence seems to miraculously lose itself in the post!

Not wishing to appear contemptuous of the public; companies, councils and organisations will from time to time issue questionnaires. Once all the responses are collated and categorised into benign categories not relating to any specific issue, the 'findings' can be published and they can then go ahead and do what they would have done all along!

I fear that I have slipped effortlessly from extolling the virtues of birdsong into another tirade about 'the system', so I will quickly haul my thoughts back to South Stack where you find us hauling ourselves back up the 400 steps. During this, my Dad displayed the best advert for not smoking that you are ever likely to see! Still out of breath when we reached the car, he immediately sparked up a cigarette, and on we pressed to Holyhead - just a couple of miles away.

It was the west pier that we were interested in, and our maps deceived us into thinking that we could drive down the hillside, avoiding the town, on lanes and tracks. These quickly degenerated into grass, and remembering my muddy byway incident, we wisely turned 180 degrees.

Our next attempt was to negotiate our way to the seafront via the suburban streets and proceed along a very narrow lane, which ran past the hotel where we would find ourselves spending the night, and what appeared to be the crumbling ruins of the harbour master's stately home. It became a dead-end but we were able to get to the gravelly approach to the pier on foot.

However, the parking arrangement left a lot to be desired, and it was a case of 'third time lucky' when we found the trackbed of an old rail line, which is now a smooth tarmac lane.

The walk to Goleudy lighthouse was an epic. This wasn't what we needed after Llanddwyn and 1120 steps. The concrete pier was on two levels and consisted of a long straight, a bend to the right, another long straight, a bend to the left and a final straight to the end. (Sounds a bit like a politician's career guide!).

Little did we know that at 7860 feet in length (almost 1½ miles), we were walking the longest breakwater in the UK. That's 820 feet longer than Southend's hyperbolic pier. It felt like it too!

The 'Great Breakwater' took 28 years to build and was completed in 1873, so we can comfortably assume that the lighthouse at the end dates from then onwards. This massive project was constructed to service and shelter the Victorian ironclads, then still in vogue, quickly rendered obsolete by subsequent history. Modern vehicle ferries to Ireland use a terminal far smaller in area - a terminal from an earlier era further to the east. Today, in sunshine, the Great Breakwater looked strangely forlorn.

The square lighthouse is seventy feet high and was built square to make the rooms as commodious as possible. The round lattice-windowed lantern sits upon a square balcony over the chunky square tower, which is white with the top third painted black.

Across the water we could see the characteristic two flashes of the Skerries island lighthouse. Tomorrow we would observe this from a closer vantage-point.

Two, at a guess, ten-year-old boys almost gave us a heart attack when one of them climbed up onto the narrow wall around the hammerhead-shaped end of the pier, and began prancing around as though completely oblivious to the vertical drop into the sea. Bearing in mind that, should he slip and fall, the nearest steps back up onto the structure are over half a mile away; and add the fact that the two gentlemen walking the end of the pier both possessed the swimming ability of a concrete paving slab, this behaviour seemed a little foolhardy. Did I say 'foolhardy?' I meant 'suicidal!'

We tiptoed back to avoid them putting on any further show of bravado. Back at the landward end, another group of children were dossing about inside some large horizontal metal cylinders. Every now and again a large bang was emitted! Anyone would think that there wasn't much to do in Holyhead!

I had gained my second wind by now, but my Dad was intent on chilling out, so we found a hotel, downed a swift pint and crashed out with 'Songs of praise' on the television. Now, if you remember the last time we had relaxed to this, it was in Washford in Somerset; and we reclined on our hotel beds with the view of a railway line outside the window, having just exerted ourselves on several long walks including dragging ourselves up a huge headland.

Things were remarkably similar in Holyhead, except that here we kept seeing cars go along the railway line!

Unlike Washford, there were no boisterous 'zoider-drinking' folk to be seen, but there was a sense of unease. Upon returning to the bar we kept receiving inquisitive glances from a twitchy young man sitting alone, chain-smoking a few tables away. He had a look of the army about him, and putting two and two together, we guessed that he was awaiting the ferry to Ireland. Not wishing to find ourselves mistakenly identified as espionage suspects, it was with some relief that we were ushered into a separate room for our meal.

I tried something I'd never eaten before – asparagus, which I found to be not too dissimilar in flavour to potato but with a refreshing crunch. I also tried a fresh local crab.

Neither of us fancied being stared at for the rest of the evening so we ventured out, but could find no establishment that looked particularly welcoming. We ended up driving past the ferry terminal, which operates ferries to Dublin and Dun Laoghaire (not a million miles apart), and parked on the fish-quay to view the round lighthouse on Salt Island.

Built on the end of Admiralty Pier, which was completed in 1824, the stumpy tower is a grey 'stone' colour with a green triangle below the balcony. The rounded top above the light compartment is also green.

Salt Island lies between the fish-quay and the west pier we had walked earlier. It is joined to Holyhead in a way that you would not recognise it as an island at all, and in spite of there being both a church and a hospital on it, we found that access was barred to unauthorised persons, which led us to wonder if the ferry companies had bought out these places of spiritual and bodily healing for their own financial edification.

I hate to say it but the town itself seemed rather grim, with a lot of grey terraces. I realise that Sunday night is perhaps not the best night to assess the nightlife in an unfamiliar place, but the undertone that we had observed or imagined gave us the illusion that entering any of these pubs could result in us getting a good kicking for being outsiders, and worse still, English outsiders!

An unfair conclusion, I am sure, but we had had enough foreboding glances for one night, and decided to finish the evening by following the disused trackbed to see where it led.

This is a road that I wish I had videoed in its entirety, and although I revile a previous Prime Minister's suggestion of turning the nation's rail lines into roads, I did particularly relish the idea of being driven along the embankment behind our hotel, through a curved cutting through rocks, and under two bridges straight towards the Holyhead Mountain.

Our terminus was a disused quarry/brickworks with a tall, thin chimney at the centre. As dusk fell, we absorbed all the info we could. An astonishing seven million tons of stone were excavated during the quarry's years of operation, and brick-making continued here until 1973.

At its peak, some 1400 men were employed quarrying and building the Great Breakwater. The noise, the dust and the smoke were difficult to imagine on this quiet evening, but as the shadows lengthened, it appeared that each one brought a laughing ghost closer to us.

We returned to our hotel feeling so enriched that we decided to forego the customary final pint, and although my Dad was soon blissfully unaware, my unease was just beginning; for I had one of those nights when one is denied the luxury of just dropping off to sleep, instead having to endure a labyrinth of bizarre dreams experienced in a half-asleep/half-awake state.

This basically involves the sub-conscious trawling through the darker recesses of the mind and throwing everything it can find into a bewildering tapestry of REM experience that one cannot fully awaken from. Every now and again, enough consciousness is regained to realise what is going on, but no matter how much you try to move, you cannot shake yourself awake and are plunged back into the 'Alice in Wonderland' experience once again. If only I could write these dreams down, we could have a Carroll-esque classic on our hands!

Just then, we were both startled by somebody trying our door. With sleepy brains not yet fully engaged in logic, it was as if that restless young recruit in the bar had been monitoring us and it was now time for confrontation!

My Father leapt from his bed, the fastest he had moved all day, and opened the door cautiously while standing behind it, to reveal an empty corridor. Too many James Bond movies! He puts the interruption down to us being in room nine and a befuddled lodger being in room six. Or vice versa.

As my heartbeat slowed down again, I realised that I would much rather write a children's story from my experience asleep, than a thriller about spies and interrogation from a real life nightmare in Holyhead!

I fell asleep and dreamed no more.

Barmouth Bliss

144) SKERRIES* (island light - 2 white flashes every 10 secs)
145) POINT LYNAS* (white occulting light every 10 secs)
146) TRYWN DU* (white flash every 5 secs)
147) ST TUDWALL'S* (island light – white/red flash every 15 secs)

The skies were dull to begin with on what we thought would be our final day. A day that would notch up the tally on our 'lighthouse odometer' to 147.

'Is there any significance to this number?' I asked myself. All that springs to mind is that 147 is the maximum break in snooker. Could this be a good omen for a 'lucky break' in getting this thing published? In actual fact, we would just end up 'snookered' with more to visit!

Our minds were as ever concerned with the finer details of the day's schedule as we ate our breakfast in exactly the same seats as we had sat in last night. Gathering our thoughts and belongings, we left the hotel and bade farewell to Holyhead, which ushered us more or less straight away onto the A55. Today we would be covering the north side of Anglesey, and soon we found ourselves on an undulating A-road, traversing the green openness, with a view back to Holyhead and its harbour to our left.

Our first port of call would be to access a better view of the Skerries' light we had glimpsed across the water yesterday. Before long, we were negotiating our way along peacefully unspectacular lanes towards Wilfa Head nuclear power station.

A little to the west of this great grey block is a short curving causeway across the small inlet of Cemlyn Bay, which can be walked at low tide. This links Wilfa Head with the point from which we wished to view Skerries lighthouse. This was another haven for ornithologists, and once again, deceptively armed with video and tripod, we parked at the end of the dead-end lane and hit the footpath, feeling a little like cuckoos invading a nest.

Pausing for a moment to read a memorial stone by the path, we learned that Anglesey's first lifeboat was launched here in 1828. At least one would assume it was from here, after all, why else would this information be found at such an isolated spot.

Crossing the Cemlyn point beside a field, we set up our photographic equipment beside the rocky shore and zoomed out into the Irish Sea, where Skerries' light was still winking at us twice in succession every ten seconds.

Across this four mile stretch of water, which appeared to be littered with rocks, we could make out the 75-foot, round, white tower with a red band around the middle. The surrounding buildings are white two-storey 'blocks'. This light was first shown in 1717. It was built by William Trench, and has been rebuilt twice and restored once. Amazingly Trinity House opposed its construction and it was apparently the last privately owned light to come under their banner (in 1841).

A blustery breeze had begun to stir the air vigorously and before long we were driving past Wilfa Head nuclear power station. To me this looked just like our own Dungeness 'A' power station had been scooped up and transplanted to hillier, more fertile terrain, complete with the long, flat block of its converter station. This observation was not far off the mark as both were built to a similar design at a similar time.

Back on the A-road that straddles around the north coast of Ynys Mon, we skimmed the edge of Amlwch, which was where we turned off. There are few places on this island that you could describe as towns. Amlwch is just large enough to fit the epithet.

The light at Point Lynas is half-way along this north coast, and the lane we approached on took a sharp turn to the right upon reaching the sea at a picturesque cove. There were a few houses dotted amongst the green shrubbery. Signs instructed us to park as we headed along the open grassy point beneath a still-dull sky, forcing us to continue along the straight lane upon foot.

Everything looks a little like something else, and this 36-foot structure looked very similar to the converted lighthouse we had seen on the Great Orme, having a turreted front and a round lamp room at ground level. Again our observations were wholly correct, for both were constructed and operated by Mersey Docks and Harbour Board. It was not until 1973 that Trinity House took this white lighthouse under its wing. An arched gateway leads to the compound at the end of the lane and at its pointed top a plaque informs the visitor that the first light was shown here in 1833 and that the telegraph and present cottage complex was built in 1879. The point was originally known as Point Elianus.

We wandered around to the front. The windowed half-cylinder of the lamp room sits at the bottom of the square tower upon which the radar revolves. The lower turreted wall marks the sea-facing side of the square compound giving it a symmetrical appearance.

As I wandered the cliff-edge to get a better view, a speedboat passed below leaving a fuzzy white trail in the water behind it. It was again time for *us* to hit the trail in pursuit of the lighthouse at the north-east corner of the island – Trywn Du.

Rejoining the A-road, the sun began to break through with its accompanying warmth. The landscape was now much less barren with houses and even villages cropping up along the route. We were headed for Beaumaris, a colourful little town on the island's east coast. Our approach was a gentle descent from a wooded area. It reminded me a little of an Irish town – instead of plain white plaster walls we had become accustomed to, the buildings were all different pastel shades from pink to orange to yellow.

We turned left at the town centre, and passed the castle as we exited. The road soon reverted into lane and skirted the flat land beside the sea, before climbing onto the embankment and passing Penmon Priory. The end of the road was nigh, and it was time for my Dad to dip into his pocket again for the privilege of parking on grass. Being a 'put money in the box' scenario, the fee wasn't paid entirely accurately due to the correct change not coming to hand.

Descending the slope to the rocky shoreline, the round 95-foot tower resembled a liquorice allsort, being predominantly white with black bands around the base, middle and below the light compartment. It was built by James Walker in 1835, and is adorned with black letters on the east-facing side. The words read 'No Passage Landward' - sound advice as the water is far too shallow to sail anything more than a dinghy. Indeed, had we stuck around for another few hours, the tide would have receded and we wound have been able to amble out to it, and perhaps even circumnavigate it (as if in some ancient Druidic ritual?).

Further out to sea to the east is the large green expanse of Puffin Island and further eastward and outward again is that breathtaking stretch of mountainous coastline from Conwy to Llanfairfechan.

A single bell pealed every thirty seconds. This fog signal was not so much a harmonious ring as a deadened metal thud.

"For whom the bell tolls", my Dad retorted, trying to sound poetic at this supposedly climatic stage in the proceedings. For with one lighthouse remaining to cross off our schedule, we left the waves lapping quietly at the rocks and tried to shift up a gear by means of a celebratory pint in Beaumaris.

With our trusty 'Good beer guide' in hand, we knew exactly where we wanted to go and promptly drove straight past it! We eventually found the car-park in a secluded courtyard. Entering the bar cautiously, we eyed up the pumps and surmised the best 'real ale' option.

Whilst sitting in a dark corner of this inn, drinking in the atmosphere (for this building was here at the height of the Wars of the Roses), snippets of conversation drifted across the slightly hazy room.

It seemed to centre around what these two middle-aged gentlemen perceived to be a very real hazard on the road – sneezing. Perhaps in Anglesey this really is the worst thing you have to contend with. My Dad mumbled something about them doing a stint on the M25, but by now the conversation had progressed to that other great tribulation – squashed flies on the windscreen! What a contrast to the murder of kings or even the setting up of the Council of the Marches (1471), which must have been topics in an earlier era here.

The road to Menai Bridge (an estranged suburb of Bangor), was an attractive drive. We crossed back to the Welsh mainland on the old bridge (unintentionally), and were soon on a vastly improved A487, heading south at a consistent 60mph.

Slicing across hill and vale, this road made mincemeat of the journey to Caernarfon, which is famous for its castle built by Edward I and used as the site for the investiture of the Prince of Wales in 1969.

Our 'Holy Grail' was the lighthouse on St Tudwall's Island, near the end of the Lleyn Peninsular, which juts out into the Irish Sea for about 25 miles. Beneath this, the Welsh coast retracts rather shyly to Barmouth and further south, Aberystwyth,

Back in 1984, in July, the Lleyn peninsular had been the epicentre of the largest onshore earthquake ever recorded in the UK. It measured 5.4 on the Richter scale and vibrated an area of 150,000 square miles.

Like Ynys Mon, Lleyn was similarly rural, but here a range of mountains crosses the middle like a sturdy backbone. This drive could be enjoyed better once we had passed the metal monster, which occupied 80% of our view, as we trawled through the interminable roadworks. Perhaps Wales isn't so different from England after all!

As I filmed the scenery we had a small debate about whether on not to leave Jimmy Young and his resident medical expert on the radio, in case we ever wanted to release an accompanying video to this novelette (preferably without releasing medical confidantes). Then with the radio on and the video camera off, we passed between these hills to the quiet crossroads village of 'Y Ffor' (Four Crosses). As we left the car to frequent the general stores, a lady with a pushchair shouted something in Welsh, not at us as we first thought, but to her friend across the road. This was apt - we knew we were back in the real Wales, for both the north coast and Anglesey had seemed strangely Anglicised.

Descending to the Lleyn's south side, we entered Pwllheli - a small seaside town which attracts a lot of visiors because of its large holiday camp.

Next along this coast was Abersoch, where the road negotiates its way around this interesting little place by means of a one-way system. Beyond this, it was lanes all the way.

We knew this was going to be a tricky one, for the island light is about half a mile out to sea. Unfortunately the only stretch of coast facing this is completely privately owned with no public footpaths and plenty of 'forbidden' signs. As the lanes around Sarn Bach got narrower, we dived up a dead end to think up a contingency plan.

Already satiated with pork pies and 'Yuk', I wandered up the narrow footpath that ran beside the muddy bridleway ahead of us, while my Dad feasted upon his.

There were tall impenetrable bushes on either side with pink flowers and small insects buzzing around. I asked a passing gentleman if it would be possible to see the lighthouse this way. He consulted his Pathfinder map and thoughtfully responded "Probably not".

But we never take no for an answer. I thanked him and continued until this bridleway/footpath combination reached another lane, then I strolled back to the car to break the news that we were lost in a network of tracks and paths all leading the wrong way.

It was Rupert Bear country again. Just like at that very first lighthouse near Fowey, we were blindly searching a maze of paths for our seldom-seen goal. Plan B would have to be implemented. This was simply to drive randomly like a rat in a maze until we were as close as possible to the sea, then abandon the car and walk the shoreline, keeping a close eye on the tide.

We eventually made the golden sands by descending some small concrete steps accompanied by the trickle of a water outlet. The view across the bay to the small hills around Pwllheli was a peaceful one. Rounding the headland, we scrambled beneath a wooden structure for launching boats at a forty-five degree angle straight from a private boathouse into the sea.

Beyond this - nothing but rocks. With the incoming tide lapping at our feet, a sense of urgency set in; the lighthouse was in view but I wanted to get closer. Progress was slow as I precariously picked out a path over the different sized boulders beneath the cliff. My Dad began calling things out from behind and I realised that this was as good as it was going to get. Out came the tripod, up went the camera, on went the zoom-lens and down went our spirits, just a little. This oblique shot across the water was to be our project's swan song. Or was it?

When I returned my Dad was sitting pensively on a rock.

"Opinion at the end of the mission?" I ventured.

"Anticlimatic" responded my Father, "anticlimatic". So what of the 36-foot high structure which occupies the highest point of this grassy little island?

Well, it is white (no surprises there), a round tower (as ever), and is a stout little structure with 'Trinity House' written all over it (metaphorically of course!). Date of construction: 1877.

The light compartment accounts for about half of its height, and there is a building next to it resembling a concrete bunker. A square, grey wall bounds the compound, and a 'sun valve' is used to switch on the light. This consists of a black rod absorbing the heat from a series of gold-plated copper bars expanding downwards to cut off the acetylene gas in daylight.

To be honest, I felt more of a sense of completion at the end of that long pier in Berwick, or even upon that grassy knoll at Trevose Head in Cornwall. I realise why now – we hadn't actually completed our mission at all! Our final resting place for tonight would be Barmouth. There seemed little point in hanging around – the earth hadn't moved for *us* at Lleyn!

We briefly flirted with the idea of viewing the lighthouse on Bardsey Island from the very end of the Lleyn Peninsular, but as we reached the top of the hill and glimpsed Bardsey's hazy presence across the water, we realised that this would be impossible, for the lighthouse is located on the far side of the island.

Beyond Pwllheli, I grew sleepy and the soothing drone of the car and the air gently blustering through the window enticed me to nod off in spite of attempts at resistance. We left the Lleyn at Porthmadoc, so called because in the ninteenth century the MP William Alexander Maddocks reclaimed the land that the town now stands upon. We drove along the embankment/bridge, which carries both the road and the steam railway (which runs here from the grey slate mountains of Blaenau Ffestiniog) across the Glaslyn Estuary.

Just the other side is Portmerion, an interesting replica of an Italian village, famously used as the setting for the 1960's television series 'The prisoner'. Being a mere 27 years of age, I have never had the pleasure of this programme, but can clearly see how this colourful place would be fitting for a surreal sixties series of this kind.

Back to today, and British television seems to have followed British music into the abyss of mediocrity. It amazes me that the telly addict is not yet an endangered species. With most factual programming banished to digital channels and the graveyard slot after 2am, we are left with soaps and situation comedies that are often about as funny as open heart surgery without anaesthetic!

Then there are two channels (one in the South-East) that seem to devote entire post-watershed schedules to the extreme deviant minority, perhaps in the hope that they will one day be the majority, for this is apparently what the people want. One feels like a 'porn' in a their game.

Even the adverts are pretty excruciating these days. They invariably contain a member of the male gender demonstrating that he has the IQ of a gnat. Apparently this appeals to the female shopper and thus, insulting the intelligence of half your potential market is a carefully planned commercial strategy.

It wouldn't be so bad if the license fee was more like the so-called 'toll' we encountered a little further along the road. My Dad wound down the window to enquire as to why two men were walking about in the road with empty plastic ice cream tubs flagging down every passing vehicle. It became immediately apparent that they were exacting the grandiose 'toll' fee of one ten pence piece!

After fumbling around in his pocket, he declared that he didn't have one. These 'highwaymen' then reduced their ransom to five pence! My Dad paid this somewhat trivial amount and continued, only to find that another toll was required to use the lane that bridges the Traeth Bach, saving us a lengthy detour on the main road. Here the sum was far more princely. My Dad protested that we had already paid a fee.

"That was for charity" came the reply.

'What charity?' I wondered, 'you're not going to liberate Wales with a handful of five pence pieces!'

A single-track railway line accompanied us across the marshy estuary between the hills. Like us, the line was bound for Harlech and Barmouth.

The approach to Harlech was interesting, as the main road split off of itself to cross the track and approach the steep hills (upon which both the town and its castle stands), from across flat farmland that looks reclaimed.

The road climbed steeply and rejoined what must have been the original route to the south of Harlech's centre - a kind of improvisational bypass.

The green, hilly scenery rolled majestically all the way down to Barmouth, a town that I grew to like the moment we entered it. The narrow High Street, which is lined with interesting old shops and buildings of varying shapes, sizes and styles, nestles beneath the wooded precipice that overlooks the town. At the bottom end of this is the harbour occupied by small fishing boats. Here the railway bridges the picturesque Mawddach Estuary to the mountains beyond. Turning right here, one encounters the seafront, which is typical of a small resort of this kind.

The inn that we stayed in was attractive and economically priced, although I think my Father would have liked somewhere a bit more regal, at least somewhere with an en suite bathroom anyway!

As we reclined on our beds, the early evening sounds drifted in through the open window, punctuated by the quarter-hourly chime of the church clock. With three and a half years of travels behind us, we wondered if serendipity would provide us with a raucous evening on a celebratory note. Perhaps if we had actually finished, it would have done!

The evening was nonetheless pleasant and after a drink downstairs, we headed for an American theme bar hoping for a nice juicy steak. The only 'juicy' going-ons were on a large TV screen, which had all the punters glued to that most American of dramas - Eastenders!

We sought solace in the back room, which looked very glitzy and transatlantic. An empty corner was floodlit as if somebody had just stolen the performer and his fifties rock 'n' roll covers band. On the wall were some gold discs, but they were not Elvis or Bill Haley but...

...Herman's Hermits!

Although it is fair to say that this particular British group were actually more popular in the States than in the UK.

After a customary look at the station, we headed for a Chinese restaurant. The odd thing is that everything is generally much cheaper in Wales than South-East England, except Chinese! Perhaps it's that little bit further that it has to travel from the Orient. Hauling large quantities of Chop Suey and Peking Duck across the Welsh mountains is bound to inflate the price a little!

Unperturbed by this, I ordered Chow Mein with beef and onions, which was just as succulent as the steak that I wanted would have been. Our Oriental hosts spoke fluent English as well as Chinese. I wondered if they could speak Welsh also – now that *would* be talented! I have yet to hear Welsh being spoken with a Chinese accent!

As dusk fell, the street lamps leant a warm glow to the town's old buildings. We were down by the harbour when I noticed an alehouse out of the corner of my eye - the aptly named 'Last Inn'.

This demanded a visit on what we believed at the time was our final night away on our mission. Inside there was a cosy candle-lit atmosphere with dark, wooden seats and photographs plastered all around the bar and beams. Space was made for us to sit at a handsome bench in a snug inglenook. Our new-found elderly companions were passing among themselves the first fully-ripened cherries of the summer, whilst we just savoured the mellow atmosphere as different conversations intertwined around us. The soporific air began to engulf us; we had to leave hurriedly or be ensnared for all time!

The main street was deserted and the night air was now cooler. We returned to our hostelry just in time for last orders. As we were served our final pint we noticed a large gentleman ordering four pints of bitter. He drained the bottom of his glass and set to work on one of them, but where were his three mates, we wondered.

As we analysed a pre-war picture of the town, he felt prompted to share a bit of Barmouth's history with us. There were now two and a half pints on the bar in front of him. It became apparent that there were no other thirsty mouths to feed – this half-gallon of ale was all his own! He told us that it had always been his plan to retire to Barmouth right from his first visit as a young man. I admired his determined approach and I don't mean to the bar to pick up his penultimate pint!

Comfortably finishing his final beer as the last punters left the bar to go home, or in our case upstairs, I can honestly say that I have never seen anybody make binge-drinking look so relaxing!

* * * * *

The bell of the church clock echoed through the night at regular intervals, giving us an excuse to get up slightly later than planned for breakfast.

Kilroy was scrutinising relationship breakdowns on TV. We began the scenic drive through the Welsh hills by following the river.

We met up with the A470, a north/south trunk route, which was recently voted as one of the worst roads in Britain (presumably by people who don't like scenery). I won't even mention the posters of bloodstained Union flags we encountered along the roadside.

After the bustling town centre of Welshpool we crossed back into England and negotiated the lanes over Long Mountain and up onto Gravel's Bank, mostly crawling along behind a large tractor!

After another visit to my Aunt and Uncle's stone-clad hilltop cottage, we bypassed Shrewsbury en route to the M54 and a clogged M6, which threw us off into a detour round some of the more pleasant parts of the West Midlands metropolis near Sutton Coldfield.

After a final 'Yuk' stop near Coventry and the most expensive snack-bar I have ever purchased, it was back onto the A14 for the three hours of open road going home.

Contrary to what we thought, this was far from the end of the road for us.

THE GRAND FINALE

Undone in London

What could be a more appropriate way to celebrate three and a half years of traveling the coastline, than a visit to the Trinity House headquarters in London?

Waiting to board our antiquated diesel train at Hamstreet station on a sunny Saturday in August, my Father made trite comments about the weather to an elderly gentleman. We were then treated, by way of return, to a resume on the derivation of the legends surrounding the number '666'. With our heads still spinning from this 'revelation', we fell into the train to be greeted by three minutes of inane spiel made over a scratchy tannoy. There were bemused looks and a sense that the guard shouldn't have bothered on the faces of all the passengers.

Changing onto the London train, it became clear that we would spend the next hour being serenaded by a gang of teenage girls, whether we liked it or not, singing everything from Beatles' classics to Popstars' disposables. My Dad buried his head in the paper.

We alighted to peace at last, at London Bridge, and our day began with a gentle walk along the Thames past HMS Belfast, the leaning glass sphere of London City Council's new building and a thousand Japanese tourists. Tower Bridge was an uplifting sight with its blue paint belying its age. Similarly the Tower of London also had the appearance of having been 'cleaned up'.

Having crossed the river and passed the tower, we got our camera out while everybody else put theirs away. We had arrived at Trinity Square EC3 just in time for our first shock. The Trinity House headquarters were not, as we had presumed, based in the towering Roman-looking building, resplendent with columns and statues, but in the less striking three-storey block to the east of this.

The front of the headquarters was bounded by a black-painted metal fence, with gates that could be locked at any time to keep the prying visitor from getting too close! We were used to this kind of thing at the lighthouses, but for the moment the gates were open. Nevertheless, I felt a little as though I was trespassing as I wandered behind the fence to read the plaques and engravings on the white block wall. Of these, there were three.

The first is a black plaque outlining the purpose and history of Trinity House, the first Trinity House being in Deptford. Next, there were three 'bricks' engraved with various names, the top one relating to the building's reopening in 1953 by Her Majesty Queen Elizabeth II. The building was partially destroyed by enemy action in 1940.

The third is a silver plaque detailing the lighthouse automation programme, which commenced in 1982. It emphatically states that North Foreland lighthouse, Kent, was the last manned lighthouse in the UK, ending four hundred years of service to the mariner by the lighthouse keepers. They have obviously not been to Walney Island, Cumbria!

Just like so many of their lighthouses, we were unable to get inside this building and had to settle for an anti-clockwise circumnavigation. This took us past Fenchurch Street station, which we had previously only encountered on a Monopoly board, and landed us beside the Romanesque structure of number ten Trinity Square. This building has three statues. The most notable is that of Father Thames, high above the onlooker enthroned by the square archway of the tower (same shape as the Arc de Triomphe). You will understand how we were mistaken, for this building clearly has a maritime connection.

As I filmed away like a lost Japanese tourist, my Dad boldly asked the doorman if we could go inside. It was then that we were informed that this sixty million pound building is now the headquarters of an insurance company. This remarkable edifice, in the style of the Vittorio Emanuelle building in Rome, took seven years to complete to its opening in 1922, its construction delayed, to some extent, by the first world war. It was the location of the Port of London Authority until 1970. With most of London's former maritime sites now similarly converted into offices, the change of use seemed inevitable.

Interesting to note is that the front of this building is the property of the crown, being within a bowshot of the Tower of London. Ancient bylaws decree that this is rented for the fee of one nosegay (posy of flowers) per year. Surely this must meet with the approval of Prince Charles, but our noses were now being drawn to the building beside. A little shocked that we had travelled sixty miles to look at an anonymous block instead of this more stately structure, a visit to a chain-pub seemed in order, especially as the prospect of a cheap pint in London was almost as surprising as what was to come.

We took a deserted tube train from Tower Hill to Embankment, where we wandered up the hill to Charing Cross. My Dad was a little distraught that there was a plaque to mark the planting of a sickly-looking tree following the 1987 'hurricane' but there was nothing here to indicate that this was the point from which all mileages to London used to be taken on the nation's signposts.

Why were we here? Well, an old map my Dad had found at home showed three lights along the banks of the Thames to the east of the Isle of Dogs along to Erith. We suspected that these had been removed during the various building projects that have taken place along this stretch of water but we had to be sure. So we headed for a comprehensive bookshop in Charing Cross Road in search of Ordnance Survey maps.

With the two that remain shown as beacons, we breathed a sigh of relief, after all we were here to celebrate the completion of our mission. It was then that my Dad came across an English Heritage book on lighthouses by Peter Ashley. Flicking through the pages, we felt a little like Captain Scott reaching the South Pole only to find that somebody else had already been there. But it wasn't until we reached the pages on the West that our hearts really sank. Not only did this show a tall chimney-like structure at Ellesmere Port, Cheshire that we had missed, but also a quayside light at Watchet, Somerset. Anyone looking at the book would have seen a picture of a red lighthouse. We just saw red!

This book even showed two old lights we had apparently missed at Hurst, Hampshire. Our hearts sank like a buffalo trapped in quicksand. The mission was far from over, and we were far from happy. Dazed and confused, we stumbled into a nearby pub for another cheap London pint before returning to Charing Cross station. We boarded a brand new train under the watchful gaze of the slowly revolving London Eye and began the journey home.

At Ashford we were herded like animals onto the two-coach graffiti-ridden diesel train for the last six miles home. With virtually every window scratched deliberately by vandals, there was little to look at as we huddled together with an abundance of German and Japanese tourists who must have thought they'd just boarded a train in the third world. It was just as well they didn't get off at Hamstreet, otherwise they would have heard the 'third world' language being screamed by a gang of teenage girls who had obviously ingested too much tartrazine! After not hearing a single risque utterance in the big city, it took me a few seconds to reacclimatise to village life. I take back all I said about Minsterley.

Sadly, when all was said and done, a day that was supposed to be a triumphant conclusion had just laid down another gauntlet for us. We would be back in the car and travelling half the country before the year was out.

Nobody said it was going to be easy.

Well-to-do Williton and Welsh Walkers

148/149) HURST CASTLE (redundant low lights)
150) WATCHET (harbour light)
151) BLACK ROCK (redundant)

This mission was becoming like one of those horror films that just won't end. Just when you think they have killed the three-headed beast, it pops up again and prolongs the showing for another fifteen minutes! Even our premise of only visiting lighthouses as shown by the Ordnance Survey was serving us badly. Lights for us to visit were popping up all over the place, and worse still at opposite ends of the country.

Gathering information from five different atlases, an English Heritage photograph book and some colloquial knowledge, we would have to either visit or eliminate two more lights at Hurst (Hampshire), along with lights at Watchet and Minehead (Somerset), Sudbrook, Port Talbot and Swansea (South Wales), Ellesmere Port (Cheshire), one in London, and yes, why not have another look at Avonmouth at the same time?

So with bags packed and another 150-mile drive under our belts, we found ourselves back at Keyhaven, south of the New Forest on the banks of the Solent.

We had no intention of trudging the mile-long spit of shingle again, and so boarded the little ferryboat, Haven Rose. This service operates in summer only and took about twenty minutes to cross this short stretch of water due to having to round the head of the spit in order to dock on the south-east side (as dictated by this morning's tide).

As the boat hit the swell, I considered it fortunate that we had not started the day with our customary 'greasy spoon' breakfast! Soon we were disembarking onto a floating pontoon and stepping out onto the familiar shingle once again. The tall, white, Trinity House lighthouse still looked the same, towering above its associated buildings a hundred yards or so from the castle. But how on earth did we miss the two low lights? Grafted onto the long castle wall, they were not out of our line of vision wherever we chose to look.

We had an hour and a half to kill so we decided to pay our fee and view inside the castle. This was worthwhile, for not only did we get to see Henry VIII's original castle, which is hidden by the huge nineteenth century walls when viewed from the outside, but we were able to get a little info on these lights as well.

The more easterly one was the first low light, constructed in 1865. This is a short, fat cylinder constructed from stone-colour 'bricks'. It has a black balcony around its polygonal light compartment.

Its replacement, built in 1911 has a far more military look about it, being a square bodied structure with a tall light compartment, which although appearing rounded is actually many-sided. Whereas the old low light is built on top of a flat-roofed brick building adjoining the castle wall, this one is actually grafted onto the wall and supported by a square metal framework. Its body, balcony and struts are all painted the same blue/grey colour, although this was not always the case - it was once entirely bright-red.

This light too, has followed its predecessor into redundancy. Two low intensity beams shown from the Trinity House high light now mark the safe channel for vessels.

The 'rooms' inside this castle are a little like air raid shelters. In one of these the acetylene gas equipment which illuminated the high light from 1922 - 1997 can be seen. Although we were able to get up onto the wall at some points, the section, which would have afforded us a single shot of all three lighthouses, was designated 'out of bounds'. After a brief look at Henry VIII's original castle (c. 1540), we caught our ferryboat back to shore. A wind had got up by now, yet thankfully, our crossing was no choppier than the ride out had been.

We stopped in New Milton for vittles, and although I shunned the usual milkshake option in the hope of being able to stay awake all the way to Somerset, I was nodding off within a couple of miles of hitting the A31.

The drive from Dorchester to Crewkerne is a pleasant one, with little villages of thatch-cottages providing enough interest to keep me conscious. Having passed through Taunton and Williton, we were soon at Watchet on the North Somerset Coast.

This fairly atmospheric little town had plenty of small boats in the tiny harbour, which is overlooked by its station on the steam railway that runs to Minehead. The accelerating huff of the last train of the day stirred the tranquility a little, as the sinking sun reflected upon the gentle incoming waves.

The bright-red hexagonal tower of this thin little lighthouse is sited at the end of the west pier; perhaps only twenty-five feet in height and with a white light compartment containing green oblong windows.

We were satisfied now and our minds turned, as ever, to lodgings. We expected far more inns and B&B places in Watchet but in the end, retired to Williton. Our hotel was located on the busy A39 right beside the mini-roundabout where it meets the Taunton road. We were offered two different rooms, each with three beds, we opted for the 'green' room. From here, we could not only hear the thundering lorries come screeching to a halt when suddenly encountering this busy junction, but we could even see the local sign by the road advertising a rally for 'liberty and livelihood'.

We had seen literally hundreds of these on our journey across country from Dorset. The title put us in mind of the well known French 'liberty, equality, fraternity', which led to the terror and subsequent bloodbath of the 1790's. Foxes beware!

Of course the vested interest in Williton would have been the Exmoor stag hunt. This ambiguous title for a march would no doubt entice lovers of country life who, thinking they were marching for rural bus services, village shops and fresh farm produce, would actually be stampeding the capital for an activity that is of no interest to them at all. Clever!

Among the ranks, I have no doubt, will also be those who, by their presence are claiming to represent rural life, yet a sighting of them using a local shop occurs about as often as a sighting of the Loch Ness Monster! The attraction of mass movement never ceases to amaze. Perhaps people need to feel that they are part of a movement, with the slim chance of witnessing a good old-fashioned punch-up being an added bonus! In the event, over 400,000 people took part, peacefully.

After an hour or so in the recovery position (flat out on the bed with a book and a cup of tea), it was time for the evening's preamble, a drink in the bar and some food. Remembering our last visit to Somerset, there now seemed to be a distinct lack of both scrumpy and 'true' locals to drink it! We were a mere four miles away from Washford; had the county really changed this much in three and a half years? Was everyone now a property entrepreneur, calculating the merits of borrowing to invest?

Our next inn was a food-orientated establishment. The value was tremendous, as was the size of the servings! Our starter was a main course in itself and we had to abandon our main courses half way through. In layman's terms, this was a 'gut-buster'.

As ever, we glanced in an estate agent's window to sum up the place. The prices horrified us – they were worse than Kent! No wonder there weren't any 'Wurzels' around.

Our final pub for tonight was just the same; there were plenty of quotations about wine painted on the walls, but there didn't seem to be anybody drinking it. I was disappointed at this gentrified version of 'Good old Zummerzet' and this lack of entertainment combined with our surfeit of food sent us reeling back to the hotel, with my Dad's pace reduced to a crawl by the physical pain that his distended alimentary canal was now causing him! This was not my idea of a pub 'crawl'.

* * * * *

After a night of ruminations and reverberations, (the lorries), we were far from prepared for the breakfast that was placed in front of us. Normally this huge platter of fried articles would have delighted us. Today it seemed more like a gauntlet was being laid down, an endurance test of over-indulgence! We would not be requiring the emergency 'dog chews' that my Dad had thoughtfully left in the car, today!

Minehead was eight miles to the west. It has a very similar feel to Llandudno, with the dark-green spectre of the hill looming over its tranquil sandy bay, and the small town centre discreetly tucked away behind the hotel-lined front. Two things were different though: to the west, the seafront became lined with picturesque thatch-cottages, and to the east was Butlins' holiday camp, resplendent with a white tented structure that looked remarkably like our designer outlet in Ashford, Kent.

But there was no lighthouse to be seen. The nearest thing, a rounded 'tower' with a green domed roof at the end of a stately Victorian building, was quickly dismissed, and soon we were motoring back to Taunton.

My Dad strayed wildly from our objectives here, wishing to check out a car showroom that he had seen advertising a special offer in a

237

national newspaper. What was special about it was that you don't get to see the car, let alone test drive it, before you buy it! Apparently, you sign on the dotted line and the next minute a brand new car turns up on your doorstep. My Father was not keen on this 'modern' way of doing business, and although he feels that his once brand-new car has been rendered a faithful old banger by these trips, we were soon back to the good old fashioned business of looking for lighthouses.

Avonmouth.

Having left the M5 after what must be one of the most interesting and pleasant stretches of motorway in the UK, we negotiated our way to Portbury Dock via Easton-in-Gordano. Aptly 'Sitting on the dock of the bay' was playing on the radio.

The lane led us into a giant industrial estate, which included a distribution centre for a supermarket and a similar holding site for new cars. Perhaps my Dad could have got a test drive here! The port itself greeted us with the usual hostility. A white van sped past the checkpoint in front of us, but as we tentatively inched towards it ourselves, a barrier was hastily lowered in front of us.

No, our best view had been from a dead-end to the east of the port, through a horrifically bright, red steel fence. We had glimpsed a structure we had not seen before but was it a lighthouse? This white cylinder with a black top had a coat of arms painted on it. At the time, I was convinced that this was the old retired lighthouse of Avonmouth Dock across the water, but now I am not so sure. It looked nothing like the picture on my 1920's set of cigarette cards. It may even have been a part of a ship! The structure would have been on the north side of the River Avon, perhaps half a mile upstream from its outflow. For all we know, it could be in Casablanca by now!

It seemed that whenever we came to Avonmouth, it resulted in frustration, we would have to give it up as a bad job.

Crossing the bridge on the M5, I glimpsed two structures on the north side jetties where the Avon flows into the Bristol Channel. Both were white topped. The right-hand one was the taller of the two; this must have been the one we had viewed from Portishead two years ago. The left-hand one was short and stubby.

There was a fuel crisis last time we were here in September 2000, and there was now a fuel crisis again: So busy was I scrutinising the docks that I forgot to give my Dad adequate directions to the old

Severn Bridge. We were now on the M49 with thirteen miles to the next services and a petrol gauge reading empty, with an increasingly bright red light on the dashboard.

As I broke the news that our quickest exit from the motorway would be London-bound on the M4 and then Bristol-bound on the M5, the swearword count began to tot up rapidly. Trying desperately to conserve our last teaspoonful of petrol, we crawled up an incline at forty miles an hour, while everything else whipped by at eighty! I had visions of us breaking down and having to resort to eating the 'dog chews' for energy as we walked to the nearest filling station!

But with panic over, we were soon heading back to the motorway from Patchway with a full tank and relieved expressions. What's more, we still had four pink and yellow canine treats to boot!

The older Severn Bridge (M48) crosses the River Wye as well as the Severn. The Wye marks the Welsh border up past Chepstow; however, the Severn was the river we were following, and we tried to stay as close as we could as we headed south on lanes. Soon we came to Sudbrook, a peculiar place where there is a solid row of terraced houses on one side of the road and old railway lines on the other.

Two planes left over from World War II flew overhead at low altitude as we left the car and began walking the path, (which I would imagine used to be a road), towards Black Rock to the north. The white lighthouse stands isolated from the shore on a mound of rocks. The side facing out into the channel appears to be painted black, although you will understand that we couldn't confirm this properly from our viewpoint. It's certainly plausible, as black is the easiest colour to spot when at sea.

This thin, cylindrical tower which rests on a slightly wider base, used to be not far from the end of the former Portskewett pier. Both this construction and New Passage pier on the other side of the channel, were connected by a two mile steamship crossing. Construction of the accompanying rail link began in 1857. Naturally the crossing would have been rendered redundant by the opening of the four mile long Severn Railway Tunnel in 1886.

The M4 lured me to sleep again. These naps seem to have been an increasingly common occurrence on these journeys. Was I becoming tired of faceless motorways and dual carriageways. Surely not!

We eliminated both Port Talbot and Swansea from our lists. Both seafronts were remarkably similar, consisting of beacons at the end of long jetties with industry to the east and modern housing springing up around. Swansea's effort was another regeneration project a la London Docklands/Harlepool and soon-to-be-seen Ellesmere Port.

Tonight we got it right: Eat early, drink late. We got a meal in a central pub where elderly boozers were baiting the female bar staff by smoking in restricted areas. Stepping in and out of the smoking zone beneath the clearly displayed hanging sign, one of these slightly cantankerous old men kept asking "Am I in it?"

"Am I in it now?"

"What about now?"

"Is this bit smoking?"

"What about over there?"

They chose to humour him, although I could tell that they did not find this easy. About as easy as getting out of Swansea at rush hour in fact. This evening, our pace was reduced to a crawl, not by overloaded stomachs, but by an overloaded A483.

The A483 is the other north/south road in Wales. Whereas the A470 runs from Cardiff to Llandudno, this one is Swansea to Chester, which was quite good as our next lighthouse was a few miles beyond Chester in Ellesmere Port. After the dual carriageway up to the M4, the road settled into its format of winding smoothly around the Welsh Hills through little towns, which were all considered as a possibility for a bed for the night.

Ammanford was a long, drawn-out affair, so long that it rolled seamlessly into another village on either side. Llandeillo was attractive but a bit quiet. Llandovery had potential but it seemed that everywhere we called in on had forgotten to turn over the 'vacancies' sign when all the rooms had been filled. Llanwrtyd Wells was next. We found an inn advertising 'real ales, real food and real staff'. We checked in as it grew dusky and we began to grow tired. The stairs were real too!

During the comatose period, I watched the news in Welsh on S4C. I noted that there are no words in this language for 'David Blunkett' 'Greenpeace' 'pornography' or 'Michael Barrymore!'

Our evening began with a stroll past two young men who were fishing for trout from the stone bridge. We almost forgot that we were standing in the middle of a trunk road, for this was not at all like the A39.

We found the pub, which seemed to be where all the locals drank, and set to work on the pool table. Having amicably decided to call it a draw at two games each, we were cajoled into trying a half-pint of the landlord's 'special' as we prepared to leave. This ale, at over 5.5% alcohol (no wonder we can't remember the name of it), was brewed especially for the pub in nearby Kington. Well, it's nearby in Welsh terms anyway.

I asked him how you pronounced 'Llanwrtyd'. His reply sounded like somebody choking! I tried to copy this sound and I think I almost got it right. Then came the hyperbole; we added Llanwrtyd Wells to our list of candidates for the title, 'smallest town in the UK'. It seemed a reasonable claim, but I wondered 'When does a settlement stop being a village and start being a town?' The logical answer is 'When it has its own town council', but if this is the case, there are some awfully big 'villages' around.

It's a little like that question 'What constitutes a beacon and what constitutes a lighthouse?' Or even, 'What is the main language in Llanwrtyd Wells, when at the local school the English-speaking children learn Welsh, and the Welsh-speaking children learn English?' That was enough 'chicken and egg' questions for one night, and we returned to our hotel for a final pint.

The place was full of walkers - serious walkers, for this town was the base for the four-day 'Welsh International' event. When we had arrived earlier, one of the rooms was full of these active types, who were all mulling over Pathfinder maps, discussing the finer points of the route. An organiser (I presume), had pounced on us before we'd even booked our rooms saying that if we didn't fancy the twenty-five mile course, there was a ten mile alternative we could trek. We said "We'll think about it!"

Mellowed a little by strong ale, my Dad was now receptive to such an ambitious challenge and decided to make conversation with some of these gentlemen at the bar. However, one of them who had a peculiar desire to wear sunglasses in a dimly-lit bar at midnight, sabotaged his efforts and looking disparagingly at my Dad, declared "You wouldn't make *three* miles!"

This would-be Roy Orbison was perhaps ten years younger than the rest of the participants and therefore seemed to think himself the ultimate walker. As he stumbled over the step on his way out, we just thought he was the ultimate....

No, we're not going to start talking like that now! We're two days away from the very end of the mission, we'd had a bucket of beer and walking was not on our agenda; be it for 'liberty and livelihood' (whatever that means), or to prove we were no wimps to a bloke that clearly wanted to look like Lou Reed in an isolated town in mid Wales!

Well, I suppose he was about to take a 'walk on the wild side!'

From Bucks' Fizz to Thames Triumph

152)   ELLESMERE PORT
153)   TRINITY BUOY WHARF/LONDON

Descending two flights of stairs in the morning, we discovered, to our surprise, that we were almost the last guests to enter the breakfast room. The walkers were already congregating outside, with their wax jackets and maps in polythene bags. Some had walking sticks and there was a general hum of anticipative conversation.

Our more mundane conversation indoors as we devoured our fried comestibles, was as follows:

"Where are you off to today?" asked the landlady.

"Cheshire" we replied.

"Oh - Cheshire Oaks! You must go there. It's a designer outlet".

I mentioned that we had one six miles up the road from home, but didn't want to dampen the lady's enthusiasm further.

We watched the athletes depart and then gathered our belongings ourselves. As we left I asked how she pronounced 'Llanwrtyd Wells' hoping for a slightly more Anglicised pronunciation.

"Lan-err-tid Wells" came the reply, "So you're off to Cheshire Oaks?"

"No, Cheshire!"

Either way, it was going to be a long drive of unrelenting A483. This particular shopping attraction must have made a considerable impact for this lady to undertake such a journey on a regular basis.

Before we left the town, we had a quick look at the station, which had been described to us as being Harry-Potter-esque. It was certainly very quaint, with hanging baskets and colourful shrubbery giving it an air of timelessness. However, with only four trains in each direction per day, not *that* many people would actually get to enjoy the site of this horticultural halt. Take, on the other hand the shabby stations we are used to in Kent, and the comparatively regular service, and one can conclude that it is only possible to put nice things where there is nobody to wreck them. Or see them!

It seemed that we had stayed in the most attractive of these mid-Wales towns, for both Builth Wells and Llandrindod Wells seemed larger, and therefore had more of the usual detractions than Llandeilo,

Llandovery or indeed Lan-err-tid Wells. Bricks were more in evidence in Llandrindod too; we had come to expect white plaster frontages by now.

All these towns seemed to crop up at regular distance intervals. After a particularly scenic section of road, winding its way through the mountains before descending with so many changes in direction that we were not sure where we would end up, came Newtown.

Newtown was the largest settlement we had encountered since Swansea. Beyond this, the route was much more heavily trafficked. At Welshpool, the road had ingeniously commandeered some of the railway tracks in order to bypass the town centre. Then bypassing Oswestry, the road joins forces with the A5, and just before Wrexham it freaks out into a dual carriageway for the remainder of the journey to the motorway.

Passing both Chester and the aforementioned retail therapy centre, we left the M53 at junction nine, which was a mere stone's throw away from both the town centre and the river. Here, the Manchester Ship Canal runs parallel with the River Mersey. The tall chimneys of the oil refinery dominate the skies, being about a mile upriver from here. Our lighthouse was at the point that the Shropshire Union Canal (now adorned with an attractive towpath walk) joins it.

This area of old maritime buildings has again been given the 'docklands' treatment: i.e. it has been spruced up and turned into sought-after dwellings for people who like gazing out onto ship canals. The locks have all been painted by the look of it, and there is a boat museum too. The area is literally a maze of rectangular inlets. This posed a problem, for although we could see the thin, brick lighthouse from across the ten or so feet width of the Shropshire Union, after such a long journey, we felt the urge to actually stand beneath it!

We eventually achieved this end by parking the other side of the motorway, and dodging the cars on the slip roads on foot. This redundant light is joined to a brick office building. The lantern is empty and its top is black and bell-shaped. The tower appears chimney-like in spite of its many-sided nature.

To consider our next options, we dropped into the least run-down looking local pub we could find. The lunchtime trade of elderly locals (who must have seen many changes to this area in the last few years), mingled comfortably with the building site surveyors.

Our final port of call would be London, but that would be for tomorrow. Our priorities now were to travel as near to the big smoke as we could get without being swept up in the grip of it, and relax.

Milton Keynes is not the obvious choice but we were drawn there by morbid curiosity.

This place was different. Normally I hate those areas you get on the outskirts of towns, which consist of flat land cut up by dual carriageways with loads of roundabouts, but here I felt as though we had just driven into a different country – the Kingdom of Milton Keynes.

The idea of building a new town with a grid layout is nothing new and certainly not American; it was even tried in the thirteenth century with Winchelsea in East Sussex, but this place really did feel like the States. Even the central business district consisted of modern 'block' buildings with a linear car-park in front, just behind the tree-lined street/ avenue. On top of this, the flatness of the land meant that no glimpse of the surrounding countryside could remind us that we were still in England. I imagined that people who live here very rarely venture outside the place. Milton Keynes was a way of life, but the thought that amazed me most is that to them, this *was* 'England'.

We stopped in a 'barn' dedicated to the pursuit of pleasures like eating and drinking, and supped an unusually bitter real ale. As we dined, we observed the indigenous people going about their daily lives. My Dad suddenly made up his mind that he did not like the place, although I was strangely fascinated by it.

Abruptly, he stood up and declared that everything in this town was 'plastic'. Whether or not the meal had upset him, I do not know. 'At least it's genuine plastic' I thought.

As we left, people in expensive sports cars used the short stretches of dual carriageway to advertise their affluent fast-paced lifestyles, completely unaware of how pointless this is when there's a roundabout every two hundred yards! Reading road signs is not easy here either; we were looking for 'Buckingham' amongst the jumble of concocted names given to each block of residential boxes.

We needed some historical vibes to pacify his mood and Buckingham seemed to be the best bet, being declared the county town by Alfred the Great (c.890) until Aylesbury usurped its position in the eighteenth century.

We have noticed on our many sojourns that if you do not have a room booked by 7pm, even in the off-season, you end up either paying a week's wage for one night, or finding somewhere where you have to sleep with your feet in the washbasin!

The usual reply is "If only you had been here half an hour earlier – our last room has just gone".

Gone where? Demolished, sold as a bijou apartment, lifted off into space! Buckingham was no exception, but at least we were directed to an alternative where our feet could remain dry all night!

We wandered the streets but found only old pubs that were now either Indian restaurants or just not open. The atmosphere was distinctly unpromising; and our dreams of sitting in a cosy inglenook, staring at replica horse brasses rapidly receded, for the only vibes *we* were getting were emanating from the open kitchen window, and they were distinctly not historic!

We eventually had to settle for a large alehouse that was obviously the young person's pub. It had a chain-like feel to it. The youngsters were having a good time whilst waiting to inherit the silver from their workaholic parents who, presumably, would be gearing up for another day on the treadmill.

Other establishments were quiet to the point of extinction. At one of these, we fed the quiz machine with coins, until the lure of watching somebody balance four glasses upon the side of an ashtray became too much. We were told that this is an event, which takes place annually at the local fair. Even we were able to balance two by the end of the evening – perhaps there are time penalties to take into account.

And so it was back to our inn for a final beer before bedtime, which like in a lot of provincial towns, was the time the place erupted into life. A lot of noise was being generated for a town of fewer than ten thousand people. Young belligerent shouts, and the sounds that you normally associate with the starting grid at a Grand Prix circuit, drifted up from the street below. We were used to this by now, but were a little surprised that it happened in Buckingham!

* * * * *

And so we arrive at the final day. This really was it.

We arose, bundled everything into the car and set off across the unspectacular but pleasant Buckinghamshire countryside to Leighton Buzzard. Breakfast was urgently required and a branch of the 'golden arches' just before Dunstable provided us with the said nourishment.

The A1 is not the best way to travel into central London, and the crawl through Highgate, Holloway and Highbury was nothing short of painful. I heard somewhere that the average speed of traffic in London at the turn of the last century was fourteen miles per hour, and after a hundred years of technical advancement it is now... fourteen miles per hour! If the government really does want to tax rail and bus tickets, I can see the whole thing grinding to a complete halt. I cannot imagine people being prepared to pay seventeen and a half percent extra for improvements that companies should be making out of their own profits. Perhaps even Charing Cross and Waterloo will end up as pretty as Llanwrtyd Wells. Pretty empty!

Arriving at Wapping, our search began for the elusive lighthouse that we'd heard was at St Katherine's Dock. This was a little like Ellesmere Port, being full of inlets and redevelopment. Here, the whole area had been smartened up into a high-class shopping complex to compliment the high-price housing.

We walked as far as Tower Bridge but were becoming increasingly impatient; all we had found was a lightship moored in one of the channels. Asking a trio of security guards if there was a lighthouse and receiving blank looks did not bode well. We had seen nothing along the Thames and nothing in this complex. While everybody else enjoyed the 'retail therapy' we were getting increasingly terse and in need of therapy.

Our therapy came just the other side of Wapping, in the form of a relaxing pint in the 'Prospect of Whitby', a sixteenth century pub steeped in history, overlooking the Thames. It was of some comfort to know that estimable personages such as Samuel Pepys and Charles Dickens had dined in this very room. Today's diners were mainly American tourists, with a few contemporary city types.

The ambience of the dark wooden interior soothed away our frustrations at having been unable to complete the mission. I had been faithfully told that this lighthouse existed, and that it had been used by Trinity House to train lighthouse keepers, yet we had failed at the last hurdle to find it.

Our resolve was to continue along the river in the hope that we might find something. As far as I was concerned, the dream was over; such was the gravity of this situation that I even prayed that we would stumble across it.

Now, I don't imagine that the Almighty physically removed this structure from St Katherine's and transplanted it several miles downstream, but somehow, this supplication was granted and my thanks are manifold. For as we sped along Aspen Way, (which to my mind really *is* the best route in and out of London), a large yellow sign with 'lighthouse' on it grabbed our attention. Instantly, our spirits were dragged out of the doldrums and soon we were parking outside a gate marked 'Trinity Buoy Wharf'. Even the name sounded promising.

Owned by 'Urban Space Management' under a lease from the Trinity Buoy Wharf Trust, this area is now a centre for arts and creative enterprise. The company name amused me a little, reminding me of the 1968 hit for the Bonzo dog Doo-dah band.

But once inside, it was more a feeling of elation than amusement. This is London's only lighthouse, designed in 1863 by Michael Farraday. It was indeed used to train prospective keepers, and had been refurbished by the London Docklands Development Corporation who owned the wharf from 1988-1998.

It is a sizeable structure adjoining a pointed-roofed, warehouse-type building and just across the water the Dome and the Canary Wharf towers could be seen. The tower is semi-octagonal and like the warehouse behind, is built from yellow/brown bricks. At the top is the round latticed light compartment, the back of which is painted white. A small black circular block tops off its roof. There are transmitters of some sort attached to it and a flag waves proudly from the balcony.

A notice on the wooden door advertises free admission to 'Longplayer'. A gentleman clearing up litter described it to us as 'the most long playing machine in the world'. I was intrigued, what was it? A never-ending tape? A perpetual motion machine? The door was locked, we had picked the wrong day. We were good at this!

We were also told that the light is still used today, now that's what *I* call a 'long-player!'

We used the Woolwich Ferry to cross the Thames. This was not like the King Harry ferry or the ferry at Studland; for it was a proper vessel, not pulled on chains. It was also free to use.

My Father had an old map with him that showed several structures along the lower reaches of the Thames. These, he insisted, had to be checked out.

I didn't really like Thamesmead that much; it was nearly all modern red-bricked housing, with more residential structures being erected at a frenetic pace. Along the riverside cycleway was its beacon, also red in colour. I wasn't expecting a lighthouse anyway, but we had to expunge the last vestiges of doubt from our consciousness before we could be satiated.

Similarly at traffic-clogged Erith, there were no pharophilic structures in evidence. Crossing the River Darent, we were back in Kent. Branching off of the busy dual carriageway, a tiny lane wound its way through the edge of the countryside to the Thames bank, but there was nothing more than a black beacon to be viewed. We were now just a matter of the well-hackneyed drive down the M20 from home.

It was over.

We had seen both the best and worst of England and Wales. Along our way, we have eulogized what is good about this country and have even found a few axes to grind. We had witnessed bacchanalia, had experienced both triumph and despair, and maybe had even received a little divine intervention at the end. There may still be omissions from our lexicon of lights, but I am confident that nobody has ever done the lighthouses of England and Wales as comprehensively as this.

"Would anybody want to?" you may ask.

This country is changing all the time. Things are lost and things are gained. We want desperately to hang on to that which is threatened. Lighthouses may not even be one of these, but we've seen a lot of things that are. If, as predicted by the doomsday merchants, sea-levels rise dramatically in the next fifty years, then certainly the flimsier lights will be engulfed, as much of the low-lying land, particularly on the eastern side of the country, will have to be abandoned.

We have seen many lights that have been forsaken, due to the silting of harbours, and the search for deeper sheltered water continues. But perhaps the biggest threat to the old lights is technology, in the form of Global Satellite Tracking (GPS). The cost of the basic equipment must be well within the range of even the most impoverished of fishermen.

A recent political leader used the lighthouse as a metaphor for leadership. Just like a political party, there had been both leading lights and disused decrepitude. All were remnants of our maritime history and thus, should be preserved.

There is still a place for them all.

Pass the candle.

Acknowledgements

The following sources of information were useful in compiling this book:

Books:
The Kentish Lights – Alan Major (SB Publications)
Shire Album 312 (lighthouses) – Lynn F. Pearson (Shire
    Publications Limited)
Guiding Lights (in association with English Heritage) – Peter
    Ashley (Everyman Publishers)
AA Book of British Towns – Philip Llewellin/Ann Saunders (Drive
    Publications Limited)
Guinness Book of Records – Norris and Ross McWhirter
    (Guinness Superlatives Ltd)
Guinness Book of Answers – Norris McWhirter (Guinness
    Superlatives Limited)
The Top Ten of Everything – Russell Ash (Queen Anne Press,
    a division of Macdonald and Co. (Publishers) Limited)
A History of England – Keith Fieling (Book Club Associates)
The Complete Beatles Recording Sessions – Mark Lewisohn
    (The Hamlyn Publishing Group Limited, a division of
    The Octopus Publishing Group Plc)

Maps:
Ordnance Survey – Explorer Series 1:25000 scale.
Ordnance Survey – Landranger Series 1:50000 scale.
AA Complete Atlas of Britain.
Road Atlas of Great Britain – Geographers' A-Z Map Co. Ltd.

Websites:
www.trinityhouse.co.uk
www.lsgb.co.uk (The Lighthouse Society of Great Britain)

Also, various newspapers, periodicals and information handouts.

Index of Lights

LIGHTHOUSE	COUNTY	CHAPTER

Gorleston-on-Sea	Norfolk	16
Great Orme	Gwynedd	32
Hale	Cheshire	31
Happisburgh	Norfolk	16
Hartland Point	Devon	5
Hartlepool Headland/Heugh (X2)	Durham	24
Harwich (X2)	Essex	17
Heysham (X2)	Lancashire	30
Holyhead/Goleudy	Anglesey	33
Hoylake	Merseyside	31
Hunstanton	Norfolk	15
Hurst Point (X3)	Hampshire	*10&36*
Kessingland/Pakefield	Suffolk	16
Killingholme (X3)	Lincolnshire	22
Leasowe	Merseyside	31
Lees Scar (Silloth)	Cumbria	29
Littlehampton	West Sussex	10
Lizard Point	Cornwall	2
Llanddwyn Island	Anglesey	33
Longships	Cornwall	33
Lowestoft	Suffolk	16
Lynmouth Foreland/ Countisbury Head	Devon	5
Margate	Kent	17
Maryport	Cumbria	29
Mevagissey	Cornwall	2
Millom/Hodbarrow Mine (X2)	Cumbria	29
Morecambe	Lancashire	30
Mumbles Head	West Glamorgan	12
Nash Point (X2)	South Glamorgan	12
New Brighton	Merseyside	31
Newhaven (X2)	East Sussex	18
Newlyn	Cornwall	3
North Foreland	Kent	17
North Shields (X3)	Tyne and Wear	25
Orford Ness	Suffolk	16&27
Ousefleet	Lincolnshire	20

Paull (X3)	East Yorkshire	21
Pendeen	Cornwall	3
Penzance	Cornwall	3
Plover Scar	Lancashire	30
Plymouth Hoe	Devon	7
Plymouth Sound	Devon	7
Point Lynas	Anglesey	34
Point of Ayr	Flintshire	32
Porthcawl	Mid Glamorgan	12
Portland Bill (X3)	Dorset	9
Portland Harbour	Dorset	9
Ramsgate	Kent	17
River Nene (X2)	Lincolnshire	15
Salt Island (Holyhead)	Anglesey	33
Saltwick Bay (Whitby)	North Yorkshire	24
Scarborough	North Yorkshire	23
Seaham	Durham	25
Seahouses	Northumberland	26
Silloth	Cumbria	29
Skerries	Anglesey	34
Shoreham-by-Sea	West Sussex	10
Souter Point	Tyne & Wear	25
South Foreland (X2)	Kent	19
South Gare	Cleveland	24
South Shields (X2)	Tyne and Wear	25
South Stack	Anglesey	33
Southsea	Hampshire	10
Southwold	Suffolk	16
Spurn Head (X2)	East Yorkshire	21
St Ann's Head	Pembrokeshire	13
St Anthony's Head/Zone Point	Cornwall	2
St Bees Head	Cumbria	29
St Ives	Cornwall	3
St Mary's/Bait Island	Tyne and Wear	26
St Tudwall's Island	Gwynedd	34
Start Point	Devon	7
Strumble Head	Pembrokeshire	13

Sunderland	Tyne and Wear	25
Tater Du	Cornwall	3
Teignmouth	Devon	7
Trevose Head	Cornwall	4
Trinity Buoy Wharf	Greater London	37
Trywn Du	Anglesey	34
Tynemouth	Tyne and Wear	25
Walney Island	Cumbria	29&30
Watchet	Somerset	36
West Usk	Gwent	12
Whitby (X2)	North Yorkshire	24
Whitehaven (X3)	Cumbria	29
Whitford Point	West Glamorgan	14
Withernsea	EastYorkshire	21
Wyre Light (Fleetwood)	Lancashire	31

Please note - former counties have been used in some cases.

Any lighthouse structure that we have been close enough to see has been listed.